Reflections on Swami Dayanand Saraswati and His Thoughts

Reflections on Swami Dayanand Saraswati and His Thoughts

H.K.Gusain

CYBER TECH PUBLICATIONS
4264/3, Ansari Road, Daryaganj, New Delhi-110002 (India)
Ph.: 011-23244078, 011-43559448 Fax: 011-23280028
E-Mail: cyberpublicationsdelhi@yahoo.com
Website: www.cybertechpublications.com

REFLECTIONS ON SWAMI DAYANAND SARASWATI AND HIS THOUGHTS

H.K.Gusain.

First Edition 2010

Published by : Asian Offset Printers

G.S. Rawat for **Cyber Tech Publications**
4264/3, Ansari Road, Daryaganj, New Delhi-110002 (India)
Ph.: 011-23244078, 011-43559448 Fax: 011-23280028
E-Mail: cyberpublicationsdelhi@yahoo.com
Website: www.cybertechpublications.com

Preface

The founder of Arya Samaj (the Society of Nobles), Swami Dayanand Saraswati was one of the greatest religious leaders ever born in India. He was responsible, to some an extent, in bringing back the age-old teaching tradition of 'Gurukul'. He advocated for the equal right of women and condemned practices such as untouchability, animal sacrifice, idol worship, etc.

To speak of, write about, and believe in a thing as it is, constitutes truth. He that is prejudiced tries to prove that even his error is truth, while the truth of his religions opponent is error. He cannot, therefore, know what the true religion is. Hence it is the bounden duty of truthful and learned men to unfold this right nature of truth and error before all men in their writings and speeches and then to leave them free to judge what promotes their welfare and what is prejudicial to their interests, and to embrace what is true and reject what is false. This will lead to the happiness of the people at large. Though the human souls posses the capacity for ascertaining truth, yet through self-interest, obstinacy, wrong headedness, ignorance and the like, it is led to renounce truth and incline towards untruth.

The search was long and arduous. Finally, at the age of thirty-six he found his mentor in Virajananda Saraswati, who was blind, but was a master of the ancient lore. The training was rigorous, and the guru was ruthless. But here was a disciple of a lifetime. As the teacher's fee (gurudakshina -- also has a sacred connotation in Hindu thought; it cannot be denied) he wanted his student to devote his life for the revival of Hinduism. The guru called him Dayananda. Dayanand Sarasvati believed that the Vedas were perfect and infallible.Dayananda advocated the doctrine of karma, skepticism in dogma, and emphasised the ideals of brahmacharya (celibacy and devotion to God).

— *Author*

CONTENTS

1

Introduction

Dayananda Saraswati; the iconic founder of the Vedic socio-religious organization; the Arya Samaj was born at Tankari in 1824; in the state of Kathiawar in modern day Gujarat in a Brahmin family of moderate means. He was neither a prodigy; nor exuded traits of the personality he would metamorphose in the distant future; and the rebel in him which would against all odds, break through the shackles of his conservative religious background remained dormant in the initial phase of his life.

However, it would be erroneous to dismiss the subliminal familial influences on young Dayandanda. His family like most Brahmins of Kathiarwar was Shaivite [the follower of Shiva] unlike the majority population which was Vaishava; devoted to Krishna and considered Srimad Bhagavatam their most sacrosanct scripture. Hence, it is not without reason that he remained one of the bitterest opponents of two of the most important Vaishnav sects holding sway in Gujarat; the Swaminarayans and the Vallabhacharyas. In contrast; in his early phase of life he remained sympathetic to Shaivism and its practices (including ritualistic animal sacrifices); and considered it more or less a much purified form of the original and true Vedic religion.

Great religious leaders are usually endowed with a maddening spiritual drive in the search for Moksha and Dayananda was no exception. He ran away from home once unsuccessfully to avoid marriage and imprisonment in the house of ignorance; his search was for a guru who would guide him on the road to moksha. Unfortunately for him; Dayananda's travails across the length and breadth of North India including its spiritual powerhouses were in vain. Although he briefly enrolled in the order of the Dandis; and flirted with Advaita Vedanta and Patanjali's Yoga destiny had decided differently; his efforts would consummate not into Neo-Vedanta but probably its variant antithesis. Dayananda's progress was hardly spectacular; he was almost close to 30 and no closer to formulating either his ideas; nor the means to unleash them in the future. A chance meeting with the blind but brilliant Swami Virajnanda helped him master the complex Sanskrit grammar like the ashtyadhyayi. Dayananda as noted was not endowed with any naturally brilliance for the subject but his conscientiousness paid dividends as he rose to prominence as Virajnanda's best pupil. Virajnanda probably imbibed into Dayananda some of his lifelong goals; to usher in the mythical golden Vedic age; peace and prosperity on the people of Aryavrta; a reign of the true religion and abandonment of the pseudo doctrines embedded in the Puranas and post Vedic Indian religious literature including Buddhist and Jain Texts.

THE REFORMER

19th and 20th century India had seen a host of great religious personalities who coupled the dissemination of their respective spiritual doctrines and dogmas with various social reform messages which could be both positive and negative in the modern sense. Calcutta and Bombay led the way; and the burning issues involved the pathetic condition of widows, female education, widow remarriage acts, restraint in child marriages and espousal of vegetarianism. Personally, I do not see Dayananda's social messages as being radically different from those of his counterparts (all except one i.e. shuddhi) as has often been alleged by some of his overzealous championeers. (Also, one cannot ignore the testimony of Jordens that it was in Calcutta that he acquired a cauldron of new ideas; many of which he would integrate in his system with some suitable modifications).

Then what makes Dayananda different; is the fact that his social message was not an auxiliary to its religious or spiritual counterpart, [2] but equally important in itself. A true believer of the Vedic religion could not reconcile himself to a disharmonious familial order where women were not respected or girls were uneducated and harshly treated. Moksha could be attained only by following the highest of the moral codes. The moral code of a man even as great as Manu must ally with reason failing which it had to be discarded. To the allegation of some modern critics like Nirad C Chaudhari who claimed that Hindu ethics were immature; Dayananda's life is open testimony to the giant potential of the Hindu ethical framework.

Secondly, Dayananda has remained silent on his spiritual and yogic accomplishments. While it may be true that many seekers remained silent on their spiritual barometer; there is nothing to suggest from Dayananda's history that he ever had a glimpse of the infinite. If the hypothesis; that Dayananda was unenlightened (from a Vedantic point of view) is true then it is remarkable as to how he maintained a dogmatic belief in the infallibility of Vedas despite his disappointments. The disappointment was there in the now middle aged Dayananda but it did not consummate in disillusionment. Instead, he remained spurred on by some unknown force into shaping a modern Vedic theory purged of all Puranic and atheistic distortions.

It is unfortunate that most Indian history textbooks, especially those authored by Marxist historians have restricted Dayananda's social reform to his critique of Hindu idol worship. While it is true, that anti image worship was an unalterable part of his doctrine it is foolish to ignore his other contributions like his criticism of the sectarianism prevalent in Hinduism which prevented it from presenting a united face to its opponents, the movement for shuddhi or re-conversion of Hindu converts to Islam and Christianity; his support for niyoga as an alternative to widow remarriage; his special schools for educating girls and his sustained appeals to the rich, powerful and princely to establish welfare states.

The view of Romila Thapar [3] that Dayananda developed his allergy to image worship as a subconscious influence of Christianity is untenable for Dayananda hadn't come under any missionary influences in the initial phase of his life. Also

Jordens informs us that Kathiawar was historically the land of the iconoclastic Jain sect; the Sthanakavasis who rejected image worship and who were probably the very first non idolatrous sectarians he ever came across.

THE RATIONALIST

Dayananda is unique amongst Indian reformers for he was not one who constantly bound himself to one doctrine. He freely revised his own ideas and theories without much ado which baffled his friends and foes alike. His unhesitant attitude in admitting his own shortcoming, learning from his mistakes and borrowing concepts from other authorities and remolding them marks him singularly distinct from a host of other contemporary religious reformers. When discrepancies from his earlier work was pointed out to him; he used to reply that it was in part due to his ignorance and after deliberate consideration he had changed his mind and revised his views. His magnum opus; the Satyartha Prakash bears ample testimony to this fact.

The first edition had a strong Advaitic bias; its critique of Buddhism and Jainism was immature and it erroneously lumped all atheistic systems into one. His knowledge of Vedas was still rudimentary and contained merely 20 quotations from the Vedas. His philosophical doctrine is essentially that of bheda abheda and irreversible moksha.

While he pleaded education for all the four castes; he categorically rejected the idea of shudras and girls being initiated into reading of the Vedas. His vitriolic attacks on popular Hinduism and its paraphernalia like idol worship, pilgrimages, rituals formed the bulk of one chapter alone. While he saw no relationship between eating and dharma ; vegetarianism was advocated but not once did he suggest total abstinence from meat.

In contrast, the second edition of the Satyartha Prakash enunciates a sound and ingenious theological position of Traitavada; dismisses Advaita in his chapter on the Neovedantins; his chapters on Buddhism, Charvaka and Jains are now rationally analyzed; his repudiation of image worship stems from his invincible position that there is no Vedic / Shruti evidence to back it up; the new edition has hundreds of Vedic quotations; he wholeheartedly supports the entitlement of women and shudras for Vedic education; his dependence on Manu is markedly diminished; and there is an appeal for total abstinence from meat. Even his criticism of popular Hinduism has been markedly toned down from its predecessor.

THE RADICAL

Dayananda's radicalism can briefly be classified under four categories

A. Theological

B. Social and Moral

C. Political and Historical

D. Methodological (with respect to preaching and propaganda)

Dayananda consistently modified his theological positions with the vicissitudes of time - he began as an advaitin and consummated into a unique traitavadin. Agents which influenced him were chiefly his own in-depth reading and self interpretation of the Vedas; his frequent discussion and debates with Prostestans, Theosophists and even Muslim clerics. Traitavada is the theory that there exists three eternal substances without beginning or end: God, the prakriti and the jivas. They are always co-existent and their nature, qualities and activity are equally eternal.

Moksha is not perpetual and Dayananda rejected the assertion that a soul when disencumbered of karma comes to a halt in the lap of infinite bliss forever. Nothing lasts forever; and moksha is no exception. Since moksha to him was a change of condition affected by human action, its effects namely bondage and liberation must be necessarily of limited duration, and therefore limited in time. Thus, Dayananda did not ally or lend support to any of the six standard systems of Indian Philosophy. Instead, he concluded that all of them were a partial expression of the ultimate truth enshrined in the Vedas.

Dayananda seemed to walk a tightrope between the two extremes of moksha.....the one of glorified earth (or a sensuous heaven) as in most Abrahamic faiths or the other extreme in the divinization of man as in the Hindu Vedanta. His preamble was that man is not a free agent; in essence he is not divine so it is a folly to conclude that he will ever realize divinity.

Hinduism is a revelatory religion but it pays minimum detail to the source of revelation. The Samhitas have remained essentially as closed subjects; and the Vaishnav sects have never hesitated to place the Srimad Bhagavatam at par with the Vedic Samhitas in being the revealed truth. Dayananda was clearly influenced by the Protestants and he was convinced by them that god reveals himself in a book. But the swami went even further and claimed that the Vedas were the repository of the totality of truth, both theological and scientific. Thus, he took an ancient Hindu tradition and gave it a new direction all of his own. Socially, he was the giant reformer of the Doab. His ideas which included cleansing Hinduism of the superstitions and myths that it had acquired through the ages; establish Vedic pathshalas for both boys and girls; and his anti ritualism which might seem run of the mill today were sufficiently radical 150 years ago.

But he did not stop at that. The plight of the widows was too moving for him; and he had to return to the Vedas to find a solution. The Vedas had a solitary one of Niyoga and Dayananda was hampered by his doctrine of Vedic infallibility in affirming with the Vedas. However, since Niyoga was unacceptable in the modern times; Dayananda accepted widow remarriage for it was a minor evil compared to the pathetic plight widows were subjected to.

Arguably, Dayananda's greatest contribution to the Hindu Social system was the shuddhi movement. It was a process to reintegrate Hindu converts who desired to be restored to their former religion. Hindus had themselves forgotten that the ancient Brahmana texts and even the late Devala and Atri Samhita contained adequate provisions for re-conversion back to Hinduism of those who had been forcibly converted out of the Hindu fold. The Atri Samhita 9th century A.D notably also made similar provisions for women who had either been defiled by their abductors or rendered pregnant by men other than their husbands. The Shuddhi movement launched in the Punjab was on its inception primarily a check on the proselytizing Christian missionaries but in the years to come it would become an active tool for re-conversion from Islam.

A common critique of Hindu dharma is that it rests very little emphasis on right ethics. Its moral ambivalence is not befitting for a major religion. Others in its defense have argued that morality is taken as an obvious fact of life; for truth is the highest morality and rest all is a derivate from it. Secondary morals need not be overstated if the primary fundamental moral value of truth is adhered to. However, popular Hinduism allows penances (for wrong moral action) that are based on certain petty ritualistic rigmaroles instead of concentrating on corrective moral action to uphold dharma. But Dayananda would put an end to the question mark over Hindu ethics for once and all!

Dayananda's conception of man evolved from the Advaitic conception of [Jiva = Brahman] into one radically different; the deepest essence of man was not a passive spectator but active and cosmic. Even in moksha; there was no inertia or inactivity but activity and freedom; both of which could result in relapse into the former state. Thus, Dayananda arrived at unheralded concept in Hindu eschatology. His salvation had to be achieved completely by his own works and by nothing else; moral action guided by reason was the one and only power effective in the process of salvation. Dayananda ruthless eliminated all other short cuts and paths to moksha; the easy rides; the instantaneous transformation that Hinduism had devised over the centuries. Dayananda said yes to free will; yes to activity and flayed the path of nivritti, even among sanyasins (those who had renounced the world).

It is best to let Jordens sum up this unique contribution of Dayananda; "No other Hindu theologian had elevated man's moral action to such a rank in the scale of human endeavour, far above the powers of ritualism, the raptures of mysticism or the wondrous effectiveness of devotion love....This conception of man is no doubt Dayananda's greatest theoretical achievement and his main contribution to Hindu speculation".

Dayananda was not a believer in a theocratic state; but he proposed an aristocratic regime; one that allows only the most able to lead the administration. He reinterpreted the verses in the Manu Smriti which divinized the king and considered them only an allegory for the traits a king should possess.

Dayananda can also said to be the first champion of an indigenous Aryan origin theory. He repudiated the Aryan Invasion theory although the means by which he arrived at such a conclusion are completely illogical. Nevertheless; his interpretation of the Vedas being universal in outlook; not bound to parochialism or sectarianism; transcending historical timelines was refreshing and a bold rejoinder to the Eurocentric indologists who attempted to construct history from myth.

The means of propaganda adopted by Dayananda included public debates; public lectures; distribution of pamphlets and sale of his literature; chiefly the Satyartha Prakasha. The use of public lectures and literature had been suggested to him by members of the Brahmo Samaj in Calcutta. The use of pamphlets was an ingenious method for dissemination of ideas. Despite his powers of oratory and logical skills he had limited success in debating and even that was restricted to orthodox Hindu pundits on image worship. The missionaries and Islamic maulvis were able to hold their own against him on most occasions.

THE PRAGMATIST

Despite his revulsion for many features of popular Hinduism; Dayananda in his later years clearly felt the need for a comprehensive and united Hindu front to tackle the threat of Christian Missionaries and Islamic fundamentalists. In 1878 he stressed the need for unity and friendship among all Hindus for the sake of well being of the whole country. He was a radical but he was also willing to compromise on certain issues. To instantiate, although he himself didn't believe in any food taboos he maintained them in the public sphere for in their absence they would be cut off from Hindu society and lose the chance of influencing its masses.

Similarly; he adopted the cause of cow protection to unite the sectarian Hindu outfits to come under one platform and struggle for a common cause. It is noteworthy that Dayananda pertinently advocated the cause for cow protection (gau raksha) not on the orthodox premise of cow being vestige to 84,000 divinities or cow as mother but due to its economic utility. A dead cow could feed only a dozen but a living cow could feed a thousand. Also, the dung of the cow was a valuable source of manure. His reasons for cow protection clearly rested on economic, ecological and probably political criterion; but not on theological or emotive ones. That the economic argument was foremost in his mind is evident from the fact that he takes great pains to show that go-medha, the sacrifice of kine, refers most of the time to bulls, whose economic value is less than that of cows. And when the texts unmistakably refer to a female animal, then a barren cow is meant.

Other instances of his pragmatism include his adoption of sanyas to run away from home; his prompt closure of his failing schools and his study under the blind Virajnanda to learn grammar.

However, it would be a grave mistake to conclude that Dayananda had any elements of opportunism in him. Dayananda sincerely subscribed to his ontological view in the infallibility of the Vedas, and them being the source of all knowledge as an axiomatic truth. The claim of the opponents of the Arya Samaj that the Swami admitted to one, Bholanath Sarabhai that he didn't himself believe in the infallibility of the Vedas, but held on to them for the sake of tactics; they being the rallying points of all Hindus according to Jordens lacks any convincing proof. Dayananda accepted the Vedas as his rock of firm foundation, he took it for the guiding view of his life and he regarded it as the work of eternal truth.

THE VEDIC COMMENTATOR

Although virtually all the six systems of Hindu philosophy pay lip service to the Vedas [especially the samhitas] as being the repository of the greatest spiritual and metaphysical truths; yet in practice the samhita portion [especially the rig Veda] have been viewed only as closed manuscripts; commentaries or bhasyas on them have been very few and far between. Sayana had written the last great bhasya on the Rig Veda in the 13th century. But interest in the Vedas revived in the 19th century due to the pioneering work of the German Indologists like Max Muller and Griffith.

Dayananda wrote his bhasya chiefly out of the old national albeit dormant instinct in Vedic superiority; a move to counter the misconceptions of these current orientalist commentaries which he claimed were inferior to his work, since the latter was based on original commentators like Yaska.

Also a bhasya would allow the Arya Samaj members to have a definite and reliable reference for all their literary queries on Vedic interpretation. Dayananda briefly concluded that the Vedas literally contained all the wisdom of god; and hence was universal in nature. He repudiated the idea of Vedas carrying any historical references since the Vedas to him antedated all history.

His second, assumption was Vedas proclaiming a pure monotheism unlike the popular view of modern indologists (then and now) that the Vedas proclaimed a henotheistic mode of devotion. Dayananda had a rudimentary knowledge of science and technology but this didn't stop him from asserting that the Vedas contained all scientific truth in them. Also, he reasoned that there was nothing in the Vedas which could remotely offend morality.

Although, Dayananda's bhasya spanning thousand of pages is not taken seriously in Vedic studies and considered outdated; the fact remains relatively unknown that it did win the approval of few of his later contemporaries whose works are considered at least intellectually far superior to his. For instance, Sri Aurobindo, arguably the most original thinker of modern India concludes "in the matter of Vedic interpretation I am convinced that whatever may be the final complete interpretation, Dayananda will be honored as the first discoverer of the right clues....He has found the keys of the doors that time had closed and rent asunder the seals of the imprisoned foundations"

Last but not the least; the bhasya constitutes the very first effort and a massive one at that in bringing the Vedas out of the sanctuary of Brahmanical dominance into the open and make them accessible to all Hindus; irrespective of caste and creed. Jordens believes this to be the strongest argument in him being called "The Luther of India"

The Hindu Nationalist

Dayananda is one of the chief figures of Indian nationalism who began as career as a British loyalist. In fact, the first edition of the Satyartha Prakasha carries a tract describing the merits of the British rule which unlike that of the decadent, intolerant Mughals was rational and scientific in its scope and expression.

When Dayananda had to face the ire of the orthodox Hindus who resented his literal iconoclasm; he had famously remarked that "If you expel the English, then, no later than tomorrow, you and I and everyone who rises against idol-worship, will have our throats cut like mere sheep".

Yet, in a remarkable transformation; Dayananda emerged as one of the paramount figures of North Indian Hindu Nationalism in Modern India. Some of his conceptualizations like a mythical golden age of the Aryans where Vedic wisdom ruled the length and breadth of not only India, but the world; where people of all classes lived in happiness and comfort; where women were respected and educated universally; where crime, poverty and adultery were unknown remain till date some core ideas of the ultra-orthodox elements of Hindu Nationalism.

The origin of this tendency in Dayananda had a multifocal origin, one of whose epicenters must have been in Punjab where he was repeatedly confronted with the missionaries. He criticized the Christians in his second Satyartha Prakasha [and to an ordinary 19th century India; Christian and British were synonymous] as being usurpers who descended on the property of foreigners.

They were so biased that when a black man is killed by a white man, they acquit the murderers in court. Since their God enjoins animal sacrifices "why should they not fill their belly with beef" They have taken delight in war; for war is their guru mantra. Dayananda's criticism of Christ for declaring war on humanity, in declaring his mission to make war between brother and brother, mother and son is denounced in the most unapologetic terms. While all this may seem to be a harsh judgment; the Swami was only paying back the missionaries in the same coin who had used even more extravagant arguments in their attacks on Hinduism.

Dayananda attempts to unite Hindus cutting across sectarian and caste lines is another feature of his ingenious attempt in constructing the idea of Hindu nationalism.

We have already noted how Dayananda had considerably toned down his attack on popular Hinduism; his tolerance for food taboos and certain other dogmas for which he cared little are an outcome of the same for he realized that dissent would lead to a forced divorce from the Hindu community which would mean inability to further influence the ignorant Hindu masses.

The protect cow movement was also more of an attempt to unite Hindus under the garb of an issue to which all had a natural sympathetic and emotive attitude. He had regretted deeply; the divide in the Hindu community which had prevented them from exerting sufficient pressure in compelling the government to enact a cow protection act.

Dayananda's Hindu nationalism was essentially rationalistic; it was not a blind espousal of all things hoary and of yore but instead an attempt to seize a vital thing out of the past and throw it into the stream of modern life, for it is the most important means of renovation and new-creation. He knew too well that the Hindu religion was the lifeblood of the nation; it was unquestionably its very identity.

VIEWS AND VISIONS

Dayananda was an extrovert; a fiery determined man who had only a singular passion in the rise of a great Arya nation. His spirituality was practical and betrayed no signs of that unfortunate tendency of ascetic voyeurism. A spontaneous power and decisiveness is stamped everywhere on his work. As Sri Aurobindo writes "what an act of grandiose intellectual courage to lay upon this scripture (Veda) defaced by ignorant comment and oblivion of its spirit, degraded by misunderstanding to the level of an ancient document of barbarism and to perceive in its real worth as a scripture which conceals in itself the deep and energetic spirit of the forefathers who made this country and nation."

He was a man of principle; and he refused to compromise on them howsoever great the peril. Neither threats of loss of influence, of ostracism, of the demise of friendship, even of danger to his life, nor promises of wealth, success in reform work could dislodge the Swami from his stand. However, it is also true that he lacked in him the ability to appreciate any shades of grey; to him all things were defined in black or white.

While his rationalism paved the way for initiating several reforms; this radical rationalism also failed him as a theologian to decipher the crucial relationship between myth and symbol. His totalitarian rejection of the Bhagavatam, Puranas and Brahmanas is a mistake, a limitation, the nadir of his genius. Even if his claim of infallibility of the Vedas tends to seem exaggerated there is no reason to dismiss his belief in Vedas being repository of scientific truths.

Sri Aurobindo reminds us that great facts of science were not unknown to ancient civilizations, and while it would be premature to affirm Dayananda's contentions there is still nothing fantastic in Dayananda's idea....He would even add his own conviction that Veda contains other truths of a science that modern world doesn't at all possess, and in that case Dayananda had rather understated than overstated the depth and range of the Vedic wisdom.

Dayananda final shortcoming can be said to be his inability to lay down a lasting legacy for the future. The Arya Samaj couldn't revivify itself through the vicissitudes of time; it has lost its potency as a reforming organization by being rooted in time; it has failed to take note and learn from its founder who constantly adapted, harnessed, and remoulded, if not modified his ideas with time.

Nevertheless, Dayananda will go down in Indian History as the most significant and radical reformer of modern India.

His humanism, courage, intellect and vision will remain an epic tale for centuries to come.

PERSONSALITY AND CHARACTER

Swami Dayanand was a man of gigantic built. He was over six feet in height, and had a compact, well-knit body, but full, which latter fact, instead of giving him a stoutish look, only contributed to make the symmetry of his person singularly perfect.

He ahs a broad and expansive forehead, considerably protruding forward, which unmistakably indicated his possession of an intellect of the highest order; while his unusually raised crown pointed as unmistakably to his kinship with the sage and saint whom the Word Divine, as the Upanishad, differentiates from ordinary mortals by, conferring upon him the epithet of dhir.

The expression of the face, when in repose, was pre-eminently contemplative and dreamy, grand in its smoothness; for deep minds are like deep waters, seldom unruffled, powerful in their wealth and abundance of depth, and carrying on their mighty operations in silence in their own all-sufficient and capacious retreats. When, however, the great Teacher was excited (and it was but rarely that he was excited), the glory of his face was the glory of a thunder and lightning.

A lion surveying the inferior herd defying his power could not look sublimer than he when face to face with, and roused against, the daring and blasphemous skeptic of little knowledge and puny intellect. And yet his withering look of scorn or of contempt was not meant for the persons themselves, for malice was utterly foreign to his nature.; it was only meant for the views, so false and mischievous in their character, which, in their ignorance and conceit, the unblushingly put forward and advocated.

He was for chastising faults as the Word Divine taught him, and as he admitted do often in his interpretation of passages from that Word, and not for chastising the individuals who had faults. His memory was marvelously capacious and retentive, the mass of facts stored in it and ever ready for sue being tremendous. What the learned Pandits hopelessly essayed to hunt up in books, he could draw forth from this mental storage-house in a minute. "His voice." In the words of the founders of the Theosophical Society, "was clear and loud, well calculated to give expression toe very shade of deep feeling ranging from a sweet childish caressing whisper to thundering wrath against the evil-doings of the priests."

He was the most self-possessed of men (speaking as men go in debate), giving the most patient hearing to his adversaries and never interrupting while they were speaking, and his replies were almost invariably given in a tone and in a language calm and gentlemanly in the highest degree.

No man could gasp sooner or better than he; he saw into the soul of things without any apparent effort, and interpreted the others' utterances with a faithfulness which left nothing to be desired. He was never irrelevant and never diffuse, and he insisted upon others' keeping to the point. Humorous and often sarcastic remarks fell upon his lips, but these were wholly free from anything offensive or gross, and were never out of character with the dignified gravity and seriousness which generally characterized his demeanor.

Though acknowledged to be one of the greatest men of his age, even by those who differed with him on many points, he was simple and unostentatious in his habits and tastes. When alone, his entire apparel consisted of a wrapper and an under-cloth (dhoti), and in public too he generally appeared in as unassuming a dress as he could get hold of.

He could command thousands and lakhs if he had liked, but though he valued wealth as a means to an end, though he regarded it as a great factor in the moral, intellectual and spiritual evolution of man, he regarded it as something absolutely worthless and positively injurious when valued for its own sake or interests of the flesh. His Will show his large-heartedness and his moral elevation.

A greater patriot, a sincerer and more earnest advocate of education and enlightenment, a truer and stronger friend of virtue in its all forms, a nobler philanthropist, Aryavarta has not produced for centuries past and will not see for ages to come.

In purity of character, in utter fearlessness, in the acuteness and comprehensiveness of intellect, in devotion to his Divine Word and its truthful Teachings he as exact prototype of his equally great predecessor, Shankracharya. Like the Rishis and Maharishis of old death had no terrors for him: it was a passage which, when traverse, let to the portals of house of immortality and everlasting bliss. Men of the type of Swami Dayanand are the making of thousands in their life and after their death, and the day will come(may it please God, that it comes soon!) when India will again shine all the glory of its pristine splendor.

2

Swami's Teachings

Swami Dayanandj was an Acharya, in the most comprehensive sense of the term. He was a teacher, a preacher, and the author of a prodigious mass of literature, distinguished for its pure and elevated diction, for its bold, uncompromising upholding of truth, for its loftiness of tone, and its depth and profundity of thought. His beliefs, as summed up by himself, were:-

1. " He, who is called Brahm or the Most High; who is Parmatma, or the Sprit who permeates the whole universe; who is Truth, Intelligence and Happiness; whose nature, attributes and doings are holy; who is omniscient, incorporeal, all-pervading, unborn, infinite, almighty, just and merciful; who is the author of the universe, its protector and destroyer; who weighs the merits and demerits of individuals according to the requirements of absolute justice and equity, - even Him I believe to be the Lord of the creation.
2. "The four Vedas, the repository of Knowledge and Religious Truth, are the Word of God. They comprise what is known as the samhita - Mantra Bhag only they are absolutely free from error, and the supreme and independent authority in all things. They require no other book to bear witness to their Divine origin. Even as the sun or a lamp is, by its own light, an absolute and independent manifester of its own existence, - yea, it reveals the existence of things other than itself - even so are the Vedas.

"The commentaries of the foure veds, viz., the Brahmanas, the six Angas, the six Upangas, the four Up-vedas, and the eleven hundred and twentyseven Shakas, which are expositions of the Vedic texts by Brahma and other great Rishis - I look upon as works of a dependent character. In other words, their authority is to be followed only so far as they conform to the teachings of the Vedas. Whatever passages in these works are antagonistic to the Vedic doctrine, I reject them entirely.

3. That which is devoid of partiality, which inculcates justice and equity, which teaches truthfulness of thought, speech and deed, - in a word, that which is in conformity with the Will of God, as embodied in the Vedas, even that I call Dharma. But that which is intermixed with what is partial, which sanctions injustice, which teaches untruthfulness of thought, speech and deed, - in a word, that which is antagonistic to the Will of God, as embodied in the Vedas, that I term Adharma.

   The immortal, eternal Principle which endowed with thought and judgment, with desire and hate, which is susceptible of pleasure and pain, whose capacity for knowledge is limited, - even that is 'Soul.'

4. God and Soul are two distinct entities. Each has certain attributes which are not and cannot be predictable of the other, and each performs certain functions which the other does not and cannot perform. They are, however, inseparable one from the other, being related to each other as the pervader and the pervaded. Even as a material object is, was, and shall always be, distinct from the space in which it exists and as the two cannot, were not, and shall never be, one and the same, even so God and Soul are to each other. Their mutual relation is that of the pervader and pervaded, of father and son. This worships and that is worshipped.

5. "Three things are eternal, namely God, Soul, and Prakriti- the material cause of the universe. These are

also known as the material cause of the universe. These are also known as the eternal substances. Being eternal, their essential qualities, their functions, and their natures are eternally the same.

6. "Things, properties, and functions, which result from combination, are destroyed on the occurrence of a separation. But the power or force, by virtue of which a substance unites with anther or separates from it, is eternally inherent in the substance, and the power will compel it to seek similar unions and disunions in the future. The unions and disunions, as well as the power by virtue of which they take place, are also eternal, in consequence of the regularity of their succession.

7. "That which results form a combination of a primary elements compounded together consistently with a thorough and complete knowledge of the distinctive properties of every separate element and with all the perfection of design, - even that, in all its infinite variety, is called creation.

8. "The purpose of creation is the essential and natural exercise of the creative energy of the Deity. A person once asked some one: "What is the purpose of the eyes?" "Why, to see with, to be sure,' was the reply. The same is the case. God's creative energy must have a play. The enjoyment of the fruit of their actions by Souls, and so on, is also the purpose of creation.

9. "The Creation has a Creator, and that is no other than the afore-mentioned God. The existence of a design in the universe as well as the fact that dead unconscious matter is incapable of forming itself into seed or any other thing endowed with life and vitality, shows that it must have a creator.

10. "The earthly bondage has a cause. This cause is ignorance, which is source of sin as, among other things, it leads man to worship things other than the Creator and obscures his intellectual faculties; whereof pain and suffering is the result. Ignorance is termed bondage,

as it involves the Soul in pain which everybody wants to escape but which he must suffer.

11. "The emancipation of the soul from pain and suffering of every description, its enjoying, unburdened by the gross physical body, a career of freedom in the all-pervading God and His immense creation for a stated period, and its resumption of earthly life after the expiration of that period, it termed salvation.

12. "The means of salvation are the worship of God or the contemplation of His nature and attributes with concentrated attention, the practice of virtue, a thorough control over the passions during the period of study, the society of the wise and learned, the love of true knowledge, purity of thought, active benevolence, and so on.

13. "Arth is wealth acquired by honesty and fair-dealing; but that which is the fruit of dishonesty and fraud, - that is anarth or unrighteous wealth.

14. Kama or true enjoyments are those which are the combined fruit of uprightness of principle and honestly-acquired wealth.

15. "The 'caste' of an individual is determined by merit and sterling worth only.

16. "He alone deserves the title of 'king' who is endowed with exalted qualities and benevolent intentions, who delights in virtuous deeds, whose mind is free from bias and partiality, who follows the dictates of justice, who loves and treats his subjects as his own offspring and who, as such, is ever engaged in promoting their interests and their happiness.

17. "He alone deserves to be called as 'subject' who, possessed of excellent qualities and actuated by good motives, delighting the virtuous deeds, free from the influence of prejudice and following the behests of justice, is ever engaged in furthering the happiness of the fellow-subjects and that of his sovereign, whom he regards in

the light of a parent, provided the said sovereign is not an enemy of the empire.

18. "He who always things and judges for himself, who is ever ready to accept truth and reject falsehood, who puts down the unjust but patronizes the just, who has as much regard for the happiness of others as his own - even him I call just.

19. "Devas (gods) are those who are wise and learned; asuras, those who are foolish and ignorant; rakshas, those who are wicked and sin-loving; and pishachas, those whose mode of life is filthy and debasing.

20. "Devapuja (or the worship of the good) consists in showing honor and respect to the wise and learned, to one's father and mother, to the imparters of knowledge, to the itinerant preachers of the true doctrine, to just and impartial sovereigns, to lovers of righteousness, to the women who are chaste and faithful to their husbands, to the men who are devoted and faithful to their wives. The opposite of this is called adevapuja or the worship of demons. To respect the good (as explained and detailed in this para.) is real worship, but he worship of dead, unconscious objects I utterly abhor.

21. "That, of which the fruit is the acquisition of knowledge courteousness and good behavior, uprightness of principle, and purity of thought, which dispels ignorance, -even that is education.

22. The Puranas (ancient commentaries of the Vedas and other works on theology) are the Aitreya Bahmana and similar compositions by the great Rishis like Brahma and others. In Itihas or history I include the kalpa, gatha, and Narashansi. The Bhagvat and other books of that sort are not the puranas '

23. "Tirth is that by means of which the 'sea of pain' is crossed. It consists in truthfulness of speech, in the acquisition of true knowledge, in cultivating the society of the wise and good, in the practice of morality, in contemplating the nature and attributes of the Deity

with concentrated attention, in active benevolence, in the diffusion of education, and so on. Bathing-places, etc., are no tirths.

24. "An energetic and active life is preferable to passive acquiescence in the decrees of fate, inasmuch as destiny is the consequence in the decrees of fate, inasmuch as destiny is the consequence of acts. A life of virtuous activity will secure the Soul a good destiny as a life of wickedness will produce the opposite result. Hence acts, being the maker of destiny, virtuous activity is superior to passive resignation.

25. "The most approved behavior of one man towards his fellow-creatures lies in his treating every one according to his worth, in sympathizing with him, from the core of his joys and sorrows, in his losses and gains. The contrary conduct is reprehensible.

26. "Sanskar or ceremonial is that which contributes to man's physical, mental, and spiritual improvement. The sanskars (ceremonies), from conception to cremation, are sixteen in number. Their due and proper observance is obligatory on all. Nothing should be done for the departed after the remains have been cremated.

27. "The performance of yajna is a most commendable duty. It consists in showing honor and respect to the wise and learned, in the proper application of the principles of the chemistry and physical science to the affairs of life, in the dissemination of knowledge, in the performance, of Agnihotra, which, by contributing to the purification of the air and the healthy growth of vegetables, directly tends to promote the well-being of all sentient creatures.

28. "Aryas are men of exalted principle, the Dasyus those who lead a life of wickedness and sin.

29. "This country is called Aryavarta, because it has been the residence of the Aryas from the very dawn of creation. It is bounded on the north by the Himalayas, on the south by the Vindhya mountains, on the east by the Attak, and on the west by the Brahmputra. The tract

within these limits is alone Aryavarta, and those that have been living in it from times immemorial are Aryas.

30. "He alone is an Acharya who can teach the sciences of the Vedas and their commentaries, who inculcates, both by example and precept, the practice of virtue and the avoidance of what is impure and immoral.

31. "He alone is Shishya (pupil) who has the capacity for assimilating knowledge and grasping truth, whose moral character is unimpeachable, who is eager to learn, and devoted to his teacher.

32. "By the term 'Guru' is meant father or mother. It also applies to all those through whose instrumentality the mind is grounded in truth and weened from falsehood.

33. "He is a Purohita or priest who wishes well to his Yajmans, and preaches to them absolute truth.

34. "An Upadhya or Professor is one who can teach certain portions of the Vedas, or who can teach the Angas.

35. "Shishtachar consists in accepting truth and rejecting untruth, realized and detected after deep and prolonged study, carried on in perfect purity of heart, and after a careful examination of the laws of nature. The man who practices shishtachar is called (gentleman).

36. "I admit the validity of proof based on ocular demonstration, and with it the remaining seven kinds of proofs.

37. "I call him Apt whose veracity is unimpeachable, who is man of pure moral character, and who labors for the good of others.

38. "Those are really principles of truth that can satisfy five tests:

    o They must not militate against nature and attributes of God.

    o They must be in accord with the teachings of the Vedas.

- o They must be in keeping with the well-known eight kinds of proofs based on natural laws.
- o They must be consistent with the thoughts and ways of men of pure lives.
- o They must be approved of by the internal spirit.

Every doctrine must be subjected to these five tests, and accepted if it can satisfy them all.

39. "That is Paropkar or philantrophy which reclaims men from their vices and alleviates their sufferings, which implies them on in the direction of virtue, and thus promotes the general weal.

40. "The Soul is a free agent, - at liberty to act as it pleases, but it is dependent on God for the enjoyment of the fruit of its actions. God is free and independent in dispensing justice and in enforcing every one of His just and righteous law.

41. "Swarga is a prolonged enjoyment of happiness and the possession of things which conduce to this happiness.

42. "Narka means prolonged suffering suffering and everything that contributes to pain and suffering.

43. "Janma or birth is the Soul's assumption of the gross, visible body. Viewed in relation to time its existence is three-fold, viz., past, present and future.

44. "Birth means the union of the Soul with the body, and death their separation.

45. When according to the rules prescribed by the Shastras, a person bestows, as the result of reciprocal affection, his or her hand upon one of the opposite sex and in a public manner, he or she is said to contract marriage.

46. Niyoga is a temporary union of a person with another of the opposite sex belonging to his or her plane or moving in a higher sphere for the raising of issue, when marriage has failed to fulfill its legitimate purpose. It is resorted to in extreme cases, either on the death of

one's consort, or when protracted disease has destroyed productive energy in the husband or wife.

47. "Stuti (or praise) is the enumeration of Divine attributes and qualities, with the view to fix them in the mind and realize their meaning. Among other things it inspires us with love towards God.

48. "Prarthana is praying to God, after one has done his own best, for the gift of knowledge and similar, other blessings which result from a communion with Him. Its principle fruit is humility and serenity of mind.

49. Upasna is conforming uourselves, as far as possible, in purity and holiness to the Divine Spirit. It is feeling the presence of the Deity in the Soul by ther realization of His all-pervading nature. Upsana extends the bounds of our knowledge.

50. "Sagun Stuti is praising God by the enumeration of qualities and attributes which He possesses, but Nirgun Stuti is praising God by those qualities and attributes which are foreign to His nature.

"Sagun Prarthana is praying to God for virtuous qualities; Nirgun Prarthana is imploring the Deity to cast out from us that which is evil.

"Sagun upasna is the realization, in the Soul, of the presence of God as possessing attributes which are inherent in Him, while Nirgun upasna is the realization, in the Soul, of the presence of God as distinct from what is foreign of His nature."

The foregoing summary of Swami Dayanand's beliefs only sums up ;the teaching of the ancient Aryan sages and saints on the subjects with which the "Beliefs" are concerned. Nothing was farther from the great reformer's thoughts than to found a new creed. In the introductory remarks to the 'Beliefs' he says:-

I believe in a religion based on universal and all-embracing principles which have always been admitted as such at present, and which will continue to command the allegiance of mankind in the ages to come. Hence it is that the religion in question is called the primeval eternal religion, which means that it is above the hostility of all human creeds whatsoever. The faith believed in by the ignorant, or by the misguided believers in human creeds, is not worth being accepted by the wise. That faith alone must really be worth being believed in which is followed by men true in thought, word and deed, of philantrophic instincts, just and learned, and of course, all faiths discarded by such men must be considered to be the reverse of authoritative.

"My conception of God and all other things in t he universe is founded on teaching of the Veda and other true Shastras, and is in conformity with the conception of the same transmitted to us by all the sages, from Brahma down to Jaimini, and this conception (being founded on absolute truth), I offer for the acceptance of all good men. My beliefs are the same as are worthy of being accepted by all men in all ages. My object, indeed, is nothing more than that I should believe in truth and make others believe in it, reject falsehood and make others reject it. Had I been biased and bigoted, I would have joined any of the prevailing Indian creeds. But I never did so. On the contrary, I reject what is objectionable and false in the institutions of this or any other country, but to that which is approved by Dharma, I cling, nor will I ever give it up. For a contrary conduct is wholly unworthy of man.

"He is really a man who possesses a sympathetic nature and fully understands what would be conducive to the happiness of others, and what is fraught with pain for them, what would bring them profit and what would cause them loss. Such a man will fear not the cruel, however strong; but his attitude towards the truly virtuous, however weak, will be one of humility. He would always exert himself to the utmost to protect the righteous, and, mindful of their welfare, conduct himself towards them worthily, even though they be feeble and helpless and destitute of external attractions.

"On the other hand, those who are unrighteous, he could constantly strive to disarm and weaken, even though they be powerful princes and affluent in worldly attractions and things. In other words, the man in question should, as far as it lies in his power, perpetually endeavor to undermine the power of the vicious and tyrannical, and to strengthen that of the good and the just. He may have to bear any amount of suffering, he may even to quaff the bitter cup of death in the performance of his duty, but he should not give up his Dharma...

" As already hinted, the Swami's "Beliefs" find their exposition and expansion in all his writings, directly or indirectly, notably in the Satyartha Prakasha and the RigVedadi Bhashya Bhumika, the most popular and the most widely studied of his works, - books which are meant for the masses and which must, in the fullness of time, influence the masses the most. We shall notice these first.

THE SATYARTH PRAKASH

The Satyarth Prakash is divided into two parts, and consists of fourteen chapters in all, the first part comprising ten chapters, and the second four.

THE FIRST CHAPTER is an exposition of the word "OM," the highest, the most expressive and most comprehensive name of the Deity in the world's religious literatures. In the course of the exposition it has been proved, on the authority of Vyakarna, that the words Agni, Vayu, Indra, etc., occurring in the Vedas, are primarily the names of the Supreme Being, expressive of His individual attributes, unlike "Om" which expresses the attributes collectively and in their uttermost perfection.

THE SECOND CHAPTER sets forth the methods which, if followed, would give parents healthy and strong children, and it further lays down rules regarding their "nurture." The greatest possible stress has been laid throughout on the necessity of the father and mother avoiding or doing or saying aught calculated to weaken the infant's mind.

THE THIRD CHAPTER is one Education. It upholds the importance of Brahmacharya and lays down rules which the Brahmacharies and the Brahmacharinies must carry out in the interests of their physical, moral and intellectual development. It refutes the assertion that the Vedas are not for women, and the Shudras, and ends with the following words:- "A country in which Brahmacharya, knowledge and the Vedic Religion receive the attention they deserve, that country is certainly blessed."

THE FOURTH CHAPTER is concerned with marriage and the Grihastha Ashrama. It lays down the rule that the girl a person contemplates marrying should not be within the sixth degree on his mother's side, nor of the gotra of his father, that the bride and the bridegroom should be natives of places distant from each other, one of the eight reasons given in support of the injunction being that the word duhita (daughter), according to the Shastras, means - native of a distant place.

The chapter then specifies the marriageable age for the maiden as well as for the young-man, and the manner in which the marriage ceremony should be conducted. No male should marry till he ahs completed his twenty-fifth year a least, and no female till she is at least sixteen years old. Mutual choice and consent have been declared as indispensable conditions of every marriage. Early-marriage has been denounced as something positively injurious, being destructive of physical, mental and moral vigor and stamina - as the bane of the individual and the curse of nations.

The marriage of virgin-widows has been upheld, and niyoga, on the authority of the Shastras, advocated. The end of marriage has been shown to be the procreation of good offspring, and not the enjoyment of pleasure. It has been incidentally pointed out that real sterling worth alone is the determinator of the individual's social status, and not birth. the five Maha Yajnas (the five daily duties) have been dealt with, and their importance fully pointed out, in the interest of the house holder.

In answer to the question :-

"Is Grihastha Ashrama superior to the other ashramas, or inferior to them?"

The Swami observes that " each ashrama is superior institution when the members thereof faithfully perform their appointed duties," and then adds:

"But as streams, both large and small, keep wandering till they find their rest in the sea, even so the three ashramas are dependent upon the Grihastha Ashrama for support. No ashrama can get on, in any way, without the assistance of this ashrama for it is the Grihastha Ashrama alone that daily, by making gifts to and supplying the Brahmacharis, the Vanprasthis and the Sanyasis with food, etc., contributes towards their maintenance. Hence, one, intensely desirous of securing both worldly happiness and moksha, should enter the Grihastha Ashrama.....Whoever runs down the Grihastha Ashrama, deserves to be denounced himself, but whoever praises it, the same worthy of being praised."

THE FIFTH CHAPTER speaks of the Vanprastha and the Sanyas Ashramas. The duties and responsibilities of both the Vanprasthis and the Sanyansis have been fully explained. It has been pointed out that no Sanyasi deserves the name that does not seek his own highest good in furthering the highest interests of others by preaching truth to them. While the idea that Sanyasis cannot accept gifts has been shown to be erroneous, the fact has been laid stress upon that their attitude towards things worldly, however precious, should be one of perfect indifference. The Brahmans alone can enter the Sanyas Ashrama.

THE SIXTH CHAPTER IS ON "Government." In order that the well-being and prosperity of a government be permanently ensured, there being and prosperity of a government be permanently ensured, there should be three distinct sabhas to carry on its affairs - the Raj Sabha, the Dharma Sabha and Vidya Sabha.

THE SEVENTH CHAPTER is on 'God and the Vedas.' It proves the existence of God, showing that the Vedic conception of God alone is perfect, and it proves the infallibility and eternity of the Vedas by unanswerable arguments.

THE EIGHTH CHAPTER deals with the origin, maintenance and dissolution of the universe. It is a most learned chapter, full of argument.

THE NINTH CHAPTER explains the nature and character of Vidya and Avidya, Bandh and Moksha and for the learning and intellectual depth displayed in the treatment of the subjects, it is fully on a level with the foregoing two chapters.

THE TENTH CHAPTER speaks of conduct, approved and reprehensible, of things that may be eaten and that should not be eaten. The chapter forbids indulgence in flesh-diet.

The remaining CHAPTERS, containing many more pages than the first ten, embody an intensely interesting account of the various creeds prevailing in Aryavarta, and a complete refutation of whatever there is un-Vedic or false and misleading in them

THE RIGVEDADI BHASHYA BHUMIKA

is a Sanskrit-Hindi work. It is an invaluable and scholarly Introduction to the Veda-Bhashya, pointing out the lofty and sublime character of the Vedic Teachings and showing how the germs of all sciences are to be found in the Vedas. The Introduction shows how the latter-day commentaries by Sayana, Mahidhar and others, Indians or Europeans, are utterly misleading and false, and justifies the need of a fresh commentary, based entirely on the ancient Niruktak system of interpretation.

We shall give quotations:-

The Divine origin of the Vedas:

1. "From that adorable Yajna have proceeded the Righ and Sama; from Him have proceeded the Chhandansi; and from Him has proceeded the Yaju." - (Yaju Chapter 31, Mantra 7)
2. "He from whom the Rig has sprung, He from whom the Yaju, has sprung, like unto whose loma is the Sama, and like unto whose mouth is the Atharva Angiras, - what is He like? Him thou declare. Reply - Know that He is Skamba." - Atharva.

From Him, the adorable, from Him who is true, all-knowledge, all-happiness, and so forth, - the Perfect Being, who ought to be the object of universal homage, and should be worshipped by all, - yes, from this almighty par Brahma have proceeded all the four Vedas, - the Rig Veda, the Yajur Veda, the Sama Veda, and the Atharva Veda. Even this is to be believed. The term Sarvahut may also appropriately be applies to the Vedas. The Vedas are sarvahut, for they are worthy of being accepted and received by all men. The object of the two verbs Jajinire and ajayat (in this mantra) is to show that the Vedas contain numerous sciences, and the repetition of the word tasmat is also to convince man that they are of Divine origin. Inasmuch as the Vedas have in them Gayatri and the other Chhandas the word Chhandansi, in the mantra, indicates the Divine origin of the fourth Veda - the Atharva. Even this is to be believed. "Yajna" is verily the Vishnu." - (Shathpatha Kand 1, Chapter 1.)

"Vishnu made this universe, and disposed the things (therein or thereof) in a three-fold order." (This is to be found in the Yajur Veda.) The creation of this universe can be predicated of God only and of none other. "He who pervades both the animate and inanimate creation, He is Vishnu, the Supreme Being." The Almighty from whom the Rig Veda has proceeded, the Great God by whom the Yajur Veda has been revealed, the Being from whom the Sama Veda and the Atharva Veda have sprung, - the Atharva being like unto His mouth, the Sama like unto His lomas (hairs on the body), the Yaju like unto His heart, and Rig like unto His vital airs (figuratively), - He from whom all the four Vedas have come forth:- what is this Deva like? - Declare Him unto me." This is the question. The answer is "He is Skamba," the supporter of the whole universe; other than this Deva (supporter of the universe) the author of the Vedas is none. Even this is to be believed.

"The Rig Veda, the Sama Veda, the Yajur Veda and the Atharva Veda, are the out-breathings of that Great Being:- (Shatapatha, Kand 14, Chapter 5).

To make this clearer : -"Maitriyi," says Yajnavalkya, "By Him, who encompasses even Sapce, the Righ Veda as the other Vedas - all four of them - are breathed forth, without effort, even as breath is exhaled without effort." Even this is be believed. Just as the vital air issuing from the body is again drawn into it, even so are the Vedas breathed out and (finally) breathed in by God. This is certain.

On this subject many people say:- "How can the Vedas, which are embodied in words, have proceeded from God, who is incorporeal and without parts? We reply: Such an objection cannot hold good when urged against an almighty God. Why? Because, even in the absence of mouth, the pranas (vital airs) and other appliances, the power to do His work is ever manifest in the Supreme Being.

And even as in the mind of man, when absorbed in silent thought, words embodying questions in answers are pronounced, even such must be believed to be the case with God also. He who is, beyond doubt, almighty, He never takes anyone's help in doing His work. We cannot do our work without the help of others, but such is not the case with God. When He, though incorporeal and without parts, made the whole world, then how can a person doubt His having made the Vedas? Yes, how? When in the world itself things extraordinary and marvelous to match the revealing of the Vedas have been done by Him. Man had to be taught from the very beginning.

(Pravadi) - Undoubtedly, no one but God has, of a surety, the power to create the universe, but one can have the power to produce the Vedas like other works produced by men.

(Vadi) - We reply: The power in man to produce any work whatsoever is possible only after he ahs read the Vedas, the production of God, and in no other way. Even at present nobody can become wise and learned till he has read something or listened to (what the wise say). Knowledge comes to men by a study of the Shastras, however slight and partial, through oral instruction, and by observing dealings of man with man.

For example, if a person (as soon as born) were removed to an isolated and secluded (though a safe place), and though regularly supplied with food and drink, etc., were never spoken or talked to by his guardians down to the hour of his death - such a person would have absolutely sure and certain knowledge of anything. And further, as people inhabiting some immense forest have all the instincts and ways of brutes, even such instincts and ways would all mankind have retained from the beginning of creation to the present time if the Vedas had not been revealed to them. To have produced a book under these circumstances is out of the question.

(Skeptic) - Don't say such a thing. God has given men intuitive knowledge, and that is better than any book. Without this knowledge it is impossible even to understand the connection between the words of the Vedas and what they connote. By improving and developing this intuitive knowledge men can produce books too. Why, then, should one believe that the Vedas are the Word of God?

(Believer) - if this is your objection, we reply to it thus: has not God given intuitive knowledge to the aforesaid child (whom we have supposed as brought up away from the haunts of men, and without any education), and has not He given the same knowledge to the people whom we have supposed as occupying the recesses of the vast forest? Why can't anyone of us become a Pandit without studying the Vedas, and without receiving instruction from others? What does all this lead to? To the conclusion, that mere intuitive knowledge won't do unless it is improved and supplemented by study and by instruction from without.

As we write books only by means of the knowledge we gain from our contact with the wise and learned and through their works, even so do mankind require (in the beginning of creation) the Divine knowledge (to get on in the world). Indeed, there being no books nor any system of education in the beginning, it was impossible, in the very nature of things, for anyone to acquire knowledge, if God had not vouchsafed his "knowledge" to the human race. How could under these circumstances, any man have produced a book? For, as far as acquired knowledge is concerned, man is dependent upon others for it; and mere intuitive knowledge can never enable him to become wise and learned.

And as regards the assertion that intuitive knowledge is better (than anything else, - this asserting too, is not based on truth. For intuitive knowledge, like the eye, is a means through which something is accomplished. Even as the eye is useless without the help of mind, even so is intuitive knowledge useless without help of the wise teachers and of Divine Knowledge.

(Prativadi): - What object has God in revealing the Vedas? This I want to be explained here to me.

(Vadi): ~ We answer by a counter-question: What object would it have served, if God had not revealed the Vedas?

(Prativadi): - I don't know.

(Vadi): ~ You may truly say this. You may now learn, by all means, what object God had in revealing the Vedas. Is, or is not, knowledge in God infinite?

(Prativadi): - Yes, it is infinite.

(Vadi): ~ For what purpose is this Knowledge?

(Prativadi): - For his own individual purposes.

(Vadi): ~ Is not God beneficient, and does not He do good to others?

(Prativadi): - He is, and does good to others. What then?

(Vadi): ~ Only this, that knowledge always exists for the benefit of him who possesses it, as well as for that of others. This is the two-fold object of knowledge. If God did not vouchsafe His Revelation unto us, His knowledge would become useless and abortive in reference to the second object of knowledge. Hence it was that He made His knowledge fruitful by revealing the Vedas. The infinitely merciful God is like unto a father. As a father ever does kind offices unto his children, even so God, in His infinite mercy, preaches His knowledge unto all men. Otherwise in consequence of ignorance and barbarism transmitted from age to age people would find it impossible to realize dharma, artha, kama, and moksha, and, hence, would be shut out from the enjoyment of supreme bliss. When the merciful God ahs created roots, fruits, etc., for the enjoyment and happiness of His subjects, how could He - bestower of perfect happiness, the embodiment of all knowledge - have left out revealing the "Veda Vidya" unto them? The happiness, which man can derive from the possession of the most enjoyable things in the universe, cannot come up even to a thousandth part of that which the possession of knowledge gives. It follows from all this that God is the author of the Vedas, and even this must be believed in.

(Prativadi): - Where did God get pen and ink and other necessary things to write the Vedas with?

(Vadi): ~ We reply: You have certainly brought forward a great objection. Just as God made this world without the help of hands and other parts of the body, and without wood, iron, and the like materials, even so He revealed the Vedas. You should never have raised the objection you have against an almighty God in reference to the revealing of the Vedas. The Vedas reveled in the beginning of creation were not, however, in the form of books.

(Prativadi): -

(Vadi): ~ (Prativadi): - How, then did God reveal them?

(Vadi): ~ He communicated them through the mind.

(Prativadi): - Through whose mind

(Vadi): ~Through the minds of Agni, Vayu, Aditya and Angiras.

(Prativadi): - All these things are dead and inert, and devoid of reason.

(Vadi): ~ Don't say such a thing. They were corporeal beings-men - in the beginning of creation.

(Prativadi): - How do you make this out?

(Vadi): ~ Because inanimate objects are incapable of thought-work. The sense in which anything is taken in any particular place is according to the context. For instance, if a person were to say to anther: "The couches are making a noise," the word "couches" here would be taken mean the "occupiers of couches." Even so must we interpret (Aditya, etc.) when we speak of them (as the recipients of Veda knowledge)."Knowledge" can be imparted only to rational men. In support of (Aditya, etc., having been men), we have the authority.

To these practisers of austerities the three Vedas were revealed: the Rig Veda was revealed through Agni; the Yajur Veda through Vayu; and the Sama through Surya - (Shatapatha, Kand 11 chapter 5)

God communicated the knowledge, termed the Veda, to these men, and through them made it known to all.

(Pravadi) - Your right. But to me it seems that God gave these persons knowledge, and by means of this knowledge they produced the Vedas.

(Vadi) ~ Don't believe any such thing. What kind of knowledge did He impart unto these men?

(Pravadi) - The knowledge termed 'the Veda'.

(Vadi) ~ Is this knowledge God's or of the men (to whom it was imparted)?

(Pravadi) - It is God's.

(Vadi) ~ Then who made the Vedas, God or they?

(Pravadi) - He made them whose knowledge the Vedas are.

(Vadi) ~ Then why did you raise the objection that those men made them?

(Pravadi) - To find out the truth. Is God impartial or partial?

(Vadi) ~ Impartial.

(Pravadi) - Then why did He reveal the Vedas to the minds of these four persons only and not the minds of all men?

(Vadi) ~ We reply: God's having imparted His "knowledge" to the minds of these four persons only cannot make Him guilty of the slightest partiality. On the contrary, this is a proof positive of the absolute impartiality of that just Being. For impartiality (or Justice) means rewarding everyone according to the merits of his deeds. And thus you must know that it was only these four persons who, in consequence of the consummate excellence and purity of their actions deserved to be imparted the knowledge of the Vedas.

(Pravadi) - The Veda was reveled in the beginning of creation; where did this excellence and purity of their previous actions come from (for as yet they had done no actions)?

(Vadi) ~ We answer: The souls are all eternal in their own essential nature, while their actions, as well as this entire visible universe, are, in consequence of the regularity of their succession, also eternal.

(Pravadi) - Are Gayatri nd othe Chhandas (metrical texts of the Vedas) also the work of the Divine Mind?

(Vadi) ~ How could a doubt like this spring up in your mind? Has not God the knowledge to produce the Gayatri Chhandas?

(Pravadi) - Certainly He has, for He is all knowledge.

(Vadi) ~ Hence your doubt is groundless.

(Pravadi) - The 'four-mouthed' Brahma originated the Vedas, - even so says itihas (history).

(Vadi) ~ Don't say such a thing, for the validity and genuineness of itihas depends on Shabadpraman and 'Shabda' is what an Apta inculcates and teaches (Nyaya Shastra), Chapter 1, aphorism 7th). Even this is what the sage Gautama says. The sage also says that shabda is itihas. On this subject Vatsayana, in the Mahabhashya, says:- "Apta is verily he who has completely and thoroughly realized and felt (in the inmost recesses of this conscious soul) the significance and glory of Dharma (truth, purity, etc.). To realize and fell in practice and sense and meaning of what a teacher has found (a virtuous principle or doctrine) to signify, with the view to make this sense and meaning known to others when the experiment is over, is called Apti, and he whom this quality exist is called Apta.

Hence itihas means what embodies facts and truths, and not falsehood. Consequently, that which has been inculcated and taught by an Apta and is true and worthy of respect, that alone deserves to be received by man (as itihas), and not what which is the opposite of it. For an evil-minded man only says what is false and untrue. Also the assertion, that Vyas Rishi originated the Vedas is unfounded, because of the worthless character of the Puranas and Tantras which assert such a thing.

(Pravadi) - Why should not we hold that the rishi, whose name heads any particular mantra or sukta, is the originator thereof?

(Vadi) ~Don't say such a thing; for, Brahma and othe such sages, too, have studied and been taught theVedas. Says the Shwetashwatara Upanishad:-

"He creates Brahma in the beginning of creation, and preaches the Vedas."

Even when the Rishis (whose names head the mantras and suktas) were not yet in existence, even at that time the Vedas were with Brahma and others:- "From Agni, Vayu and Aditya the three eternal Vedas - known as Rig, Yaju, and Sama - were milked."

Manu and:- "The boy Angiras taught the Vedas to his elders," even so says Manu (Chapter II). When even Brahma read and studied the Vedas with Agni, etc., how could Vyas have originated them?

OF WHAT IS VEDA THE NAME?

(Pravadi) - Now to what is the name Veda applies?

(Vadi) ~ To the mantra bhaga only, is our reply.

(Pravadi) - Why do you not, according to the saying of Katya ana, that the name Veda is applicable to the mantras and Brahmanas alike, accept the name Veda for the Brahmana bhag as well?

(Vadi) ~ Don't say so. The Brahmanas cannot be called the Veda.

(Pravadi) - Why?

(Vadi) ~ Because the Brahmanas are called the Puranas (histories); because they are the expositions of the Vedas; because they are the compositions of the Rishis (sages), and not the Words of God; because the Rishis, Katyayana only excepted, have refused the name Veda, to the Brahmanas and because they are the productions of mortals. The histories of men which the Brahamanas contain - these histories are not to be found in the Vedas.

(Pravadi) - Brother! Texts like:-

Treble the age tha is of Jamdagni, the treble the age that is of Kashyapa, the treble the age that is of the sages, even that treble the age be ours, bearing the seal of the names of rishis are to be seen in the Yajurvedada, and in the other Vedas. Then, why do you refuse to give the name 'Veda to the 'Brahmanas' also?

(Vadi) ~ Don't labor under such delusion. Here the words Jamdagni and Kashyapa are not the names of individuals or corporeal beings. On this there are the authorities:- [Kashyapa is koorma, which means the vital airs - the pranas]

Hence koorma and kashyapa are the names of the vital airs (pranas), because of their tortoise-like form in the regions of the navel. With the mantra God alone is worshipped and praised. It means :- "By Thy grace, O Lord, may our eyes (jamdagni) and our pranas (kashyapa), attain treble the usual age -i.e., last for a period of three hundred years."

[The word chakshu (eye) stands here, figuratively, for all the external organs, and the pranas for the internal organs (mind, etc.)]

Yaddeveshu tryayusham" - on this part of the mantra there is the pramana.

[Even the wise are the devas.]

Hence the wise are called the devas. The meaning:-

"The treble the age which the wise attain to by virtue of their knowledge (tanno astu tryayusham) even that, with the physical organs and the mind, sound and yielding righteous enjoyment, be ours, so that enjoying felicity we may live this treble the age."

[The eye is the Jamdagni rishi, because with the eye man sees and understands this world. Hence the eye is the jamdagni rishi.]

Hence the sotires which Sanyanacharya and other have related in their commentaries on the Veda, should be looked upon as the outcome of delusion. Even this should be looked upon as the outcome of delusion. Even this should be believed.

[After this the Swami proceeds to show, on the authority of Yaska, Panini, Vatsyayana and others that the Vedas are the mantra bhaga only, and do not include the Brahmanas, and in conclusion answers the question, 'Should the Brahmanas be regarded as authoritative as the Veda?' thus:-]

It is not proper to regard the Brahmanas as authoritative as the Vedas , for the Brahmanas do not come from God. Of course they are to be regarded authoritative so far as their teaching is in conformity with that of the Vedas. Hence they should be regarded as secondarily or dependently authoritative only. The Vedic conception of God.

(Pravadi) - Are, or are not, all the sciences contained in the Vedas?

(Vadi) ~ The germs or principles of al sciences are to be found in the Vedas. Of these sciences Brahmavidya (science of theology) is the first and foremost of all sciences. We shall notice it briefly here in the Rig Veda:- "We invoke the protection of Parmeshwara(the Supreme Being), who is the Maker of the whole universe, the Lord and Master of the stationary and the moving, and the illuminator of the intellect. He bestows strength and energy upon all, and is our support. O lord! Thou are the increaser of knowledge, wealth, prosperity, etc. Do thou, in Thy mercy, guard and sustain us."

"He who is the most exalted of all, who is worthy of being adored by all, who pervades the entire universe, the Omniscient Being, who supports the firmament, who survives the dissolution of the world into its primary atoms even He is Brahm. The vasus and other devatas (i.e., the entire universe) are supported by Him, even as trunk supports the spreading boughs" - (Atharva, Book 10th, Chapter 23, mantra 38.)

"There is only the One Supreme Being - there is neither second, nor third, nor fourth, nor fifth, nor sixth, nor seventh, nor eighth, nor ninth, nor yet tenth Deity." - (Athrva,Kand 13, chapter 4, Mantras, 16 - 18 and 20 - 21)From these mantras it is clear that God is one and that there no other besides Him - not second god, no third god, no fourth god, no fifth God, no sixth god, no seventh god, no eighth god, no ninth god, neither any tenth god. By means of these nine negatives, commencing from the figure "2" and carrying he calculation up to the knot the existence of God has been declared, and the existence of a God other than Him has been utterly denied. For this reason the worship of aught else than one God had been totally condemned.

"He, the Supreme Being, pervades the entire universe even as space. He is on infinite might and the creator of all. He is incorporeal and exempt from birth and death. He is indivisible and impenetrable by the minutest conceivable object. He is free from the bonds of nerves and muscles. He is wholly absolutely above ignorance. He is free from sin and every sinful desire.

He is omniscient and privy to our in most thoughts. He presides over all, in self-existent and the efficient cause of the universe. He imparts His knowledge to His eternal subjects in the beginning of every creation." - (Yajurveda, Chapter XL, mantra 8.)

THE VEDIC DHARMA

The Vedic teaching in reference to Dharma shall be set forth briefly. The Supreme Being declares in the Rig Veda:

"(Sangachhadhwam) O morals! The dharma which has been declared by Me, which is characterized by justice, is devoid of partiality, which is distinguished for its true qualities, - even this dharma do ye accept and embrace. (Samvadadhwam) in other words, having given up all mutual differences and dislikings for the acquisition of this dharma, do ye be united with the other, to the end that your true joys may ever be on the increase, and your pain and suffering may be destroyed. (Samvo manansi janatam). Being united with each other, had having given up idle and fruitless controversies and disputations, do ye discuss among yourselves, in all love and charity, (on subjects affecting your welfare) by the agency of questions and answers, so that (by means of such discussions) true knowledge may go n steadily increasing among you, in the most commendable manner.

"Do ye develop your thinking faculty, do ye exert yourselves in the most befitting manner, to the end that your minds may become affluent in knowledge. Or, which is one and the same thing, ye should make such a use of your energy and resources that it may fill your minds with a sense of joyful tranquility and peace. Ye should always follow and act up to the dictates of dharma, an not to those of that which constitutes adharma (ignorance).

"In connection with this an illustration shall be given: (Deva bhagam yatha, etc.) As your predecessors, having became men of exalted knowledge before you, are doing their work in life, or have quitted the word's stage; - just as they worship the Being who possesses the attributes of omnipotence, etc., and just as they follow and act up to the dharma declared by me, even like them does it behove you to conform your lives to the same dharma, to the end that the dharma declared by the Veda the Veda may become known (to all)."

"(Samano mantrah, etc.) O mortals! Let your mantra [that exercise of the intellectual faculties through which, by the agency of speech or preaching, a knowledge of all objects with their powers and properties, manifest or latent - of all objects from me, the Creator, down to the earth - is acquired] be alike, equally weighty, and free from all antagonism. When many people getting together would deliberate over matters in respect of which there are doubts, the individual opinions all that is best and essential, calculated to promote the well-being of all sentient beings and distinguished for its absolute truthfulness, that should be chosen and thoroughly known, - to be laid up in the mind to regulate each unit's practical life, to the end that it may make him more happy day by day.

"(Samitih samani) Let yoru social code or maryada [that which inculcates justice, which gives importance and knowledge to man, which renders the observance of brahmacharya, the acquisition of learning and sciences and the attainment of good qualities possible, which provides, through legislative bodies, for good government and so forth, which guides aright one's temporal and spiritual affairs, which increases the strength and health of body and mind - even that constitutes social code or maryada be good and the same: in other words, it should be perfectly uniform, to the end that it may add to the happiness of all by bestowing upon them the blessings of liberty and independence. (Samanam mahah) Let your minds be free from mutual antagonism, and harmonious. Let your chitta (the power which recollects things done in the past and meditates on the Creator] be the same. In other words, ye should exert yourselves for the destruction of the pain of all sentient beings and for the augmentation of their happiness.

"(Sah, etc.) Ye must exert yourselves to the utmost to do good and to be useful to all.

(Esham etc.,) Those of you who, in their dealings with all sentient beings, care for their welfare as they would do for the welfare of their own souls, unto them - the benevolent and the augmenters of the happiness of others, I am gracious and (abhimantriye vah etc.,). I desire you all to follow the dharma already declared. Even so should all of you do to the end that truth may never become extinct among you nor untruth prosper.

(Samanena vo) The gifts that ye receive from others, and those that ye present them with - these also must be regulated according to the behest of dharma. Hence I unite you each with the other by a universal dharma, and therefore, dharma that has been declared by Me, even that ye should observe and follow, and naught else than that."

O mortals, the energy and strength that is in you, the same in its fullness, having been made amenable to dharma and mutually harmonious and concordant, do ye employ in promoting the general well-being.

"(Samani va' etc.) Let your enthusiasm and your good and righteous ways, by virtue of advancing the weal of each other, contribute to the happiness of all. In whatever way the dharma preached by Me be preserved from extinction even so should ye proceed.

"(Samana hridyana vah) Let all those actions of yours which are connected with the heart, this is which have to do with the mind, be characterized with profound love, calculated to bring about and establish harmony and concordant and harmonious.

(Samananmastu vo manah). Let the mind, which is distinguished by the possession of all these things, be harmonious in all."

"(Yatha vah susahansati, etc.) O mortals! Ye should so proceed and exert yourselves that your actions, assisting mutual co-operation may contribute to the well-being of all, and ye should seek your own happiness in the happiness of others. Ye must not by joyful when other are unhappy; on the contrary, ye must act as to enable everyone to be independent and happy."

"(Drishtva, etc. Prajapath, the Supreme Being, declares the Dhaama: all men should ever have perfect faith in truth and disbelief in untruth.

(Prajapatih styanrite rupe, etc.) The Lord, by means of his omniscience, differentiated Truth from Falsehood or Virtue from non-Virtue, each distinguished by its attributes hidden and manifest. How? To this is the answer; He planted in the constitution and nature of all men an abhorrence of Untruth, non-Virtue and Injustice; In other words, - He enjoined disbelief in adharma (non-virtue). Similarly, the all-knowing Prajapatih, the Supreme Being, enjoined belief in truth se forth in the Shastras, and in Justice and Virtue, tested and proved by ocular demonstration and so forth, and free from all tinge of bigotry and prejudice. Hence, it behoves all men to keep their minds firmly fixed on dharma and totally estranged from adharma."

"(Drite Drinha, etc.) All men should deal kindly and affectionately by one another, in every possible way and on all occasions. All men should accept and follow the dharma (system of faith) declared by the Lord, and to Him they should ever pray, so that they may learn to love dharma. O Lord, the destroyer of pain in all its phases, have mercy on me, to the end that I may know the true faith.

(Mitrasya, etc.) With their minds free from all prejudice, and with hearts pure, let all men see in me a friend; in other words, let them retard me as their friend.

(Drinha, etc) With my mind filled with this laudable desire, make me constantly richer and richer in truth and in exalted qualities.

(Mitrasyaham, etc.) Similarly, may I, O Lord, with my understanding permeated with love and the eye of a friend (sarvani bhutani, etc.) see all sentient beings rightly and well.

(Mitrasya chakshusha, etc) Even so may we all see each other with the eye of a friend, free from ill-will, and so conduct ourselves one with the other, that it may lead to the furtherance of mutual good."

Let us all practice tapa. Tapa means:- "To worship Brahma only, and to acquire true knowledge; to speak truth and act truthfully; to hear and preach true knowledge; to prevent the mind from doing evil, and to set it to the performance of duty; to employ the organs and senses in Dharma, and to prevent them from taking a wrong course; to control the mind and to make it intent upon Dharma, to disseminate true knowledge under all circumstances."

"Also, O man, thou shouldst worship and believe the omnipresent, all-pervading Brahma only and naught else. To speak truth and to act truthfully is the most essential condition of Dharma, because it is truth only through which man obtains happiness and Moksha and through which he never falls from the pedestal.

All men should, therefore, practise righteousness. They should practice Dharma as directed (in the mantra commencing with rita). Similarly they should acquire knowledge by observing Brahmacharya, and should employ their wealth in disseminating knowledge and other virtues. Contemplation is the characteristic of the wise and learned. The wind blows through satya (truth). The sun shines through satya. Men are respected for righteousness and satya.

The wise know God by purifying their mental faculties and thus do they acquire happiness."

The following further injunctions may be given in this connection from the Taittiriya Aranyaka:-

"Men should acquire knowledge and continue the study of the Vedas and other Shastras; they should speak the truth, believe in truth and study the Vedas, etc.; they should observe Brahmacharya; they should keep their organs and passions under control; they should always keep the mind and soul intent upon the performance of Dharma (virtuous deeds); they should acquire Dharma; Artha, Kama and Moksha through the help of the Vedas, fire, etc.; they should perform Agnihotra daily and thus purify air, water, etc., should honor and serve wise men who may happen to visit them, should manage human affairs properly, should educate their children and subjects well, should beget children by paying due regard to bodily strength, and should pay due attention to the health of children."

[The frequent occurrence of the word Swadhyaya pravachane in the different parts of the above passage is to show that the study of the Vedas is incumbent under all the twelve kinds of circumstances.]

[Rathitaracharya is of opinion that the practice of truth and study of Vedas alone constitute Dharma. Paurusheshti holds the observance of Brahmacharya and the study of the Vedas as the only Dharma. Maudgalya alias Nak gives preference to the study of the Vedas.]

The acharya, teaching the Vedas, should instruct his pupils as below during the course of, and after the completion of, instruction, _

"Speak the truth; observe Dharma and attend to the dictates of Duty.

"Do not neglect the study of Vedas, etc. After having pleased your teacher by valuable gifts, take to grihastha and beget children. You should never disregard Dharma, should always strive to better yourself, should never give up righteous ambition, should never be lazy in the study of the Vedas, should never give up Deva Kriyas and Pitri Kriyas, i.e., should always perform the duty towards the wise and the elders.

"Worship your mother, father and the atithis.

"You should do only good actions and not other than these. You should imitate only such of our actions as are good, and not those that are otherwise. those that are virtuous amongst us are Brahmans, then you should trust. You should give them things as best you can, you should give them presents out of respect or shame, fear, or promise.

"If you have any doubts about my actions, you should do as wise and virtuous Brahmans do in similar circumstances, - you should act according to the dictates of wise and virtuous Brahmans. This is the advice, this is the exhortation, this is the injunction of the Vedas, these are the instructions they embody. You should observe these and obey these."

"God can be known through truth, righteousness, Brahmacharya, and knowledge. He the Fountain-head of light and wisdom, is visible within themselves to sages whose passions are completely under subjection and who are free from vice.

"Victory is always to truthfulness. If true, a man always comes off triumphant, but if not true and not a follower of true Dharma, defeat is his fate. (The wise man's path of eternal bliss and Moksha, is so called because of its truthfulness.) It is by that path of truth and virtue that the sages attain to their object and reach Brahma, the Fountain-head of truth and Dharma, and reaching Him acquire eternal bliss and Moksha, and not otherwise.

"All men should therefore follow true Dharma and avoid untruth and adharma. (chodana) The Dharma taught by the Vedas is the only true Dharma as it is free from untruth and unrighteousness, and deserving of being termed Dharma. That prohibited by God and deserving of being termed Dharma. That prohibited by God should be considered improper and shunned by all men as adharma.

"(Yatobhyu) Dharma is that the observance of which grants worldly happiness and Moksha, and that which does not fulfill these conditions is adharma. This also is the teaching of the Vedas.

"God has taught Dharma to all mankind in many other similar mantras in the Vedas. All men should understand that this is their only Dharma, and none else."

3

Birth and Early Life

EARLY YEARS

Swami Dayanand was born at Tankara (Morvi), a town situated on the bank of the Machhooka Mahanadi, IN Kathiawar (Gujrat), in the Vikram era 1881 (1825 A.D.). His original name was Mool Shankar, and his father's Karsanji.

He was the head of an eminent Brahman family of the village and was rich, prosperous and influential. Karsanji was in service, holding the position of Jamadar, which office was hereditary in his family. The post of Jamadar was one of great responsibility, being much like a Tehsildarhip, the principal duty of its incumbent was the realization of State revenue. Karsanji had under him a number of sepoys to assist him in the discharge of his duties. The family over which he presided had lands of its own, and the income from these was largely supplemented by the interest on sums regularly lent to the neighbours in need of money.

We are told that Karsanji was man of stern disposition, having no faith in half measures. When he set his heart upon doing a thing, or when duty called upon him to undertake anything, he would set about his task with a will, and would not rest till it was accomplished, or till it was proved that, for some reason or other, it was in spite of the best he could do, impossible of accomplishment. He was a religious man, almost austere in life, and so thoroughly orthodox and uncompromising was he in is views, that slightest departure from the practices and observances which his faith enjoyed, was, in his opinion, unwarranted and deserving or lacked sympathy with his fellow-creatures at large: he had a large share of both; but, when anybody crossed him in anything or criticized his doctrine, he had, for the time being, and perhaps for many days to come, nothing but contempt and hatred for the offender, and thought that he had no title whatever to his love and his good offices.

Dayanand's mother, on the other hand, was, like the mother of Nanak, nothing but a personification of patience, gentleness and sweetness. While her love for her child was unbounded, she had a genuine kindly feeling for all around her, ready to share their sorrows and to participate in their joys on all occasion. She was an ideal Hindu woman, unlettered no doubt, but the soul of simplicity, purity and goodness, a veritable queen of the "home".

From such parents had Dayanand descended, and it was therefore but natural that while he had, on the one hand, the immutable resolves of his father, on the other, he possessed a heart embracing the whole world in its circle of sympathy.

Dayanand was five years old when his education commenced and this is the age at which, according to the Shastras, a child should be put to his letters, by his own parents if possible. He proved and extraordinary apt pupil, passing from one elementary book to another in rapid succession. In his eighth year his Yajnopavita Sanskara was performed, and the investiture with thread of the "twiceborn" was forthwith followed by his initiation into the sandhya and upasna. Karsanji though a Samavedi Brahman, was a follower of Shiva, and as such he taught his son, Rudri, following it by the Samhita. No pains were spared to impress Dayanand with the sacredness and superiority of the Shaiv faith, and the importance of keeping of the fasts peculiar to the creed was continually made clear to him. The worship of Shiva, as the supreme, unapproachable deity, was specially insisted upon, and, in order that the deity might be always close by, it was hinted that a clay image of him could serve the purpose just as well as one made of stone or metal: the father's intention being that Dayanand could have a fresh idol as often as he pleased and should worship it daily without fail.

When Dayanand had reached his tenth year, he was fairly regular in his adoration of Shiva, but beyond paying this homage at stated hours, he did not concern himself much with Shaivism. The father, however, was not to be satisfied with this much. He was always for his observing the more rigorous fasts his elders kept, for his hearing the katha and for keeping long and trying vigils at night. The mother might protest that the boy was unequal to the hardship sought to be imposed upon him, that it was physically impossible for him to bear so much strain; yet the father was not to be easily dissuaded from his purpose. With all the allowance he made for his tender years, as result of the loving mother's pleadings no doubt, he would take him frequently into Shaiva temples to see what was going on there, and he would never visit a brother in faith but Dayanand was with him, to listen to what the men had to say about the excellence of the Shaivism. Whatever disappointment the father might have experienced on seeing Dayanand not up to the mark in austerity, he must have felt more than compensated for the disagreeable feeling by the progress which Dayanand was making in learning. By the time Dayanand was fourteen years of age, he knew the whole of the Yajur Veda Samhita by heart, some portions of the remaining three Vedas and some minor works on Sanskrit grammar. He understood but little (as also his father) of what he could repeat, but even is oral knowledge was worth much: it was to prove of service later on.

The fast of Shivatri approached, and now that Dayanand was his fourteenth year, there was absolutely no reason, said his father, why he should not keep it. Dayanand was at first reluctant to comply with his father's wishes, but when the katha, setting forth the meritoriousness of the fast, was recited to him, he consented.

The mother strongly protested against her son being subjected to such a trial, saying that if he went without his usual morning breakfast and remained without food for the rest of the day and the night following, he would fall ill; but her expostulations were of no avail. Karsanji was bent upon having his way, and so the fast had to be kept. As the evening set in, the father and son went to large Shaiva temple outside the village, where the rules in connection with the worship of the presiding deity of the sacred shrine were duly explained to him. One of the injunctions was that the devotee who kept the fast of Shivratri, must remain awake the whole night, as otherwise the fast would bear no fruit. Dayanand found the temple fairly crowded with worshippers and priests, some in a state of excitement, while others sober, silent and thoughtful. Presently, the worship began with the chanting of hymns, to which many of the laymen present cheerfully joined in singing.

The first quarter of the night passed off very well, the entire congregation remaining awake and displaying all the fervor and enthusiasm which could be expected of them. In the second quarter the proceedings became less animating, but the majority continued to keep awake and go one with the rites. As soon, however, as the third quarter came, the devotees seemed to have well nigh exhausted and were unable any further to resist sleep. Nodding of heads was visible all around, and one man after vainly endeavoring to battle with drowsiness and after fruitlessly exhorting his neighbor not to give in so easily, stretched himself, at full length, on the floor and commenced snoring heavily.

Dayanand's father was one of the batch which was the first to fall asleep, nor were the priests long in following his example. Finding that the dread Jamada was "safe," they stole out of the temple and lying down were soon ranging free in the land of dreams, though and lying down were soon ranging free in the land of dreams, though more nervous of them, no doubt, now and then found themselves suddenly deprived of their newly-acquired freedom by the sight of the apparition of their stern village official.

Dayanand was surprised at the scant respect which these worshippers of Shiva seemed to have for the fast by practically going against their professions, but he was determined that nothing should induce him to lose the reward which his leaders had deliberately forfeited. To prevent himself, therefore, from dropping into a slumber, he took to vigorously sprinkling water over his eyes, and to thinking. While thus employed, he saw something that drew him out of his abstraction and riveted his attention on itself.

A mouse creeping out of its hole began to take liberties with the image of Shiva, and make free with the offerings which had come to it from the worshippers. For many moments the boy watched the doings of the little creature, possibly amused a little, but serious thoughts followed, and he mused: "Is this the Mahadeva whom the katha represented as deity with human shape, with a trident in his hand and playing upon the drum - the God who bestows a boon upon one and pronounces a curse upon another, and who is the Lord of the Kailash mountain? This image has not the power to drive away even an insignificant mouse from its presence!"

Dayanand thought long and hard and intently, and this thinking laid the foundation of that great, all-embracing religious revolution which he subsequently wrought in the land of his birth. Thousands upon thousands of men and women remain awake the whole night of the 13th of Magh, but who ever sees the deity which is the object of his or her adoration or receives the reward which he or she aspires? Shiva, the real, all-pervading and all-powerful beneficent Being who rules the Universe, did, however, answer the prayers of a child, saying, "The boon sought after shall be thine, but here is work for thee to do, and that must be done before thou can reach thy goal.

Study the primeval Veda and enrich thyself with knowledge and wisdom, and, by means of these, bring thy brethren back to the adoration of one and the only true Lord of the creation, tearing them away from the worship of the created inanimate thing." Dayanand's soul heard the words and took in the inspiration in a vague, dreamy, half-conscious fashion, to be realized and worked out in the gradually increasing light and enlightenment of coming years.

The late Sir Sayyad Ahmad, referring to Dayanand's reflections, skeptical in a sense no doubt, but like the intensely dark moments heralding the approach of happy dawn of light and life, turn his face from idolatry and seek out had study those portions of the Vedas which are concerned with the unity of the formless, self-effulgent God and with His other attributes?"

The question, " Is this shapeless stone the Mahadeva?" again and again pressed it self upon Dayanand's mind, but no satisfactory answer was forthcoming. At last, finding himself baffled, he awakened his father and requested him to resolve his doubts for him. That gentleman, unceremoniously aroused from a refreshing, half-finished sleep, demanded in a tone of surprise and anger: "Why do you ask such a question?" Dayanand replied: "The mice are running over this image of stone, and taking unwarranted liberties with it. The Mahadeva, of whom the katha spoke, is an animate being, how he can permit mice to run over his body? This idol cannot so much as move its head, much less protect itself from others. It appears to me that it is utterly impossible to reach the living omnipotent Deity through the agency of or through medium of this image.

Dayanand's father, perceiving his son's earnestness, found himself compelled to answer his question. He said: "The Mahadeva, who lives on the Kailash mountain, is represented by and invoked through this image, for he cannot be seen face to face in this age of Kaliyug. By being imagined as inhabiting an image of stone, metal or wood, etc., and by being worshipped through it, he is as much pleased as though he were actually present in the idol and were himself adored."

The parent added, "Your habit of raising objections is anything but praiseworthy. Why, this idol is nothing more that an image of the God?". Dayanand had to remain content with the answer, but reasoning like this could never set his doubts at rest. The only effect which it produced upon his mind was to shake his faith in idol-worship, to make him look upon the institution as false. And his resolution was made then and there, that he would never in future worship Mahadeva till he had seen him face to face.

Shortly after the termination of the conversation between father and son, Dayanand craved permission to go home, for he felt tired and hungry. The permission was give (as it could not but be given under the circumstances), and a sepoy was ordered to escort him home. Karsanji, however, thought it his duty to warn Dayanand at parting not to eat anything during the night. But the moment Dayanand reached home, he told his mother that he was hungry and would have something to appease the his hunger. The good woman at once brought him some sweets, and while handing them over to him, said: "Did I not tell you that you would not be able to bear the hardships attendant on keeping a fast? But you would have your own way, and you see the consequences. Eat these sweets and don't return to your father now."

Dayanand ate the sweets and went to bed at about 1 A.M. sleeping soundly for over seven hours. When Karsanji came home and hear how Dayanand had disregarded the parting warning, he was greatly annoyed and took his son to task for disobedience. Dyananand replied that the image in the temple was not identical with the Mahadeva spoken of in the katha, and consequently he did not feel bound to recognized its sanctity. At this the father could only utter a growl of displeasure, and then kept quiet, hoping to win over his son to his views on some subsequent occasion favorable for the purpose.

But this was not to be. Dayanand ha san uncle greatly attached to him. He complained to him of the pressure that his parent was bringing to bear upon him and pleaded his intercession, backing up his appeal by declaring that keeping fasts and attending to the worship of the God interfered adversely with his studies. The uncle interceded, supported by the boy's mother, and the result was that Dayanand ceased to suffer from the galling restraint. Being now, in a manner, his own master, Dayanand threw himself wholeheartedly into his studies, reading, with a Pandit, Nighantu, Nirukta, Purva Mimansa and works on karmkand (ritual). His leisure was now devoted to his books.

THE EFFECT OF THE SAD EVENTS ON DAYANAN'S MIND

While Dayanand was busy with his books, often revolving in his mind, in the midst of his lessons, the question which the affair in the temple had been instrumental in confronting his mind with, and accident happened which made the seriousness of the problem still more apparent to him. He was at the close of his sixteenth year when the event in question occurred and no one need doubt that he was wholly unprepared for the said occurrence.

Dayanand had two brothers and two sisters, all younger than himself, and fro whom he had great affection. One night, while his father, in company with himself and other male members of the family, was attending a nautch-meeting at the house of a friend, a servant came with the news that his eldest daughter, now fourteen years of age, was suddenly taken ill with cholera. Everyone hastened home, the physicians were summoned, and nothing was left undone that promised to afford relief, but all in vain.

The condition of the patient grew worse every moment and she expired after four hours of great agony. Weeping and lamentation commenced, the bereaved mother rending the air with her cries. It was terrible shock to Dayanand. He felt like one utterly unnerved and stupefied. "Ah!" Said he to himself when he was able to reflect, "who can defy death? Not one of the beings, that ever lived who could escape the cold hand of death. I, too, may be snatched away any time and die. How, then, shall I be able to fulfill my resolve of alleviating human misery, and where shall I find the assurance and means of attaining Mukti, the final beatitude?" It was then that he made a resolve of seeking the way to release himself from the bonds of life and death and go out in search of Truth.

He know that man's happiness and sufferings are the results of his actions in his previous birth. Those who had led a noble life in accordance with the scriptural injunctions are born in noble families, while others, whose previous life had been spent in perpetrating evil and falsehood, take birth as lower creatures.

The saints and virtuous people, perched, as the result of karma, on the highest plane of existence, will think in this fashion, and average man is apt to misconstrue their words and actions. The fact is, that they do not look upon the world as something discardable: no, the very reverse of it, but the world is not an end to them, but a means of gaining what is higher than the world, what is infinitely more valuable and more glorious. They think, as Dayanand thought, in the strain of the Divine verse:-

SAMBHOOTINCHA VINAASHAM CHA
YASTADDE DOBHAYAM SAHA.

VINAASHENA MRITYU TEERTVA
SAMBHOOTYAA MRITAMASH NUTE
- Yajur 40: 14.

"Whoever thoroughly understands the nature of the visible creation and of the imperishable atom from which the visible creation springs at one and some time, the same shall, by virtue of his knowledge of the primal atom, triumph over death, and shall obtain beatitude by virtue of his knowledge of the visible creation and by reason of his virtuous activity in that creation.".

These thoughts which filled Dayanand's mind, he did not express to his parents, but confided to his friends.

The nature of the aspirations which now filled Dyanand's breast was not long in being known to his father and mother. They were alarmed, particularly the latter, and began to devise means for preventing their son from carrying out his purpose. They were not to blame, they were actuated by love - not the enlightened love of the saint but the intense blind love of the world's children. A plan suggested itself for frustrating the boy. It was resolved that he should be married as early as possible. " Once he is secure in the toils of grihasthashrama (married-life), " said they, "he can never give us the slip." They soon disclosed their intentions to Dayanand, who was so frightened at the idea of marriage that he flew to the friends of the family with an earnest appeal to prevail upon his parents to delay the function. They listened to his prayer, and succeeded in inducing Karsanji to postpone the marriage for a year.

BRAHMACHARYA, EARLY MARRIAGE AND FLIGHT

A year's respite was great thing. The present danger was warded off, and who could say but affairs might take a favorable turn at the expiration of the period? But after all, if Dayanand found that his parents were inexorably resolved upon giving him a wife, he could use his legs and put a distance between himself and the place of his birth. In the absence of immediate danger he must go on acquiring knowledge, to fit himself for the life which he must come to leas sooner or later. He read on therefore, with all the passionate ardor of a true student, enlarging his acquaintance with the Sanskrit language and giving in keeping to a most retentive memory a mass of facts which, though calculated to help him to recognize and appreciate, by contrast, all the better the real truths in the fullness of time, even as darkness helps one to recognize and appreciate the worth of life all the better.

The twelve months slipped by quickly enough, the suspicious parents must renew their importunities as regards an early time to approach on him on the subject, Dayanand commenced importuning them for increased facilities for the acquisition of knowledge. He said that it was absolutely necessary that he should go to Kashi to prosecute his studies further with advantage. It was the great seat of Sanskrit learning, and experts in different subjects could nowhere be found in larger numbers.

The request took the parents' breath away, and they told him shortly that they would not accede to it. To weaken their opposition and to ultimately bring them to comply with his wishes, Dayanand spoke to them of the value and excellence of brahmacharya, drawing upon the Shastras and ancient history for quotations and examples to illustrate his meaning. But al would not do. They would not listen to his representations, and informed him that he must be a householder before many days were over!

Dayanand's parents acted after the fashion of other parents in India when they insisted upon his marrying. Indeed, they showed themselves vastly more prudent than the majority of parents in their country do. This majority, as we are well aware, is only too fond of seeing their children married before they are ten or twelve years of age, and some, overpowered by their love for their offspring, will go so far as to get them bound in the holy bonds of wedlock in their eight year. Dayanand was now fully twenty years old, and, to judge from what he was when he appeared before the public, he must have been a healthy and powerful youth at this time, or even a year or two earlier. But for al this, it cannot be denied that Dayanand's parents were also short-sighted like many more others in their situation. They could not rise to the height of realizing the greatness of perfect brahmacharya, of conceiving the vast possibilities of the vow. Dayanand looked to the ideals of ages gone by. If not one married in those days till he had completed his twenty-fifth year, and if large numbers never married till they had reached their thirty-sixth or forty-fourth year, he could not understand why the descendants of these men should be hurried into marriage before they had reached even the minimum marriageable age. And, further, why should not an individual be permitted to forego entrance into the grihasthaashrama when, swayed by a natural, intense, overpowering impulse, he would rather be wedded to a life of study and contemplation? The Shastras allowed such a concession in rare cases, and were not wholly unacquainted with Brahmacharis and Brahmacharinis of the type in question. It was, however, clear that the young men's parents were fully determined to disregard the rules of brahmacharya in their son's case.

One of the greatest causes of India's greatness, in times of youre, was its adherence to the law of brahmacharya. It secured each individual a perfectly developed body and a well-disciplined mind, cultured in various degrees. The result of this was that every individual was a man, even something of a hero, physically and morally, and serviceable to himself and others, intellectually. India was certainly low in the days of Magesthenese, but even then the land was very loyal to the requirements of brahmacharya and every town and city and village abounded in the right sort of men and women. The present national degradation will never cease till the nation is once more affluent in true Brahmacharis and Brahmacharinis. Where the body and mind are weak, there must be cowardice, physical and moral, and all the innumerable evils which are born of these. Mark what the Upanishat takings its inspirations from the Word Divine says of brahmacharya.

> *"There are three kinds of brahmacharya, the ordinary brahmacharya, the middling brahmacharya, and the highest brahmacharya. The ordinary*

brahmacharya is the living of a life of perfect celibacy, devoted to study, up to one's twenty-fourth year. The student must bear in mind that keeping this brahmacharya secures one an exemption from physical and mental ailments and a life of peace and tranquility ranging over seventy or eighty years. The middling brahmacharya is living a life of perfect celibacy up to one's forty-fourth year. This brahmacharya conduces to the fullest development of the physical powers, gives the mind a thorough control over the body and the senses, and makes one a terror to the wicked and the sinful, physically, morally and intellectually. The teacher should impress the value of the forty-four years' brahmacharya upon the student's mind by pointing out its advantages. The highes tkindof brahmacharya is the living a life of perfect celibacy, devoted to study up to one's forty-eighth year. Even as the perfection of the alphabet lies in forty-eight letters, even so does the perfection of brahmacharya consist in forty-eight years. This brahmacharya conduces to the fullest and harmonious development of all the powers of man."

Finding that nothing that he could say would move his parents, and that his mother in particular was dead against his leaving home, Dayanand, in despair, asked to be permitted to reside at a village a few miles from his own, and where the landed property of the family principally lay. The father thought that Dayanand would not object to taking care of the property, and he proposed that he should take upon himself the work and the responsibility of a superintendent. But Dayanand was disposed to do such thing. He wanted to reside in the other village because a learned man resided there, and if he was not to be allowed to God to Kashi, he might as well study for some time with this learned man. This request was granted, and Dayaand was thankful that it had not been refused, for, apart from the fact that his removal to the neighboring village would enable him to continue his studies for some time, it would be a distinct relief to him to be away from his parents. They were continually talking of his coming marriage, which was annoying to him, and he knew that if he ever ventured to intimate that he preferred remaining as he was, he was bound to be severely taken to task for harboring such a foolish (!) idea.

Dayanand commenced his studies with the new Pandit, and the latter was delighted with his progress. One day, in the course of conversation, Dayanand openly confessed to his teacher that he had no intention whatever of marrying, and that he positively disliked being a "householder." The teacher reported Dayanand's words to his father, who had him immediately recalled to his native village, and ordered that preparations for his marriage should be made without delay. Dayanand was at a loss what to do. He consulted his friends, but they, like his parents, being unable to sympathize with his lofty aspirations, advised him to marry.

After much reflection, he was convinced that his only means of escape from marriage lay in flight. He had already counted upon the possibility of such a contingency, and now it must become a fact. Any hesitation, when affairs had come to such a pass, would be fatal. He must bid farewell to home and friends once and forever - in that lay his salvation. Just as the preparations, which had been pushed on with startling vigor during a whole month, were complete, and when a week or so more would find him married, Dayanand braced himself for a final effort, and so soon as the shades of the evening came on, he stole out of the house, with hismind fully made up never to se5 foot in it again, if he could help it!

RENUNCIATION

His Pursuit and Capture

Dayanand left his father's home in the Jyeshtha of Vikrama Samvat 1903 (1846 A.D.), and he was at this time over twenty-one years of age, a lively youth with intellect stamped on his forehead, but, withal, simple and artless in the extreme. The first night he passed at a village some eight miles from his own, and long before it was dawn, he was speeding along by-ways and unfrequented paths again. When the evening se in, he had done about twenty-five miles, and being too tired to proceed farther, he put up in a temple of Hanuman, in a certain hamlet.

He did well to have avoided the highway, for his father, interpreting his absence only too correctly, had dispatched servants in pursuit, and they were searching for him. Even before he had time to leave the temple, and this he did on the third day after quitting home, he heard from a petty official that a party of horsemen and footsepoys had visited the village to which the temple was attached, looking for a lad named Mool Shanker.

Dayanand thanked Heaven for the narrow escape and resumed his journey. He had gone not gone far when he fell i with a party of begging mendicants, who engaging him in conversation. So wrought upon his simplicity as to prevail upon him to surrender all his ornaments and various other things to their idol. "As long as you don't give up everything of value, you possess, to the image," said they, "so long you need not expect to rise above worldly attachments." Dayanand believed the impostors and parted from them considerably lightened of his valuables.

While pursuing his flight, Dayanand heard here and there from people about Lala Bhagat at Sayle, a town some six miles from Mooli, a well-known station on the Wadhwan-Morvi line. Dayanand turned his steps towards this town, which he duly reached, finding the house of Lala Bhagat, a distinguished saint, crowded with wearers of ochre-colored clothes. Here a Brahmachari conferred upon him the privileges of the order to which he himself belonged, and named him Shuddhachaitanya (pure-minded), making him put on ochre-colored garments and keep a Kamandal (the beggar's gourd) as his constant companion.

Following in the footsteps of the Sadhus of the place, Dayanand began to practice austerities. He held idol-worship in abhorrence, but he was still under the influence of superstition in various ways. As an instance of this, he was one night sitting under a tree and practicing under a tree and practicing yoga, when, all of a sudden, a curious noise, made by some birds roosting on the tree, broke upon his ears. He was alarmed, thinking that the tree was haunted by evil spirits, and getting up in haste joined his group! Leaving Sayle, Dayanand arrived, in his new habiliments, at a town called Koutha Gangada, in small principality, near Ahmedabad (Gujrat).

The town was alive with the presence of numerous Bairagis, who had managed to entangle a princess in their toils. The worthies, seeing Dayanand habited in reddish-yellow garments, had a derisive laugh, their secret object being to win the new-comer over to their order, Dayanand would not be caught this time, though he suffered himself to be persuaded so far as to part with his stock of silk-dhotis to them and to buy three rupees worth cotton ones instead. Here Dayanand stayed for three months, known to all his neighbors as a Brahmachari.

Ere turning his back upon Koutha Gangada, Dayanand learnt that the annual fair at Siddhapur, a Railway station on the bank of the Saraswati, would take place in a few days. Thinkig that he might come across some yogi there who could point out to him the way to salvation, Dayanand set off towards the locality. In the way he encountered a Bairagi whom, on nearer approach, he recognized to be one perfectly acquainted with his family. When the eyes of the two met, tears rolled their cheeks. On the Bairagi's asking why he saw him dressed in ochre-colored garments, Dayanand told him all.

The Bairagi was at first moved to laughter, but soon assuming a stern and serious tone he tole him that he had made a great mistake in taking the step he had. After this the pair separated, each pursuing his different way. On reaching Siddhapur, Dayanand put up in the temple of Nilakanth Mahadeva, already crowded with Dandi Swamis and Brahmacharis (students). The fair came off. Wherever Dayanand hear was a learned and pious man, there he would go and converse with the worthy soul. in his ecstasy he little dreamed, that something umpleasant was in store for him and that he must soon face it.

The Bairagi, whom Dayanand had met on his way to Siddhapur, had communicated with his parents, telling them, in his letter, where Dayanand could be found. We won't say it was treachery on his par: on the contrary, it may be that he was actuated by the best motives. Perhaps, like many others he could not understand Dayanand (it was apparent from his parting rebuke to Dayanand that he did not), and he thought he was doing the youth good in informing his parents of his whereabouts. But whatever the real facts, certain it is that it was his communication that once more set the father on the son's trail.

Karsanji came accompanied by several sepoys and went through every part of the fair making inquiries about his missing son. His efforts were at last crowned with success. Entering one morning the temple of Mahadeva, he found himself suddenly face to face with Dayanand. Seeing him dressed in ochre-colored clothes he flew into a passion and, in a voice of thunder, asked: "What means this?" So terror-inspiring was his visage that Dayanand dared not meet his gaze. He raved and stormed at the youth, calling him the disgrace of his family, the cause of eternal shame to his race, and so on. Dayanand was in a mortal fright, and moving from his place, fell at his sire's feet, saying that he had done what he had by evil counsel of others, and that he fully intended to return home from Siddhapur.

He humbly craved forgiveness for any offence he might have given, and said he was thankful to his father that he had taken so much trouble on his account. This show of contrition and humility failed to appease the anger of Karsanji. Taking hold of his garments, he tore t hem to pieces, and dashing his bowl on the ground smashed it to fragments. Then having dressed him in new suit of clothes he took him to where he had put up, and said, "Will you kill you mother by running away from home?"

In spite of all that Dayanand had said to set his father's mind at rest, the old man had no faith in his words. He stationed the sepoys upon him, giving them strict orders not to let him go anywhere. Night came and still Dayanand found himself watched as closely as ever. He was helpless, not knowing what to do, and bitterly thinking of turn which affairs had taken. For he had, as his father rightly suspected, no mind to go home. It was fright that made him tell an untruth: in his heart of hearts he resolved to regain his freedom as soon as he saw a chance of doing the same. While he lay in his bed, despondent and musing over his fate, what did he find on stealing a look at the guard but that he had fallen a sleep? "Now or never," said Dayanand, and creeping out of the room he ran with all his might. He had gone about half a mile, when he saw a temple with a lofty papal tree growing near it, and shading the building on all sides by its huge branches. He could not but see that the guard would soon awake, and, missing him in his bed, would give an alarm, upon which his father and his attendants would be again after him. Under the inspiration of the moment, Dayanand climbed up the huge tree and hid himself on a lofty branch just near the top of the building. He had not been settled many minutes in his "retreat" when several horsemen came dashing in the direction of the tree but, though they looked closely in every nook and corner of the temple, they failed to find any trace of their master's son.

The priests of the temple wer interrogated, but they could give no information. At last disappointed with their fruitless search, the pursuers turned up back and were soon lost to view. During the time the search lasted, Dayanand had sat closely "packed up" and did not so much as breathe, for fear that his presence might be detected by anyone. The sun at last rose, but Dayanand would not leave his hiding-place yet. He ws in fear of the priests, of his father and his men and even of a causal way-fearer whom he might meet in the event of his leaving his retreat before night-fall. He had nothing to eat but he had a lota full of water, and this water he partook when the wanted to refresh himself. When the livelong day had at last ended he slipped down the tree, halting at a village some four miles from the temple. Early in the morning he started off afresh, and passing through Ahamedabad, arrived at Baroda. Here associating with the Sannyasis and Brahmacharis of the Non-dualistic school he himself became a Vedanti, believe in the identity of God and soul. During his residence here he heard that a meeting of learned Sadhus was shortly going to be held on the bank of the Nerbada, and no sooner did he hear this than he set off towards the place specified, to be present at the conference. Reaching there, he had a talk on the Shastras with Sachchidanand Paramahansa. At this place hearing that large number of learned Brahmacharis and Sanyasis lived along the bank of the river, Dayanand pordeeded in search of the same and met several. With one of these - Paramahansa Parmamand - he resumed his studies, and, in the course of a few months, had gone through Vedantasara, Arya Harimede, Totaka, Arya Harihara, Totaka, Vedantaparibhasha, and similar other works.

WANDERINGS AND STUDY AND INITIATION INTO SANYASA

As Brahmachari, Dayanand, in conformity with the usual practice, had to cook his meals himself. This greatly interfered with his studies. To be rid of this trouble, he made up his mind to enter the Sanyasa Ashrama. The initiation would be, moreover, useful to him in another way: it would give him a name which would completely hid his identity and would minimize the chances of his being reclaimed by the members of his family. They knew him as Shuddhachaitanya, but when the name had been dropped in favor of a sanyasa name, a great clue to his whereabouts would be lost, and he could then count upon the enjoyment of greater freedom in his movements. With this idea in his mind, he requested a Sanyasi named Chidashrama to initiate him into sanyasa. His request was refused on the ground of his extreme youth. The refusal, however, had no discouraging effect upon Dayanand.

He was firmly resolved upon being initiated, and he stayed a year and a half on the bank of the Nerbada, studying and waiting his chance. In the meantime, a Dandi Swami and a Brahmachari came and halted in a forest near the town of Chanod. The name of the Dandi Swami was Purnanand. A Dakshini Pandit, a friend of Dayanand paid a visit to this learned Sanayasi, along with Dayanand and introduced him to the Sanyasi, and a conversation on Brahmavidya ensued.

Dayanand could not but perceive that the Sanyasi was a man of profound learning, and he moved the Dakshini Pandit to request him to initiate him into the Sanyasa. The Pandit conveyed his wishes to the learned Sanyasi, making a powerful recommendation on his behalf. The young man, he said, was passionately devoted to the study of Brahmavidya and valued it above all things, but, as at present circumstanced, he could not fully satisfy the craving of his soul. for, as a Brahmachari, he has to prepare his food with his own hands and to attend to other similar sundry things, which took away a large portion of his time.

In order that his entire time and leisure be at his disposal, to be exclusively devoted to study and reflection, it was necessary that he should enter the sanyasa and might it not be hoped that the erudite Swami would grant his application? Swamim Purnanand's first answer was much the same as that of the Chidashrama Swami. He declared that he could not see his way to initiate one so young, and he added: "I belong to the Maharastra. The young man ought to wait upon some Gujrati Sanyasi and get initiated by him." To this the Dakshini Pandit repliedThat when the Sanyasis belonging to the Deccan went so far as to initiate into the sanyasa even men of inferior castes, Swami Purnanand should have no objection whatever in bestowing the privileges of the order upon one who came of a prominent Brahmin family. After much discussion the Swami prevailed upon to entertain the young man's petition, and on the expiration of the third day after the meeting, the important function took place, and Shuddhachaitanya came to be named what we have called him from the very beginning of our sketch - Dayanand (Saraswati).

Dayanand was sanyasi in twenty-fourth year, but his initiation did not mark, as in most cases if does and ought to, the completion of his education. To al intents and purposes, he was still a Brahmacharyi, and he himself felt that he was such. His initiation had, however given him one thing - made him absolutely his own master, and this was a privilege, for which, as we are aware, he intensely longed with the one, sole object that he might drink his fill at the fountain of knowledge.

In the course of the new trip which Dayanand had undertaken, he came to hear of one Swami Yoganand, and adept in Yogavidya. He went to him, and commenced with him the study of the highest branch of metaphysics. When he had gone through some elementary works on the subject, he proceeded to Cinor, where he came across a Brahman named Krishna Shastri, who was well-versed in Sanskrit grammar. With this Shastri he reas for some time, and then left for another town, where he studied the Vedas with a certain Pandit.

Here after some time, he met two Yogis, named Jwalanand Puri and Shivanand Giri. Associating with them he resumed the practice of yoga, and he would often hold discussions with them on the science of yoga.

Eventually, the two Yogis left for Ahmedabad, telling Dayanand that if he would learn something more of their science, he should follow them shortly to the place they were bound for. After the expiration of a month, Dayanand left for Ahmedabad and rejoined the Yogis. They were true to the great mysteries of Yogavidya. Dayanand fully availed himself of their instructions, and he always thought of the two Yogis with a feeling of profound gratitude.

At Ahmedabad, Dayanand hear that the Koh Abu was the abode of many distinguished Yogis, and he set off thither. On reaching the top of the mountain he found that the report was not unfounded. Many Rajyogis dwelt there, and he waited upon them. These Yogis, Dayanand declares, had deeper insight into their science than even the first two Yogis, from whom he parted at Ahmedabad. He stayed with them, and learnt many more valuable secrets.

Thus wandering about, Dayanand met many more Yogis and Pandits, deriving considerable benefit from their company and improving himself physically, intellectually, and morally. He made a point of staying wherever a truly learned man was found, and of studying with him in the capacity of a humble student. He was thirty years old when he visited the Kumbha Fair of Haridwar. (1912 V.E.).

As long as the fair lasted, Dayanand remained in the wood surrounding the Chandi Hill, practicing yoga, and on the termination of the fair he went to Rishikesh, where he had interviews with many Yogis and mahatmas and learnt more of practical yoga from them.

THE TANTRAS, ANIMAL FOOD, AND VISIT TO RISHIKESH AND SHRINAGAR

Ere long Dayanand withdrew from the society of his teachers at Rishikesh, and passed some days in solitude, dividing his time between study and contemplation.

One day, in a solitary ramble, he came across a Brahmachari and two Sadhus natives of the hills, and joining them, the party left for Tehri a famous seat fo learning. While staying here one of his new acquaintances sent him an invitation to dine at his house. At the appointed hour a servant waited upon Dayanand , who, accompanied by a Brahmachari, repaired to the house of his would-be host. On arriving there, he saw a Pandit was cutting up meat, and that a few steps farther on, several Brahmans were engaged in cooking the same article. Heaps of bones lay beside them, and head of several animals ready cooked. The sight greatly disgusted Dayanand, and thought the master of the house extended to him a cordial welcome and pressed him to enter the best room in the house, he found himself compelled to return to his dwelling at once. "Don't let me disturb you," said he, "but go on with your work," and uttering these few words he came back to his cottage and felt at case.

Before many minutes, however, had gone by, a fresh man waited upon him, and informed him that everything was ready and that his presence alone was wanting. "Every variety of meat-dish," explained the messenger, "will be served to your holiness, it has been prepared expressly for yourself, and the master hopes it will please you." Dayanand replied that the very sight of meat made him sick, to eat the same was out of the question, and hat if the man's master must have him share his hospitality, he could send him some flour and vegetables, and his own Brahmachari would do the cooking. The disappointed host had to comply.

Shortly after this, Dayanand asked the two Pandits for a loan of the books whose praises they so warmly sang, and the Pandits willingly agreed to lend him the entire lot. Dayanand, however, chose those only which go under the name of the "Tantras". No sooner had he opened one of these than he was astounded at the nature of its contents. They were so obscene, so utterly subversive of the moral and social relations which have ever existed and ought to exist between one member and another of a family and between one member and another of society at large, that no one, not absolutely and hopelessly depraved and debased, could help recoiling at the bare contemplation of what they taught.

And one book was as bad as the others, teaching little else than what will vitiate and degrade, what will demoralize. Things, many and various, have brought about the fall off India, but nothing has perhaps contributed more to prostrate the Indian community morally and intellectually than the Tantras. Alas! That such a literature should have ever come to exist in the land of the saints and sages. Dayanand's soul sickened as he turned over the leaves, and at last he threw them away with a loathing. During the rest of his life he never thought or spoke of these but his heart was filled with indignation at the villainy of those who had brought them into existence.

From there Dayanand set off towards Sri Nagar, and, on reaching there, put in a temple on the Kedarghat. Here had occasional discussions with the Pandits, and whenever he found one of these too warm an admirer of orthodoxy, he would quote from the Tantras and so completely seal his lips. Of the Sadhus whom Dayanand met at this place, Ganga Giri pleased him the most. Dayanand came to have great esteem and regard for him and stayed with him for two months. As soon as the autumn set in, he, in company with the two hill-sadhus and his Brahmachari, left for some other locality, and visiting Prayag (Allahabad) and other places arrived at the tomb of Agastya Muni, thence proceeding to a hill named Shivpuri.

This is the place where some people (the Jains) believe salvation is attainable while one is yet living. Dayanand passed the dour months of winter here, and then separating himself from his companions, bent his steps towards Kedarghat alone. Passing through the Guptakashi, Gourikund and Bhim ganga, he reached the temple of Triyugunarayana. He did not seem to like the palce at all, and consequently returned to Kedarghat without delay.

When he had seen sufficient of the inhabitants of this place, he thought he would visit the neighboring hills. These hills are covered with perpetual snow, but the fact fid not daunt Dayanand. He had heard that these were the abode of mahatamas, and he must seek them but in defiance of every inconvenience and danger. He went and commenced making his inquires. But not useful information was forthcoming. The people interrogated would ether deny all knowledge of the existence of men Dayanand was after, or would tell such stories regarding them as no man with a grain of common sense would believe. Dayanand did not know what to do. After fruitlessly wandering for twenty days exposed to the piercing, intense cold of the mountains, he retraced his steps to Kedarghat.

His recent excursion in the hills, though attended with much suffering, had created in Dayanand a great liking for the free and bracing mountain air, and one day he ascended the Tunganath Hill. The temple on the summit he found crowded with priests and crammed with idols, andnot much pleased with sight, he prepared to descend the same day. He saw before him two paths, one leading to the west, and the other to the south. He took the one leading to a jungle, and before he and gone far, he found himself in the midst of a thick wood. Sharp stones and huge boulders lay strewn everywhere, and the streams and rivulets were wholly destitute of water. Laying hold of the grass and of the dried-up bushes, Dayanand made a shift to reach the bank of a stream, and mounting the ridge of a hill ran his eye in every direction. Nothing but inaccessible steeps and jungle were to be seen.

The sun was near setting, and Dayanand could not see how he would manage to pass the night in such a dreary place without food and water. At last he resolved to seek some habitation. His progress was slow, and the thorny bushes through which he had to pass tore his garments to shreds and drew blood from his body. He, however, went on limping along with wounded legs and lace-rated feet, and, after undergoing many hardships, lighted on the highway. He had to grope his way in the darkness, and in time, the signs of habitation appeared. It was an insignificant, uninviting hamlet, and

Dayanand set off towards Okhimath to which it led. Here he passed the night, and as soon as it was morning, proceeded to Guptakashi. Desirous of exploring Okhimath at leisure, he returned to it again, and found that almost all the caves were inhabited by imposters. Here a great Mahant wanted to make Dayanand his disciple, offering him wealth and assuring him that he should succeed him to the gaddi.

Dayanand rejected his offer, saying that if he wanted wealth he should not have left home and separated himself from his parents and friends. At the same time he told him hat even the event of his settling down with him, he could not gain the object for accomplishment of which he had severed his connection with the world. The Mahant urged Dayanand to stay with him for some time, he refused, returning to Joshimath the very next day. Eventually, he met many learned Sanyasis and Yogis here, and he took further lessons from them in connection with practical yoga.

LOVE OF SCIENCE

Difference between Great and Common Men

Parting company with the mahatamas of Joshimath, Dayanand set off towards Badarinarayan, and on arriving there visited the great temple. It afforded him great pleasure to discover, in the person of Rawalje, the Mahant of the temple, a man deeply reads in the Shastras, and he conversed with him for several days on the subject of the "Vedas and the Darshanas."

Dayanand was informed by the Mahant that learned Yogis, adept in the science of yoga, were not to be met in the neighborhood of Badarinarayan. The information was extremely disappointing, but as such men now and then came to visit the temple (so his host assured him), he determined to look out for these, and in the meantime to explore the neighboring hills, to make certain if these were wholly destitute of the presence of Sadhus and Sanyasis of the right type. Early one morning he left Badarinaryan, and, proceeding along the foot of the hills, arrived at the margin of a stream called Alakananda, and following the direction of its current struck in to a wood. At this time, the entire mountain was wrapped in a covering of snow, and it was with the greatest difficulty that he reached the source of the stream. He place appeared to walled in by lofty hills on every side, and no path was visible which might be followed. Dayanand was in great distress. He was very lightly clad, and the cold was so intense that he could hardly stand it. He had nothing with him so subsist upon, and his exertions had so sharpened his appetite that, as a last resource, he began to eat ice. But such food was anything but satisfying and Dayanand had to give up on with his repast. "Let me see, if I can cross the stream," said he; "I might find a way out of the difficulty on reaching the other side." In pursuance of this resolve he descended into the stream, but it was not joke to cross it.

The water was shallow in some places, but very deep in others, and pieces of ice with sharp, piercing edges were whirled down the current in hundreds every minute. And the bed of the stream was strewn with stones, some lying fault, with surfaces extremely slippery, and others planted upright with points that would penetrate the flesh like a sharp piece of iron. The attempt was made and when Dayanand reached the other side, his feet were wounded and bleeding and utterly benumbed with cold, and he felt like one in a state of stupefaction. For many moments he sat all but forgetful O himself and of what was going on around him, but there was danger in continuing as he was, and with a vigorous effort he roused himself from his torpor. Finding that his legs and feet refuse to work, he tightly wrapped both in his torn garments and essayed to move forward, but the attempt was unsuccessful. "Oh! That some fellow creature would come to help me." He exclaimed; "if I stay longer where I am, I should certainly perish without realizing the dream of life - accomplishment of the object for which I left home."

While he was looking wistfully in every direction to see if he could espy some one who might be of service to him in his trouble, his eye lighted on two-hill-men advancing towards him. They made their obeisance to him and offered to take him to their huts. Dayanand, while begging to be excused form accepting their kind offer, told them what had brought him in that dreary region. Upon this, the hill-men offered to lead him to a place named Sadpat Tirath, which offer he thankfully accepted. The next instant he had to refuse it. "I am perfectly exhausted," said he, " and at this moment can't move a step. You have better leave me to my fate." The two hill-men sadly bade him farewell and ere long were lost to sight. In time, Dayanand, by the grace of God, came to feel better and resumed his wandering, and passing through Vasudhara, a Tirath, and skirting Managram, he reached Badarinarayan at about 8 P.M. His prolonged absence had made the good and learned Mahant very uneasy, and as soon as the latter saw him, he felt that load had been taken off his heart. At supper Dayanand ate sparingly, and then retired to rest. With the appearance of morning, he tool leave of his hose, and proceeded towards Rampur. On the way, he stopped with a Yogi and passed the night at his cottage. This man, according to Dayanand, was deeply learned in Sanskrit literature, and his words had a most encouraging effect upon him. As soon as the day broke, Dayanand set forward, and traveling through jungles and over hills, he arrived at Rampur, putting up at the house of Ramgiri.

This Sadhu commanded great respect in Rampur by virtue of his pure character - a commodity which one's worst enemies will seldom fail to appreciate. He was an eccentric man, passing sleepless nights, and often talking to himself in loud and lusty tones. One not in the secret would think that he was talking with somebody in his room, for he always seemed to address a second person. Often he would commence screaming and if anyone rushed to his rescue on such occasions, he would, on entering the Sadhu's room, find that there was nobody there but himself.

Dayanand sought an explanation of this singular conduct, but his disciples could give him none except that such was their preceptor's habit. Dayanand sought a private interview with the Sadhu himself, and learnt that he was engage in accomplishing the siddhis of Yoga-vidya. His conversation, however, led Dayanand to the conclusion that his knowledge of the science and practice of yoga was imperfect. Leaving Rampur, Dayanand turned his face towards Kashipur, and from there went to Daronasagar, where he passed the entire winter.

during his residence here, it, one day, came into his mind that seeking the heights of the Himalayas he should destroy himself.; but with reflection better counsels prevailed. It was a cowardly act, he confessed to himself, a true manly soul ought to fight to the end, acquire all he can of knowledge and wisdom and then resignedly wait for the call.

The most vigorous and elevated natures are not wholly above the weakness of giving away to despair, but, unlike average humanity, they will not surrender themselves to it body and soul; they will get over the fit and will re-enter upon their wonted energy and with a renewal of their determination either to reach the goal, or to perish nobly in the attempt. Syanand felt, in the light of Shastric teaching and in the glow of the light within, the heritage of past karma, that his was to try, in faith, and not to be impatient for the fruit: God would grant the fruit in His own good time, if he was true to himself and to his mission.

From Daronasagar, Dayanand pressed on to Moradabad, and visiting Sambhal and Barhmukstestar reached the banks of the Ganges. One day, as he sat near the water's edge, thinking he espied, all of a sudden, a corpse being carried down by the rapid current. Dayanand had with him, along with other books some works on physiology and anatomy, and he had often given time to the study of these. But his knowledge was mere book-knowledge, untested and unverified by actual observation and experiment.

The sight of the corpse reminded him that here was his opportunity, and he forthwith plunged into the river and dragged the body to shore. Taking out a sharp knife from his pocket, he cut open the body near the heart which he tore, and began to examine it closely. He found that the description of the heart, as given in his books, was totally wrong. After that he cut open the head and the neck, and, as formerly, discovered that his books did not describe their anatomy correctly. He was disgusted with the spurious composition, tore them to pieces and flung them into the river along with the corpse. The incident shows

Dayanand's love of knowledge and research. To the Sanyasi the touch of even some living men is pollution, and they will on no account bring any part of their body into contact with a corpse. Dayanand deliberately and of his own accord handled a corpse, proving thereby that true knowledge is worth more the mere sentiment and that true men of science will have it in spite of sentiment.

THE SOURCE OF NERBUDA AND HIS ENCOUNTER WITH A BEAR

Dayanand stayed for a short time on the bank of the Ganges, and then left for Furukhabad. Before the nest year (V.E. 1913 or A.D. 1856) had quite run its course, Dayanand had visited many places lying between Allahabad and Kanpur. Subsequently proceeding to a place in the vicinity of Benaras, he put up, on reaching his destination, in the temple of Vindhyachaleshvarji, where he spent one whole month. Then going to Benaras proper, he stayed there for twelve days in a cave. Here he came across many individuals profoundly versed in Sanskrit literature. Chandalgarh was the next place he visited. Here he put up in the temple of Durgakouhar, and applied himself whole-heartedly to the study of Yoga-vidya and to the practice of its teaching.

In the Chaitra of 1856, Dayanand set off in search of the source of the Nerbada, having heard that the tract around was the abode of learned Sanyasis and Yogis. Proceeding along the bank of the stream, he found himself in a great jungle, not wholly destitute of huts at irregular intervals. Stopping in one of those he drank some milk and then resumed his journey. He had advanced about a mile and-a-half when he found himself in a wood still more drearier, abounding in plum trees and prickly shrubs, and choked with tall grass which completely hid the path from view. While making his way through these, he suddenly found himself confronted by a huge big black bear. The ferocious animal reared it self on its hind legs, and with a terrible roar advanced towards him. For one instant Dayanand stood rooted to the spot, but the next he was calm as ever, and taking up a stick bit the bear on the nose. The blow was dealt with a tremendous force, and proved effective. The animal ran away shrieking with pain. The men in the huts, hearing the noise, hurried out with clubs and hunting dogs, an finding a Sanyansi in trouble (as they thought), offered him help and service, adding that the jungle was the abode of numerous, bears tigers, elephants, etc., and advising him to cut short his journey.

Dayanand declined their assistance with thanks and informed them that he was bent upon proceeding forward and taking his chance. The villagers at parting presented him with a stout club, saying that it would be of great use to him in his dangerous trip. Dayanand accepted it, but the next moment he threw it away and fearlessly advanced on his track. For hours he traveled on. At last the sun went down and everything was enveloped in gloom. At last the sun went down and everything was enveloped in gloom. No light indicating habitation could be seen anywhere. Now and then he stumbled against trees rooted out by elephants. To add to his distress, he soon found his passage blocked by a still more awful and almost penetrable jungle. Nothing but thorny hedges and prickly pears were visible on all sides. To turn back was out of the question.

Dayanand crept into it on his knees, and, following a zig-zag track, at last emerged into open space. He felt utterly exhausted with the effort. His clothes were torn to threads, and his body was wounded in twenty places and bleeding profusely. It was, however, no time and no place to make a halt. The darkness was gathering apace overhead, and it was no longer easy to distinguished objects even at short distances. Dayanand moved forward as best he could, and having steered clear of many dangers through continuous masses of rank vegetation, lighted on some straggling huts girt round with heaps of cattle-dung. A stream of clear, transparent water flowed not far from the huts, and the sheep and goats were still grazing on its bank. Dayanand saw a neat cottage standing under a tree and wished very much to go into it and rest, but then it would inconvenience its inmates, and to inconvenience them he did not like. So he climbed up the tree and passed the night on it. As soon as it was dawn, he alighted from the tree and, going to the margin of the stream, washed his wounded feet and other parts of the body, and then prepared to engage in upaasana. Before, however, he could sufficiently compose his mind for his devotions, he heard a noise resembling that of the roar of wild beast, but it was nothing but the sound of a tom-tom. A party of villagers, composed of men and women, was advancing towards him with a large number of cows and sheep, on its way, no doubt to some temple to celebrate a religious festival.

When the procession was sufficiently near to where Dayanand sat, it came to a halt at the sight of a stranger in such an isolated locality, and an old man detaching himself from the rest came forward and asked Dayanand where he had come from. Dayanand replied that he had come from Benaras and that he was proceeding towards the source of the Nerbada river. On hearing this answer the party departed, and Dayanand became absorbed in contemplation. About half an hour after this, a man, who appeared to be a person of consequence, followed by two servants, came and sat down near Dayanand. He invited Dayanand to go home with him, but Dayanand begged to be excused, saying that he was all right where he was. When, in answer to his inquires, he made known to the chief what he was after, the old man was pleased and ordered his servants to stay with him and show him every attention.

Learning that he Sanyasi abstained (at present) from the use of solid food), he had a large bowl filled with milk brought to him. Dayanand partook of the refreshing drink, and with the setting of the night retired to rest. To guard against the attacks of the wild beasts, the chief had a fire lit around the stranger, and Dayanand slept soundly till morning, under the watchful eye of the assiduous chief's servitors. On getting up, he performed his ablutions and then did his sandhya, after which he proceeded on his way, eventually reaching his destination. For three whole years he wandered along the banks of the Nerbada, and it was during these wanderings that he came to hear of the great Sanyasi Virjanand at Mathura. Something whispered into his ear that this was the man he had been looking for in vain for so many years, and towards Mathura, accordingly, did Dayanand bend his steps.

A SKETCH OF SWAMI VIRJANAND

Virjanand belonged to that part of India which has, from times immemorial, been pre-eminently the birth-place of the saints and the sages, which has produced, in the course of the ages and centuries untold, some of the most distinguished thinkers and teachers and representatives of heroic and chivalric impulse and instinct, with whose names the annals of Aryan antiquity are familiar. He belonged to the Punjab, being a native of Kartarpur, a small town situated on the Beas, one of the two rivers which enclose the extensive tract known as Duaba Bist Jullundur. Long before Virjanand was born, no less than two centuries before that an event took place, Kartarpur had come to be associated with the last years and the death of one of the greatest benefactors of his mother-land in her days of suffering and sorrow. Guru Nanak, the founder of Sikhism, the reviver of that pure theism which the primeval Scripture of mankind inculcates, passed the closing decade of his life in this place.

Virjanand was born in 1854 V.E. (A.D. 1797) at a time when the Maharaja Ranjit Singh sat on the throne of the Punjab, and when the Sikh empire was in the zenith of its glory. He was Brahman by birth, his father's name being Nararyan Dutta. He was hardly more than five or six years of age when he had an attack of small-pox, which left him blind for life. The parents were totally unprepared for the misfortune which had overtaken their younger and favorite child, and their grief was unbounded. But the inevitable had to be accepted.

As will almost always happen in such cases, the helpless condition fo the boy only contributed to intensify the parents' consciousness of the claims which he had on their tenderness and care, and he became a greater pet with the than ever. The father, who had already taught him something more than his letters and who had abundant proof that he was a child of remarkable intelligence, eager to learn, came to the conclusion, after much thought and reflection, the best course for him to adopt in regard to his blind son's interests, both temporal and spiritual, was to continue his education. The resolution was carried out, but Virjanand was not to reap the fruit thereof long. He was destined to face another calamity in the near future, and the calamity came, leaving him an orphan at the age of eleven.

By the death of his parents, Virjanand was thrown on the mercy of his elder brother and his wife. The elder brother might not be naturally unkind, but he was weak-minded and entirely guided by his wife, who was cruel to the extreme, hating her brother-in-law with all the hate of a woman. She was always tormenting the poor boy, flinging the most cutting taunts at him, and boldly hinting that he would be better out of the house than in it.

Virjanand would often reply, which rendered he still more savage, and she would beat him unmercifully. At last the crisis came. Convinced that his sister-in-law was bent upon getting rid of him and that his brother also, led and intimated by his despotic spouse, was arrayed against him, deliberately conniving at her faults of omission and commission, he parted company with his father's home and cast himself adrift on the wide world.

God, however, will care for His own, and, in obedience to the promptings of a happy impulse, Virjanand, though no more than twelve years old yet, set off towards Haridwar. It was painful journey, extending over weeks and months and exposing the boy to numberless hardships, but at last it was accomplished. After halting at various places for periods varying in duration, he found himself, in his fifteenth year, at Rishikesh. There he commenced a life of study, more specifically of contemplation. Going to the bank of the river he would sit there for hours together, repeating that noblest of the Veda-mantras - the gayatri - and meditating on the nature and attributes of the Divinity of which it so comprehensively speaks. For three years did he thus employ himself, being .hunger and thirst and inclemency of weather, and utterly regardless of the dangers which beset a place like Rishikesh in those days. Verily the fiercest denizens of the forest become as lambs when brought into contact with the rue worshippers of the Lord.

At any rate, such worshippers fear naught but the Lord, and they will be loyal to Him under the most trying circumstances. Having reached is eighteenth year, Virjanand returned to Haridwar, to be initiated there into Sanyasa, in response to the summons he thought he had received in a vision he saw in his former place of residence. He sought out a worthy Sanyasni named Paramanand, who, according to his wishes, admitted him to his order, bestowing upon him the name with which we are already familiar, namely, Virjanand (Saraswati). Virjanand now applied himself to his studies with renewed vigor, and had, in a short time, made sufficient progress to be able to compose original verses in Sanskrit. He had real esteem for the Brahman who helped him in his studies at Haridwar.

After a few years spent exclusively in his own improvement, Virjanand began to take in pupils himself, and was pleased to discover that he was a complete master of the Madhyakaumudi, and could teach it with ease. But an occasion now and then arose when a wider and more comprehensive knowledge of Sanskrit grammar was demanded than that which an acquaintance with the Madhayakaumudi, however thorough, places at one's disposal. To make up his deficiency, Virjanand removed to Kahkhal and went through the Siddhantkaumudi with a competent man, teaching it at the same time to his own pupils. As soon as he had finished the book, he left Kankhal and following the course of the Ganges, arrived in time at Kashi. Here he stayed for over a year, studying and mastering Manorama, Shekhara, Nyayamimansa, and works treating of Vedantic philosophy, astonishing, all around him with his intellectual acumen and the depth of his learning, and gaining from the appellation of Prajnachakshus Swami or the Swami "with eyes of understanding"." On completing his twenty-second year, Virjanand bade farewell to Benaras and proceeded to Gaya. On the way he was set upon by robbers, but before these miscreants could do him any personal injury or strip him of what little he had with him in the shape of money, a Sardar, attracted by the tumult, appeared on the scene and made the fellows take to their heels.

A few moments were sufficient for the nobleman to appreciate the worth of the Sadhu to whom he had been of service, and he kept him in his tent for full five days, showing him every attention and profiting by his teaching. On the sixth day Virjanand resume his journey and reached his destination without meeting with any further adventures of an unpleasant character. At Gaya he continued to live for a considerable period of time studying the Vedanta Shastra (of Vyasa) and other kindred works, and then left for Calcutta. How long he stayed at this place is not known, but certain it is that, on his return from the great city, he resided for some time at the town of Swaron.

It was while Swami Virjanand was stationed at Swaron, that he made the acquaintance of the Maharaja Vinay Singh of Alwar. More correctly, it was the Maharaja (king) that fell in with the Swami and made his acquaintance. While the latter was one morning standing in the Ganges, reciting the Vishnu Stotra of the great Shankara, the Maharaja, who had come to bathe in the river and was actually having a wash at the time, felt as if fascinated by the rich and thrilling tones in which the song was being poured forth. As the melody died away, much to the regret to the listeners in the neighborhood, and the Swami came out of the stream, the Maharaja approached the Sadhu of marvelous voice and, entering into conversation wit him, was struck with his erudition and with the loftiness and purity of his ideas.

The request was not long in coming that the Swami would accompany His Highness into his dominions, but, to the surprise of the Maharaja, it was refused: "You are a Raja, and I am a recluse," said the Swami; "how can I live with one of your station and surroundings?" The Maharaja, instead of taking the refusal in ill part and turning away, became more determined that ever to have his desire realized, and one day going into the garden where Virjanand was putting up, pressed his request with so much humility and earnestness, that Virjanand at last yielded, but not till His Highness had agreed to the condition that he should read with the Swami fro three hours daily, and that if he missed but a single lesson, unless under circumstances beyond his control, the Swami was at liberty to at once leave his court.

Having reached Alwar, the Maharaja assigned the Swami a palatial building to reside in, and commenced his studies. He proved a very good pupil, taking his lesson regularly and treating Virjanand with all the respect due from a disciple to his preceptor. The courtiers remarking their master's faith in the Swami and perceiving that he was really a man of sterling worth and deep learning - one who could only influence his associates for the better, became his sincere admires and availed themselves of his counsel, and company as of the as they could.

Not so the illiterate and selfish Brahmans around the person of the prince! They scented in the new-comer an enemy who would spare no pains to weaken the hold of superstition on the Maharaja's mind and to thus render him les liable to be led astray by them. Virjanand heard of their machinations, but caring neither for prince nor peasant but in the prince and peasant's own interests, he was, perfectly indifferent as to what they thought of him and as to what plots they formed against him.

Virjanand had been teaching he Maharaja three years, when one day, His Highness, forgetting that it was time for his lesson, joined a party of pleasure and spent several hours in enjoyment. The result was, that it was extremely late when he put in an appearance at the house of his preceptor, whom he found in a temper. "You have broken your promise, Maharaja," said he, "but I will not, and I now thingk myself absolved from my engagement."

His Highness expressed regret at his conduct and promised a better behavior in future, but it was in vain. Virjanand set off from Alwar for Bharatpur without so much as informing the prince that he was going. Possibly, he was convinced that the Maharaja found study no longer pleasant, and this being the case, there was no reason why he should not be strictly uncompromising in adhering to the condition of his engagement in his dealings with His Highness.

Having arrived at Bharatpur, Swami Virjanand stayed there, at the request of Maharaja Balwant Singh, the ruler thereof, for six months, and, when taking his leave of the Maharaja, he prepared to depart to Mursan, a small town, the

Maharaja presented him with four hundred rupees in cash and a shawl.

At Mursan, the Swami, stopped for some time with a wealthy reis named Teekam Singh, and then returned to Swaron, where he fell dangerously ill, the physicians actually going so far as to give him up. But the Supreme Healer came to his assistance, for a nobler mission was yet in store for him, and he must live for many years yet to accomplish it!

It is not known how long Swami Virjanand stayed at Swaron after he had recovered his health, or what places he visited after he had left Swaron the second time; but what is positively certain is, that late in the year 1893, V.E., (A.D. 1836) he arrive at Mathura, and taking up his quarters in a temple resume his work of teaching. As one day after another passed away, the liking of the Swami for Mathura grew stronger and stronger, and finally he became resolved to permanently settle down in the place. Accordingly he rented a suitable building, and, reorganizing his classes, formally opened a school.

His fame, as a pre-eminently competent and successful teacher, spread in the city and in its vicinity, and he was ever ready to measure his strength against all who should dispute his learning. Only a single instance would suffice. Rangacharya, the famous leader of the Vaishnovites, came on a visit to Mathura, and his guru, Krishna Shastri, also soon followed him, from the Deccan. The pupils of Virjanand and those of Krishna Shastri met, and a discussion took place between the parties as to t he nature of the smasa (combination) in AJATUKTI.

The disciples of Virjanand held that it was shashtitatpursha (Genitive Determinative Compound), while those of Krishna Shastri contended that it was saptamitatpurusha (Locative Determinative Compound). Neither of the two parties would yield, and each referred the question to their guru for a decision. Virjanand assured his disciples that they were in the right while Krishna Shastri told his that truth was on their side. The result of this was, that a discussion was arrange between the teachers, Seth Radha Krishna being assigned the position of Madhayastha, or of one who was to declare, on the termination of the debate, as to which of the two parties had been victorious. The condition of the Shastrartha was, that the party who should come to be defeated should lose two hundred rupees to the other, the Seth supplementing the amount due to the winner by an additional hundred from his own pocket. The news of the approaching discussion spread through out the city, and the people flocked, in crowds, to the place where it was to be held. The vidyarthis on both sides took their seats, the presidential seat was duly occupied, and the representative youths from each group stood up to have tilting before the principal combatants should arrive and the shastrartha proper should commence.

Several vidyarthis of Virjanand had express orders to come and inform him at once when the Shastri arrived, so that he might be on the spot without delay: but the worthy Shastri never put in an appearance, and the Swami waited for report of his arrival in vain. The Seth being rather partially inclined towards the Shastri and probably well aware how trying it would be to the Shastri to make good his position in an encounter with the prajnachakshus Swami, finally giving it as his judgment that Virjanand has been worsted in the struggle. The bulk of the huge gathering was astonished at such a verdict.

When Krishna Shastri had failed to make his appearance and when no shastrartha had taken place between him and Virjanand , how could the Seth, in justice, declare that Virjanand had been routed? Full of indignation at the conduct of the Seth, the Swami say the Collector, Mr. Alexander, and requested him either to get a Shastrartha held between Krishna Shastri and himself, or, in the absence thereof, to compel the Seth to make the total sum of five hundred rupees to him (Virjanand).

Mr. Alexander counseled the Swami not to bother his head about the money, for the Seth was rich and powerful and could, if necessary, spend thousands to vex and harass him even though he was in the right. In the meantime the Seth had not been idle. He go the Pandits of Agra and Benaras to certify, in writing, that Virjanand had been defeated by the Shastri, and was, of course, the winner of the sum staked on the issue of the encounter.

Virjanand deeply felt this gross injustice, and he wrote to and called upon the Pandits of Benaras (Pandit Kaka Ram Shastri, Gaur Swami, Kahsi Nath Shastri, etc.), to solemnly declare as to who was in the right. These pandits confessed that the right lay on his side, but added: "We have already signed the Seth's paper, and we can do no more?" Pitying these selfish men, the Swami went to Agra, but the reply of the Pandits of that place was the same as that of their brethren of Mathura, and he returned from his fruitless trip utterly disappointed.

To make his assurance doubly sure, he commenced an investigation of the question which had given rise to the shastrartha that never came off, and, while yet busied with his books, he heard one day, early in the morning, a Dakshini Pandit repeating the Panini. He listened attentively, and as the Brahman's recitation progressed, the conviction force itself on his mind that Krishna Shastri was wrong and that he was in the right. From that day, Swami Virjanand transferred his allegiance entirely to the works of the Rishis, and began to instruct his disciples too in the same.

Six months after the Swami had been so shabbily dealt with, Lakshamana Jyotishi (astrologer), a disciple of Krishna Shastri, fell dangerously ill. The astrologer thought it was the Dandi Swami's curse that was at the bottom of his illness, and, being under such an impression, he sent a request to Seth Ram Krishna to see the Swami and, by making him a reparation, to secure his forgiveness. The Seth duly waited upon the Swami and made known to him the Jyotishi's request, adding that he was willing to offer the Swami double the amount he had lost if he would but grant the forgiveness sought for. Swami Virjanand, in reply, bade the Joytishi and told to disabuse their minds of the impression they were under for man could do nothing and everything rested with God. "You have nothing to apprehend from me," added he; "indeed, I would go so far as to give a thousand rupees from my own pocket to save Jyothishi." The Jyothishi died on the following day. Virjanand had uttered words of truth, for God alone can save.

In the beginning of Samvat 1918, 1861 A.D. a grand Durbar was held at Agra, in which almost all the leading Native Princes took part. Maharaja Ram Singh of Jeyapur was one of those who attended, and hearing that a Dandi Swami of no uncommon type was present in the city, requested him to pay him a visit. When the Swami came, the Maharaja rose to advanced as for as the door to receive him, and conducting him to his own singhasan seated him thereon. After the two had talked a little, the Maharaja expressed a wish to learn Vyakarana (grammar) from the Swami. The Swami replied; " I should be only too happy to accede to your Highness's wishes, provided you would bind yourself to study with me for three hours daily. Works like the Ashtadhyayi are a hard reading, and need sustained application.

On second thoughts, His Highness decided not to read Panini or any other similar book. Ti would) as the Swami had kindly considerable time daily to be finally mastered, and His Highness doubted if he could stand the strain or regularly spare the time. "If you would kindly prepare an easy book to your own grammar," said the Maharaja, " I should be glad to learn it." Of course, the could not do it, for that would be an insult to the Rishis, and there was an end of the matter.

At parting the Maharaja presented the Swami with two hundred rupees, two gold mohars, and shawl, but he Swami refused to accept the gift, saying that it was not from interested motives that he had accepted the Maharaja's invitation. The Maharaja did not think it prudent to insist, but after six months sent the things back to the Swami from his own dominions, assigning him further an allowance of rupees fifteen monthly. Another prince allowed the Swami four annas ad ay and on the income thus accruing the Swami principally lived.

Swami Virjanand was distinguished figure at Mathura, being looked upon, and rightly, as one of the greatest Sanskrit scholars of his time in India and a person of real sterling worth in every respect. whenever any stranger of consequence visited Mathura, he was sure, he be a Native or a European, to call upon the Swami and have a talk with him on advocacy of what he thought right, won him the respect of all but the selfish. If a European or a Native misquoted the Scripture, or did not take care, or was unable, to be correct in his pronunciation of

Vedic words, he was snubbed there and then. And as we have seen, the Swami was ever ready ot vindicate his views when anyong took exception to them and nothing gave him so much pleasure as a public discussion with the supporters of the false orthodoxy of modern times.

The books which, among many others, he held in the greatest abhorrence, were the Puranas. His contempt for these was so absolute that he would sleep with the Bhagwat placed under one of the legs of the couch. And he was not much to blame for his attitude towards the Puranas. Apart from the fact that they are childish and unscientific productions, they are in many place, as immoral as the Tantras, and hence can produce no effect on the reader's mind.

Is it possible that any moral can tolerate the supremely disgusting and insufferable stuff to be found, for instance, the Linga Purana? The feats of the Linga, though heroic (!) indeed, are a record of shame, a tale of utter indecency and obsenity. Do such books teach religion? If the reply be in the reply be in the affirmative, then we say that they teach a religion which can only debase the people.

Further, a scholar like Swami Virjanand could not but feel that it is the Puranas that have been chiefly instrumental in holding up the true Vedic religion. To the ridicule and contempt of a large portion of mankind. For it is they that evolved a jarring and inharmonious multiplicity out of a perfect, all-embracing Unity.

In a spirit of rivalry and swayed by selfish motives, they relegated the Supreme Being , of whom the Veda speaks, to the background, and set up each of the various names and from under which He appears in the Scripture, as an independent and absolute Deity. Shiva, Vishnu, Brahma, Devi, and so on, are no longer names of the same all-wise, all-powerful and all-pervading Lord, but figure in the pages of the Puranas as separate and distinct personalities perpetually at war with each other and fiercely disputing or ignoring each other's claim to the sovereignty of the universe..

And thus, thanks to the Puranas, idolatry had sprung up where the worship of the one and only God originally existed, the many false gods have come to usurp the place which rightfully belongs, has always belonged, and shall ever belong, to the Paramaatma alone. No genuine follower of the Vedas can help resenting the perfidious concoctions of the authors of the Puranas, and of Swami Virjanand nothing less could have been expected. An anecdote is told of the Swami, which shows hoe he felt towards the misleading modern compositions. Mr. Priestly, the officiating Collector, and a really worthy European, calling upon the Swami one day, asked if he could do him any service. The Swami replied that the greatest service the collector could do to him was to get hold of every copy of the Kaumud existing in the land and have it thrown into the Jamuna. Such is the value which the jeweler will always place on all false brilliants!

Swami Virjanand was of medium height, saprely built, and fair in complexion. He lived principally on milk and fruits. He would often put some saunf (aniseed) into his milk before drinking it. Once, through mistake, he swallowed arsenic, in sufficient quantity to kill a man. Prompt measures were taken as soon as the mistake was discovered. By having water, in copious quantities, but slowly and in the form of a thin stream, poured on his head, by lacing the body in a particular position, and by the force of will-power on the internal apparatus he was at last fortunate to escape the great danger that threatened his life. Swami Virjanand died of colic pains in Samvat 1925, 1868 A.D. at the age of seventy-one. It is said that two years before his demise, he had foretold his disciples that he should die on a certain day and of such a disease. He left this property worth Rs. 525 to Pandit Jugal Kishore, on of his pupils. When Swami Dayanand heard of his teacher's death, he exclaimed: "Verily, the sun of Vykarana has set!"

Virjanand's entire life passed in teaching, but the only man who came up to his ideal of a pupil, whose heart beat in response to his own, who promised to realized the aspirations of the Blind Swami's great soul, was Dayanaand.

At Mathura -studies under Swami Virjanand.

Dayanand reached Mathura in any part of the year 1916, V.E (1859), and put up in the temple of Lakshmi Narayan. the accounts he had heard of Virjanand's learning proved only too correct, and he immediately sallied forth in quest of his dwelling, which he was not long in finding. For there was scarcely anyone in Mathura who was unacquainted with the name of the Dandi Swami, who had not heard of his vast learning, and who did not know that the stern old Sanyasi alays lived with his doors shut. Dayanand knocked at the door, and the question came in sharp tones from within, "Who is there?"

"A Sanyasi, Dayanand by name," was the reply.

"Do you know anything of Sanskrit grammar?"

Yes, I have studied Saraswata, etc."

At this reply the door opened, and Dayanand went in. Virjanand examined Dayanand, and, on the termination, told him that there was a vast difference between the true Aryan Literature and the books composed by common mortals, and as for himself, he had absolutely no respect for the latter and never taught them. Dayanand could not disabuse his mind of the idea he had clung to for years, in a moment, but he arguments of the Swami prevailed, and he eventually consented to have nothing to do with the works which had the stamp of true science and true wisdom on them.

He even went so far as to throw in the Yamuna his old stock, so that Vrijanand might be pleased, and admit him as his pupil. But, though all this was satisfactory enough, the fact could not be lost sight of that Dayanand was a Sanyasi, and Virjanand could not see how a Sanyasi could afford to carry on his studies with him. "I am not in the habit of teaching Sanyasis," said he; "but if I take you in as a pupil, how will you manage to live?" Dayanand replied that he would find himself food somehow or other, no matter if it was the coarsest possible: all that he cared for was knowledge, and that, hoped, Virjanand would not refuse him. Finding him persistent in his entreaties, Virjanand at last granted Dayanand's prayer, and having raised a subscription of thirty-one rupees got him a copy of the Mahabhashya to commence his studies with.

Shortly after Dayanand had come and taken up his abode at Mathura, a severe famine spread in the land, and even the well-to-do become sparing of their gifts to the suppliants. The hospitality extended to the vidyarthis began to be more or less withheld, and they were often hard to put to it for a meal. Dayanand behaved manfully in this period of trial, living on roasted gram, or on dry bread made of the same article, from day-to-day. These came to him from the house of Durga khatri, Dakawala.

Nothing less can be expected of a true Sanyasi, or of a true Brahmachari. In whatever character Dayanand may be regarded, he proved himself fully worthy of it. An austere life is an essential condition of true brahmacharya, and a Sanyasi that is not perfectly contended with whatever the householder gives him in the shape of victuals, belies the traditions of he order to which he belongs.

In course of time, a certain Pandit Amar Lal, a man of philanthropic mind and of unbounded charities, struck with the virtues of Dayanand, took upon himself to supply him with food and with books. He made a point of taking him daily home and of seeing him take his meals in his presence.

If ever he had invitation to dine at a friend's house: he would never obey the call till he had first fed his guest at his own house. Dayanand waa deeply beholden to this generous man, and his gratitude lasted till death. It is said that the Pandit feasted no-less than one hundred twenty-five Brahmans daily at his dwelling! Another person, to whom Dayanand was indebted fro pecuniary help, was one Hardev, who used to give him two rupees monthly for "milk."

A money-changer, named Govardhan Das, also assisted him according to his means, defraying his expenses on oil, which came up to four annas a month.

Dayanand's life at Mathura was a life of incessant toil. He read day and night, spending hours in thought and contemplation, and frequently holding discussion with his fellow-students on various subjects of importance. In his moments of leisure, he would speak to those around him on the value of Brahmacharya, and exhort them, the Brahmans to particular, to be regular in the performance of their sandhya and their agnihotra. His extreme thirst for knowledge, his quick and clear perception of the nature of things, his lucid and convincing expositions of Shastric teaching, and, above all, his righteous ways made him a favorite with the vidyarthi community, and his company was sought after by them, one and all.

Dayanand's reverence for Virjanand increased daily. He loved and served him with his whole heart, performing most cheerfully the humblest offices to please him and to make him more comfortable. He would sweep the floor, and bring pitcher after pitcher of water from the Yamuna, so that the dirt might be effectually washed out of the house, and his preceptor have his daily bath liberally.

Virjanand was often cross with his foremost pupil, and, in his anger, would order him to be driven out of the house; but Dayanand would not mind his roughness and would re-gain his favor by his humility and his attentions. Whenever he found that his own entreaties were of not avail, he would get some influential man to intercede fro him with his teacher, and the desired forgiveness was eventually obtained. Swami Virjanand, it is daid, would frequently inflict corporal punishment upon Dayanand.

One day he dealt him such a blow with hs stick as to seriously injure his hand. The only reply which Dayanand made to his guru was to address him as follows: "Most holy Sir, you should not give yourself so much trouble on my account. My body is hard as iron and cannot be hurt much with your stick. Your own delicate hands might suffer by the exertion, and that would give me real pain."

The mark of the blow remained on Dayanand's hand as long he lived, and whenever he looked at it, the remembrance of the debt of immense and endless gratitude, which he was under to his guru, would make his whole being thrill with emotion.

Dayanand read with Swami Virjanand for two years and-a-half, and during this period he had mastered Ashtadhyayi, Mahabhashya, the Vedanta Sturas, and many other works. And when his course of education was finished, and he thought it was time for him to leave, he, in conformity with the usages of olden times, approached his guru and, laying half a seer of cloves before him, asked permission to depart. Virjanand gave him his blessings and called upon him to produce, after the fashion of the students of yore, suitable dakshina (present) marking the termination of his course of education. Dayanand made answer that he had nothing that he could venture to offer to his most revered guru. "Do you think I would ask you for anything you have not got?" was the rejoinder. Being silenced by the loving rebuke. Dayanand said: "Most holy Sir, I am ready to lay at your feet whatever you thing I have really got in my possession."

"Dear son, you have got it, and that is true knowledge. If you would pay me my dakshina, give this knowledge to thy mother-land. The Vedas have long ceased to be taught in Bhraartavarsha (India), go and teach them; teach the true Shastras, and dispel, by their light, the darkness which the false creeds have spread. Remember that while works by common men are utterly misleading as to the nature and attributes of the one true God, and slander the great Rishis and Munis, those by the ancient teachers are free from such a blemish. This is the test which will enable you to differentiate the true, ancient teaching from the writings of ordinary men."

Dayanand bowed his head in aquiescence, assuring his guru that he would do his best to accomplish the task assigned to him, upon which the guru once more gave him his blessing and permitted him to depart. How far Dayanand kept his word and how far he succeeded in redeeming that word, is known to the world. Few men have labored as Dayanand did. His self-sacrifice and his patriotism wer of the highest possible type, almost who can but say that they might once more prove the making of India? Verily, they will!

Five-year Review of Past Studies

Dayanand's life, as we are well aware, had, for years been the life of a Brahamchari and a Sanyasi combined, and anything but lacking in the vanaparastha stage. He had from his childhood onwards been passionately found of study, profoundly meditative and wholly indifferent to the comforts and attractions of the world. We may, in the contemplation of his personality, before, in obedience to a welcome summons from a great teacher, he appeared on the arena of great reforms, recognize in him almost exclusively the Brahmachari, but what of that? His was an ideal brahmacharya of the ancient type, identical with and embracing both the Vanaprastha and the sanyasa.

He devoted long periods to reflection and self-subjugation, and he was formally initiated into the sanyasa, and was thus Vanaprastha and the in one. But we maintain that even if he had not gone through the forms, even if he had not put on ochre-colored garments and sought the forest and the cave, he would still be a true Vanaprasthi and a true Sanyasi, for it is the spirit which imparts life and reality to all distinctions, titles and appellations. Henceforward, we shall know him as Swami Dayanand Saraswati.

Virjanand's great pupil entered upon the work which he might take in hand as of right; but it was not much that he accomplished during the first five years (Samvaat 1920 -25), A.D. 1863 - 68 the greater part of this period being applied to a revision and review of his past acquisitions. The strongest man when preparing for a leap would go back several steps to be able to put the success his entire energy into the exertion awaiting him, and so it is with the preacher and the teacher.

However able and gifted these may be, they must take stock of all their resources before they burst upon the public, to brave and to bend it to their will and to thus accomplish the great mission of their life. Whatever little we know of the work of Swami Dayanand during the five years specified, may be described in the compass of a few chapters.

Soon after parting with his teacher, the Swami visited Agra. Here he put up in Lala Gulla Mal Aggarwal's garden, giving himself up to his books and preferring retirement. One day, a wealthy Sanyasi, named Kailas Parvat, came and halted in this very garden and commenced a katha. The Gita is no easy book, and it were no surprise if an average Sadhu, acquainted but imperfectly with the Shastras, should break down when expounding a particularly difficult verse.

Kailas Parvat, in due course coming to one of the difficult couplets, failed to explain it to the satisfaction of his audience.

Some one among the gathering humbly requested Swami Dayanand, who happened to stay there at the time, to interpret the verse. The Swami complied, and his exposition was so learned and beautiful that the listeners were charmed. Kailas Parvat joined in the applause, praising the Swami's superior learning and advising those desirous of study to come to him for their lesson. The counsel was gladly followed by the individuals to whom it was given, and several of them commenced coming to Swami Dayanand for instruction.

At the request of the people, the Swami began here a katha of the Panchdashi. But he had not gone through many pages when he came across a passage which said that God himself is subject to the power of maya (delusion!) Hastily throwing down the book the Swami informed the congregation that he should no longer have anything to do with such mischievous and misleading stuff. It was the composition of a common man, and he could not, in defiance of the express orders of his guru, teach a book prejudicial to the works of the Rishi's. the Swami got the Sandhay (the Arya Prayer-book) first published at Agra, and the publication pleased his admirers so much that a gentleman named Rup Lal had thirty thousand copies of it distributed.

During his residence at this place Dayanand was in constant correspondence with Swami Virjanand, who remove the doubts that arose in his mind from time to time. He sometimes waited upon him in person, to have answers in full.

In Samvat 1921 (1864 A.D.), after about two years residence at Agra, Dayanand set off towards Dhaulpur in search of the Vedas, and from here he repaired to Lashkar Gwaliar. Early in 1865 A.D. the Maharaja had the saptah or seven-days katha of the Bhagwat set up. No less than four hundred Pandits were to take part in and conduct the rites connected with katha. Hearing of this, the Swami, who was then on the Abu Hills, came down with four or five vidyarthis, and began to fearlessly expose the absurdities and the immoral teaching of the book.

The Maharaja wa not long in being informed of the Swami's arrival. He once ordered some of his men to wait upon him and ascertain his opinion as regards the desirability or otherwise of the katha which the state Pandits had commenced. The Swami's reply was that such a thing, as the result would show, could be productive of nothing but pain and suffering. "If His Highness is sincerely desirous of doing something meritorious," added the Swami, "he should have the Bhagwat discontinued in favor of "Gayatri-recitation." When the reply was communicated to the Maharaja, he burst out laughing, remarking playfully that it was not for him to contradict a Sanyasi like the Swami; but as for himself, he could not revoke his order, as the preparations in connection with the katha were complete.

The katha came to an end, but, strange to relate, the very night the reading terminated and the royal drums beat to announce the joyful event, the Maharani was prematurely confined to give birth to a still-born child. And only a month or two after cholera of a virulent type broke out in the city, carrying away thousands, including the Maharaja's son, Of course, the Swami was no believer in miracles. When he spoke unfavorably of the Bhagwat, he did so because the book is really an execrable production and an outrage upon the glory of the Supreme, who alone should be worshipped and adored. Honoring and reading such books can do not good to any one either in this world or for the next. If a series of misfortunes befell the Maharaja, they were not effects of the Swami's prophecy. The Swami must have spoken of the veil of reading the Bhagwat, in like terms, in many other places, and it may be presumed that the announcement did not lead to anything like the disastrous consequences which followed his declaration in the Gwaliar State. Enlightened men will always be careful how they connect as cause and effect events not linked together by any such relation, events which are mere accidents and nothing else.

The Swami repeatedly sent challenges to Ramacharya, Gopalcharya and others for a shastrarth, but no one came forward for a discussion.

Leaving Lashkar Gwaliar, Swami Dayanand proceeded to Karoli, and thence having passed onto the capital of the Jeypur State, in company with three Brahmans, put up in a garden.

There or four shastrarths were held here, on a minor scale, and in each of these his deep learning and acute reasoning exported admiration from all present. In one of the discussions, held in the presence of Vyas Baksshi Ram, in a State Mandir, the Raj Pandits went so far as to deny that the Mahabhashya was an authoritative Vyakarna! When the Swami called upon them to put the same in writing, they looked foolish and said nothing.

At the request of Thakur Ranjit Singh of Achrol, conveyed through Thakur Hamir Singh of Bekaneer, the Swami visited the former and the two conversed on dharmic subjects. The Swami's words produced the desired effect on the Thakur's mind. He gave up idolatry, and going daily to the residence-place of the Swami, would hear him explain the Manu Smriti and the Upanishads. The katha was attended by many other people besides.

The expositions of the Swami were so clear and so conviction-carrying that his listeners could not fail to be influenced for the better.

Witness are not wanting, even so late as now, are not wanting, even so late as now, whose sense of gratitude compels them to depose that they were real gainers by the Swami's presence in their midst. If they were addicted to drinking, it was that noble individual whose comments on the words of the Rishis weaned them from their evil habit. If they were loose in morals and were wont to set the dictates of virtue at defiance, it was he who taught them to behave better. And so on. Every man who had occasion to come in contact with the Swami, felt all the better for having been in his company.

The Swami, though a believer in one God and teaching Him alone, had still the symbols of Shaivism on his person. He converted thousands of people to his own purer from of Shaivism, distributing rudraksas (necklaces or rosaries) to al his admirers. It was he who initiated the Maharaja Ram Singh into the creed.

In Samvat 1922 (March, 1866 A.D.) Swami Dayanand left Jeypur for Pushkar, where a great fair was going to be shortly held. Having reached this place, he put in the Brahma Mandir, and, inviting discussions, commenced a vigorous refutation of idol-worship. Many Brhamans took up the challenge, but were invariably worsted in the struggle. Seeing how utterly unable they were to cope with the Sanyasi, they, in their despair, waited upon a learned man named Baikuth Shastri, and solicited his help.

The Shastri promised to hold a Shastrarth with the Swami at his own quarters, but failing, for some reason or other, to keep his appointment, the Swami himself repaired to his abode, and the contemplated discussion came off in the presence of four hundred Brahmans.

The Shastri spoke in favor of the Bhagwat, and the Swami against the teaching of that book. So scathing was the Swami's criticism on what the Shastri had not alternative but to take shelter, like average Pandits, in mere "word-controversy." But here also he found in his antagonist more than his match.

As a last resource, the Shastri conducted the Swami to his guru, who, on hearing the arguments of both parties, gave his verdict in the Swami's favor. Baikunth Shastri bowed to his master's superior judgment, and had the frankness to acknowledge in public that Dayanand was in the right.

It would appear that during his continuance at Pushkar, the Swami had ceased to be even a nominal adherent of Shaivism. He advised the people to cast off the great symbol of Shaivism - the necklace, and to have nothing to do with the creed. As a result of this, Baikunth Shastri was deluged with complaints against the Swami, but that good man replied that he failed to see why he should meddle with the Sanyasi's doing. "But, said he in conclusion, "whatever" the worth of Dayanand's teaching, he will never succeed in his mission till he has gained some prince as his disciple."

AT AJMERE - THE AGRA DURBAR

The next place which Swami Dayanand visited was Ajmere (30th May, 1866). Here, as usual, he commenced exposing the Bhagwat, proclaiming it as an immoral book out and out and false in its teaching. He denounced the temples also, and fearlessly gave it out as his opinion that religious necklace and rosaries were nothing better than so much wood. The Pandits of Ajmere were horror-struck at the views of the Swami, and went into paroxysms of rage over them, but, being unable to meet him to argument, they could do no more than send him the following writing;-

1. A Sanyasi should not stay more than three days in an village or city.
2. He should never drive a carriage.

These were the questions though not in the usual interrogative form, and the Swami replied to them in writing, pointing out, at the same time, the mistakes with which the composition of the Pandits bristled.

At Ajmere the Swami had a discussion with the Rev. Mr. Grey, the Rev. Mr. Robinson and Rev. Schoolbred of Biawar, on "God, Soul and the Laws of Nature, and the Vedas." The discussion lasted for full three days, and the Rev. gentlemen found it hard to face their antagonist. As an interchange of civilities, the Swami saw Mr. Robinson at his own house.

On this occasion, Padri asked the Swami if it was true that Brahma, influenced by lust ran after his own daughter.

The Swami replied that the story was a libel on one of the greatest of Rishis, that if the deed, of which the story spoke, was ever done in the world, it must have been done by a depraved mortal, scarcely deserving the name of "man".

Rev. Mr. Robinson was a great admirer of the Swami. He gave him a certificate, stating that the Swami was profoundly versed in the Vedas, and that he had never seen so learned a man in his entire life. Such individuals, wrote the Padri, were rare in the world, and their company could not but be productive of good to all.

The document enjoined upon all who wished to see the Swami to treat him with all possible respect. The Swami also called upon Mr. Davidson, Deputy commissioner of Ajmere, and , in the course of conversation, said to him: "People of false creeds are plundering your subjects. The king being like a father, it behoves the representatives of Government to take steps to remedy the evil."

The Deputy Commissioner's answer to this was that the policy of Government was perfect neutrality in matters of religion. The Agent to the Governor-General in Council was anther European gentleman wit whom Swami Dayanand had an interview at this place. The Swami talked to him on the necessity of protecting the cows, setting forth, in detail, the benefits which Government and the people would derive from the adoption of the measure recommended. The Agent admitted thee force of the Swami's arguments but said he was sorry he could do nothing in the matter.

This worthy gentleman gave the Swami a letter, saying that it would secure him an introduction to whom so ever it was shown. He further sent a letter to Raja Ram Singh of Jeypur, in which he expressed regret at His Highness having given but an indifferent reception to a man of the Swami's stamp.

Hearing that a grand Durbar was to be held at Agra (November, 1866 A.D.), Swami Dayanand felt that he could not miss such a splendid opportunity for the determination of truth, and consequently left for the place in the company five vidyarthis. The Dubar came off, and was a magnificent affair, all the Native Rulers of the country wit their followers being present on the occasion. The Swami commenced his updesh (lectures), publishing at the same time; in Sanskrit, and eight-page tract, sowing the puerile character of the teachings of the Bhagwat. Thousands of copies of this publication were distributed free among the gathering to the real delight of all true inquires, particularly of those who could understand Sanskrit.

In the meantime, receiving from the Maharaja of Jeypur an invitation fro a discussion with Rangacharya, the Swami left for Mathura to have an interview with his guru before obeying the call from His Highness. The meeting between the teacher and the pupil was most cordial. Laying two gold mohars and a muslin-piece at his preceptor's feet, and presenting him, moreover, with a copy of his tract on Bhagwat, the Swami at last asked for leave to depart, informing the great man that he should next preach at the approaching Haridwar Fair,

Virjanand, with his heart overflowing with joy at the work that was being done, blessed his noble disciple, wishing him the fullest measure of success in his mission. The two were not destined to see each other in life again!

From Mathura, the Swami proceeded to Jeypur. The Maharaja expressed a wish to see him early, but before the wish had time to be realized, some on informed His Highness that the Swami was an enemy of Shaivism and of idolatry. On hearing this he was deeply offended, and determined not to admit the Swami to an audience. It was, therefore, nothing strange that the Swami, ignorant of the change that had taken place in the Maharaja's mind, should, on reaching he place, be informed that His Highness was 'out'. The swami guessed the truth, and observing that a Sanyasi like him could affor to dispense with the company of princes, returned to his quarters.

AT KUMBHA FAIR - HARIDWAR

Haridwar is a place situated amidst surroundings of surpassing beauty, in the midst of a scenery the most glorious and bewitching of its kind. The rock and hill about is covered with vendure of superb loveliness and generally wrapped in a mantle of clouds developing new shapes and new colors every moment. The river Ganges, round which Nature has wrought itself to such exquisite charm and fascination, lends, as it speeds on its eternal course, an attraction to the locality which is simply irresistible.

No place could be more welcome to a person of a contemplative and devotional turn of mind than Haridwar. The climate is bracing, and as regards the water of the Ganges, it has been testified by men of science that it is the purest imaginable. No disease-germs or bacilli can flourish in it, kills them immediately after they are thrown into it. Epidemics, no doubt, now and then break out even at Haridwar in these days; but man, when acting in ignorance, or under guidance of a perverted judgment, will turn best gifts of God into a veritable curse.

The Ganges has always been a favorite with the best representatives of the Aryan nation in Science and literature. Many of those writings which embody the highest and most valuable thoughts of our saints and sages were produced on the banks of the Ganges or in its vicinity, and much of that poetry which bears on it the stamp of true genius and of which we are deservedly proud, was give to us by those who were familiar with the noble stream and its environments.

The name of every grotto and cave, of every tank and fountain in the neighborhood of Haridwar, bears witness to the sincere and genuine character of the regard in which the place was held by the illustrious Aryas of yore.

For ages and ages was Haridwar the residence place of the sage and saint, and of the literary man who taught, and inspired with lofty thought and high resolve, all who came in contact with them, and life in India was a life of happiness and peace, of righteous activity and continual progress.

But a time came when the true thinker, the true instructor, and the true writer had all but ceased to exist in places like Haridwar, and when the impostors of every description sat bold and conspicuous on the vacated seats, in hundreds and thousands. It is difficult to say when precisely the reign of "sham" commenced, but there is ground to believe that it commenced long before the commencement of the Christian Era.

When Heinen Tsang, the Chinese traveler, visited India, and he came here in the seventh century after death of Christ, he found Haridwar much the same thing as it is in these days. Among thousands of pilgrims that came to bathe at Haridwar in these days, the belief was common that a plunge in the Ganges was sure and certain means of obtaining salvation. There was never perhaps a time when fairs were not held at Haridwar; but while originally the people flocked to the place from motives born of an enlightened.

Perception of the real factors in the evolution and development of the soul, - from the consciousness that the company of the wise and good was indispensable for spiritual elevation, they came in the latter ages (which followed soon after the great battle of Kurukchhetra had permanently crippled, almost utterly paralyzed, the Indian intellect), to make it their periodical rendezvous mainly led by hankering after a bath in the waters of Ganges, believing, in their ignorance, that no more was required to wipe out all moral and spiritual sins and to secure endless bliss in the world to come.

Swami Dayanand knew what Haridwar once was, and what it latterly had been, and he made up his mind to pay it a visit on the approaching Kumbha Fair (Baisakh, 1924, B.E.), to do all in his power towards exposing imposture, and to disabuse the layman's mind of the impression that Haridwar was a Tirath in the true sense of the word. He was there a month before the actual date of the Fair, and he found place choked with votaries of a thousan-and-one false creeds stiff with self-conceit and engaged in fierce disputation with one another, purely worldly consideration being at the bottom of most of the quarrels.

The Swami fixed upon Sapat Sarover, a palce at a distance of three miles from Haridwar, and right on the path which lead to Rishikesh, and having constructed some thatch-work on the spot chosen, took up his abode therein. He named his quarters - Pakhand Khandni or the "exposers of sham and imposture," telling all who came to hear him that bathing on the steps of Haridwar was, spiritually, entirely, useless, and that the worship of God alone, as taught in the Scripture and the Upanishads, could give them salvation.

Along with preaching, a katha of the Upanishads was commenced, and the tract on Bhagwat was once more distributed in thousands. Offerings came to the Swami in cash and kind, but these were invariably distributed among the poor at the close of each day. Pretended Sadhus and Sanyansis, the apostles of Vammargism and Jainism and of other kindred systems of faith, whose principal object seems to be more or less to sap the foundation of all that is calculated to raise humanity Heavenward, generally kept their distance from the Swami's quarters, calling him all manner of names and denouncing him as innovator of the worst possible type!

Maharaja Ranbir Singh of Jammu and Kashmere was one of those notables who went to see the Swami during the Durbar-days. A friendly discussion took place on the 11th mantra of the 31st Chapter of the Yajur Veda.

BRAAMHAANO ASYA MUKHAMA ASEEDA BAAHOO RAAJANYAH KRITAH

OOROO TADASYA YADDAISHYAH PADBHYAAM SHOODRO AJAAYATA

The Swami explained the meaning of the mantra at length, showing how the metaphorical language of the Veda, when translated in plain terms, meant no more than that the Brahmans or those well-verse in Divine knowledge occupy the highest position among all the varnas, the Kshatriya the Vaishayas and the Shudras, standing below them, and above or below each other in the order of their varying degrees of merit and sterling worth. Those who held that the Brahmans had proceeded from the mouth of God, the Kshatriyas from His arms, and so on, were in the wrong for God has neither mouth nor arms, nor thighs, nor fee; he is the incorporeal progenitor of the entire universe.

The Maharaja's spokesman, the faous Vishuddhanand, hast to accept the Swami's exposition, though he would not acknowledge as much. It is certainly and utterly futile attempt on the part of the idolators to seek in the Scripture for authority in favor of idol-worship. The Word of God emphatically declares:-

NA TASYA PRATIMAA ASTI YASYA NAAM MAHAVIDHYASHAH. Yajur Veda 32:3.

"He, the Supreme, of infinite glory, has no likeness, weight or measurement."

Other similar discussions took place, the Swami doing his best to give the inquirers an insight into the teachings of the ancient sages and leaving nothing unsaid that would destroy the hold of superstition on their minds. The rich and the poor, the high-born and men of humble birth, were al equally welcome to hear his words of truth, of right and justice.

Haridwar -Shastrarth

The Kumbha Fair had left the saddest impression on the mind of Swami Dayanand. He had gone there with great hopes, had put his whole energy into the work that had carried him thither, but for all that, the Fair left his spirits weighed down and depressed. So much idolatry, so much degrading and debasing adoration of the temporal, so much chicanery and fraud, so much of all that is low and mean, he had never before seen in one single spot, and is soul sickened at the sight.

It was not any ignorant and illiterate that clung to and cherished error, that did what should not be done, that followed and worshipped what should not be followed and worshipped, but even learned Pandits, and Sadhus deliberately went in for practices and advocated views that reason and authority alike condemned as objectionable and injurious. Could one individual vorrect the perverted the judgment of millions, could he cope with any success with the hydra-headed monster of unwisdom and delusion that sat enthroned on the heart of the mighty, myriad-manned Hinduism and regulated its life of thought and action?

The specter of doubt rose in Dayanand's mind and he felt 'despondent' "The nation is leagued against itself, knowingly courting its destruction, and hard it is to help it," mused he. As might be expected, the fit of despondency did not last long, the great man's soul rose above doubt and despair, and he exclaimed, "I must go on; all that I need is more force - moral and spiritual discipline (tapa)." The realization, by the Swami, of the need of having more tapa (force) was followed by his distributing among his followers all he had in the shape of clothes and utensils and cash, sending out of his money Rs. 35 together with a copy of the Mahabhashya, to his guru at Mathura. Kailas Parvat Swami who happened to be with Dayanand when the distribution took place, asked the meaning of this strange behavior. Dayanand's reply was, that he wanted to be perfectly independent and unencumbered, to be absolutely simple in life, and to teach unhampered and unfettered. All this took palce about a week or two after the Fair had come to an end.

Swami Dayanand had now nothing but his kopin on, and his kamandal, and he began to be much alone. But it would not do. Many people who knew him, sought him out, and disturbed his devotions. One day, some one, a selfish Brahman, no doubt, writing on a slip of paper in Sanskrit the words - The

Vedas are nowhere compared to the Bhagwat, pasted the slip agains the door of Dayanand's hut. When the offensive words caught the Swami's eye, his heart filled with indignation and he commenced denouncing and exposing the Bhagwat again. Not that his in any way affected his recently-formed resolution. He would wander along the banks of the Ganges, he said, till his tapa was complete, and during these wanderings he would speak in Sanskrit alone.

Leaving Haridwar, Swami Dayanand repaired to Rishikesh, and, after staying there for four or five days, he returned to Kankhal, and following the course of the stream, arrived at Landhora. He had not eaten wnything for the last three days, and felt terribly hungry. When he found that he could hold out no longer, he asked a peasant for something to eat. The man gave him three baingans (fruit of the egg-plant), and with these he appeased his hunger. Self-denial and self-control of this kind was practiced day after day, andwith the greatest cheerfulness.

At night the Swami would lie down on the bare ground, on sand, wherever it was to be had. If anybody wanted to speak to him, he would answer him in Sanskrit only. Now and hten a shastrarth would be held, and on such occasions also, the remarks he had to make would be made in Sanskrit alone. He would not stop long in one place: on the country, his movements were always rapid, and if he was here to-day, tomorrow he might, be found miles away. But wherever he went, his virtue and profound learning drew crowds. He taught Gayatri to al who came to him, and gave the Yajnopavit to the "twice-born" in large numbers. At Miranpur (a village 20 miles from Roorkee) he had a discussion with the Pandits for two days.

At the request of the Thakur Sher Singh of Karmvas (a village) the Swami, assisted by some forty pandits from Anupshahar, Danpur, Karnvas, Ahmednagar, Ramgarh, Jahangirabad, etc., helped in the performance of a "Yajna" on a grand scale. So well was everything managed and so faithfully the ancient ritual followed, that the function produced the happiest effect on the mind of the population in the neighborhood. A desire to tread once more in the footsteps of the sages O yore was aroused in the mind of the Twice-born classes, and Brahmans and Ksahatryas and Vaishayas thronged around the Swami from all sides, with a prayer to be invested with the "sacred thread." Nothing oculd give him greater pleasure than to comply with such a prayer. But at the same time he did positive work, he took caere that the negative was not left undone. The preaching of the Gurumantra and the investiture with the sacred thread and similar other things were uniformly followed (provided the Swami's leisure permitted) with a merciless exposure of the Puranas, and of the Tantras, Vammargism, polytheism, and so on.

"Whatever makes you forget virtue in the most comprehensive sense of the word, he would say, addressing the people, in the course of his observations, "whatever makes you take to drinking, to adultery, to stealing, to lying and so on, the same is the destroyer of the soul, and must be shunned."

At Anupshahara discussion on idol-worship took place with Shastri Hira Vallabha. It lasted for about six days and as the condition of the shastrarth was, that whichsoever of the parties was defeated, the same should accept the beliefs of the other, the Shastri, on finding the victory declare itself for Dayanand, rose from his seat, and, in the presence of the full assembly, acknowledged, in Sanskrit, that the learned Sannyasi taught nothing but the truth, and that the worship of stocks and stones was false.

After this taking up the chauki on which the thakurs (idols) were placed, he flung it into the Ganges. On the same day, on Pandit Tika Ram, who was a priest in a temple situated on the bank of the stream, severed his connection with the temple and idols for good, and got employment for which his literary attainments fitted him.

Also four more individuals renounced idol-worship, and, casting away their necklaces and rosaries, became the worshippers of the one true God!

Well has Mehta Aminchand sung:- "The Dandi has appeared, the hypocrites have betaken themselves to their hiding-places, the vain and conceited are in a fright, the vile and the unjust (with them).

"Shining with the effulgence of knowledge, has the sun come forth, dispelling the gloom and ushering in the light.

- The Swami, known by the name of Dayanand, has come into meeting, with the thunder-roar of the lion.
- He advocates truth and denounces fraud, thus holding up the signs and symbols of superstition to the contempt and ridicule of the world.
- The idle talkers, the disbelievers in God, and the believers in Mythology, are rending the air with their cries.
- Great atheists have become theists and wait upon him with folded hands.
- By his Veda-given strength and his cogent argument he has transformed Kaliyuga into its opposite.
- By the force of unbroken austerity and by the splendor and might of his spiritual power, he has struck terror into the hearts of he wicked.
- He is Yogishwara, a great Rishi, perfect in self-knowledge, one who is triumphant everywhere by the might of his truth."

AN ATTEMPT ON THE SWAMI'S LIFE

The shastrarth at Anupshahar had been far-reaching in its effects. Thakur Mukand Singh, of Chhalesar, a Chauhan Kshatrya by caste, had been, throughout, present at the discussion, and was one of those who, at the termination of the discussion, had been compelled to come to the conclusion, in spite of their long-cherished belief to the contrary, that the worship of idols was degrading and sinful in the extreme.

As soon as he returned to his village he informed his kinsmen that it was his intention to have all the family-temples-some thirty in number and scattered in different hamlets - thoroughly "overhauled" and relieved of the presence of idols for good. And in pursuance of this resolve he had all the images lying in the temples in question removed form their strongholds and thrown into the Kali Nadi or the Black Stream. This action was deeply displeasing to his caste-men, as many as sixty villages in the neighborhood actually went the length of indulging in the threat that the perpetrator of such a sacrilege should be outcasted without delay. The threat somehow or other was not carried out, the Thakur's caste-men being wise in their generation, as persecution, in the majority of cases, will only add fuel to the fire and strengthen and invigorate where it seeks to crush. Verily the preacher of truth is a mightier and more irresistible iconoclast than kings and princes with unlimited brute force to accomplish their purposes with!

While Swami Dayanand was yet staying at Karnvas, the report went round that a remover of the "forehead-mark" has made his appearance in the vicinity, and it was nothing surprising that a conservative man like Rao Karn Singh, a reis of Baroli, a disciple of the Chaivite Rangacharya, who had come to bathe in the Ganges, should, on learning the nature of the doctrines which the Swami preached, become his mortal foe. One day the Rao was condescending enough to pay a visit to the Swami, accompanied by twelve armed men. The Swami received him with great courtesy, though he could not help smiling as soon as the mark on the Rao's forehead caught his eye, and asking him further, in Sanskrit, why he, a Kshatrya, had put the beggar's sign on his person. This made the already angry Rao still more angry, and he enquired in a gruff voice, "Where shall I sit?" "Wherever you like," was the reply. As he and come with the sole object of venting his rage, he declared that he should sit just where the Swami sat. The Swami answered that he was welcome to please himself, and he made room for him at the same time, on his own seat.

As soon as the 'big' man was squatted down, he turned his blood-shot eyes towards the swami and exclaimed in wrathful tones: "Mendicant! You are not doing right things in disbelieving in the Ganges and the Tiraths. If you say anything against them in my presence, I shall deal with you severely." The tearful (!) words failed to move the Swami, and, after the fashion of true Sanyasis, he calmly replied: "If you want to fight, you had better go to the Rajas of Jeypur and Dhaulpur; but if, on the other hand, you want to hear truth sifted and differentiated from falsehood, then invite your guru

Rangacharya here, and we shall be ready for him." Having said this, the Swami entered upon a vigorous exposure of the Chakrankit Faith, of which the Rao was a follower.

At this the Rao was beside himself with passion, and laid his hand on the hilt of his sword. Before, however, he could use the weapon, a follower of his, one Baldev Parshad, a wrestler by profession, stopped him, saying, "don't' trouble yourself, Sir; I shall finish with the audacious Sadhu in the twinkling of an eye."

The wrestler raised his hand to strike, but Swami Dayanand was too quick for him. Seizing his arm, he gave him a push which sent him several paces back, reeling!

The men around the Swami (there were some fifty of them) were astonished at this sudden attack on an inoffensive person, and that too a Sadhu, and one of them Rao Karn Singh and his band meaningfully in these words: "If you molest this Sanyasi, you will only carry from here a broken skull!" Crest-fallen and gnashing his teeth in impotent rage, Karn singh rose and beat a hasty retreat, vowing to be even with his enemy at some other time.

After he had gone, many of the assembly stood up and gave it as their opinion that such conduct should not be left unreported to the Police.

The Swami, while thanking them for their regard for him, observed that if Karn Singh had failed to acquit himself as a true Kshatriya should, it did not follow that he too should prove himself false to his Brahminism. "I have, moreover," added he, 'received no hurt. The same of the thing is enough for the Rao. If he is wise, he won't repeat his feat again."

This was the first attack on the Swami's life, but, as we might suspect, it was not the last, even on the part of Karn Singh. Soon after this, he tried to incite some Bairagis to assault the Swami, promising that if they brought him his head, they should be liberally rewarded.

"You are, each of you," said he, to make his persuasion the more effective, "single and alone in the world. If you do what I tell you to, you will have dharma from being defiled." The

Bairagis, however, refused to commit such a horrible deed, telling him to keep his money to himself.

ANOTHER DASTARDLY ATTEMPT - A SHASTRARTH

Swami Dayanand was well aware of the value of winning young men over to the Truth, and consequently whenever he came across these, he made a point of addressing them a few weighty words which never failed to lead, sooner or later, to results of a most gratifying character. One day, while, during his wanderings, he sat on the banks of the Ganges, thinking and enjoying the bracing breeze, two young men, approaching him from behind, commenced rubbing ashes over his naked body. Turning round, the Swami fixed his piercing gaze on their faces and, pleased with the results of his survey, asked them how they passed their time.

They replied that they were students, studying the Bhagvat and the Kaumidi. The Swami, while commending their studious habits, informed them that the books they were reading were utterly worthless productions, and advised them to go on with the Ashtadhayai, the Manu Smriti, and the Upanishads instead. At the same time he spoke to them on the true Vedic religion, showing, in the course of his remarks, how mischievous and false the Chakrankit Faith was.

The students were greatly impressed with the Sanyasi's words, and going into their village, repeated to their elders what had been said to them. They also succeeded in inducing a Pandit of the Chakrankit Faith to accompany them, with a view to hold a discussion the Sanyasi, but the moment the Pandit set his eyes on the Sanyasi, he turned upon his heel, and entering a temple, hid himself there. Evidently, it was not the first time the Pandit had seen the Swami, he was well aware how he should fare in a discussion with such a man.

The people were displeased at his precipitate retreat, and the majority were convinced that the Chakrankit Faith, which many of them were going to embrace, was not worth their acceptance. The Swami was unwearied in pointing out the excellence of the Vedic Sanskars to the "twice-born" and, as we have seen, he invested many a member of his community with the "triple sacred thread." Of those who received the Yajnopavit from the hands of the great man, the largest number belonged to the Kshatriya castes, inhabiting the villages situated in the neighborhood of Karnvas.

The priestly class was in despair, and exasperated beyond measure, at finding their tricks exposed and their influence undermined, and they again and again asked themselves the question: "Are we really powerless to get this man out of the way, once for all?" Perhaps not as a Brahman of Anupshahar undertook proves very nearly succeeded in proving.

The unsuspecting Swami lectures on "Idol-worship" becoming intolerable, a priest, with his hear filled with hatred but yet suppression his real feelings with a powerful effort, came up to him with a smile and presented him with a betel-leaf. The unsuspecting Swami took the leaf, but before he had eaten it many minutes, the poison swallowed with it began to show its effects. Realizing his danger, he sought the bank of the Ganges without delay, and descending into the water set about doing the Neoli-karm, or swallowing large quantities of water and passing out the same, according to a prescribed method, from the intestines, so as to carry away gradually all hurtful matter from the stomach.

The process was successful, and the Swami's life was saved. But according to the fashion of great men, and in keeping with the traditions of the order to which he belonged, the Swami did not so much as administer a reproof to the murderous Brahman. Others, however, were not so forgiving. When Sayyad Mohammad the Tehsildar of Anupshahar, heard of the Brahaman's doing, he was very angry, and had the scoundrel sent to prison in a case pending in his Court against him, though lighter punishment could have fairly satisfied against him, though lighter punishment could have fairly satisfied the ends of justice. The Swami had great regard for the Tehsildar, but when the later came to see him, after the Brahman had been incarcerated, and told him how the fellow had been dealt with, the Swami felt annoyed and would not talk to the official. On the Tehsildar's inquiring what had done to displease the Swami, the answer was given in these words: " I have come into the world to release people from captivity and not to see them sent to prison. If the Brahman would be base, why then let him have his way; why should I be false to my own self?" It is said that Brahman was shortly acquitted in an appeal.

At Anupshahar, the Swami had also a discussion with Sadhu Krishnanand Saraswati, on "Idolatry." The Sadhu finding himself unable to maek good his position on the authority of the Scripture and the ancient Shastras, became irrelevant and sought shelter in Nyaya. But the Swami was a greater and truer logician than the Sadhu, had here also he found himself driven to the wall. However learned our Pandits may be, they set the slightest possible value on 'relevancy.' The fact is, that they are seldom conversant with the works of the sages. No wonder then that the Swami always spoke of the authors of Chandrika, Kaumidi, and other books, in terms of absolute contempt.

Austere in life, seeking, even during intensely cold nights, no better bed than a heap of rice-husks, defying sickness of all sorts or taking in sickness, if he ever did take, his only sovereign medicine, the tulsi leaves ground with pepper, remaining days and nights wrapped contemplation on the bank of the Ganges, giving good counsel to al who came to him, and constantly distributing the Gayatri Mantra, written with his own hands, among high and low, Swami Dayanand lived out the five years from Samvat 1920 to 1925. he did little int heway of teaching during this period, sending those who seemed really desirous of study to his guru at Mathura, with letters of recommedation. While at Shahbazpur, he received the news of Swami Virjanand's death, and, in tones of deep grief, exclaimed, "The highest authority on Vyakarna is not more." It was after the demise of his revered preceptor that Dayanand set regularly to work, and of this we shall know in the following pages.

THE ESTABLISHMENT OF SCHOOLS

It was about the close of the Samvat 1925, that Swami Dayanand, now resolved to have more system and regularity in his work, arrive at Farrukhabad. He had, as the result of prolonged reflection, come to the conclusion that schools and seminaries of a superior type were badly wanted in the country, and that preaching and shastrarth-holding, though extremely valuable in their way and indispensable for the success of his propaganda, could not alone achieve all and everything.

One great object, therefore, which his lectures at Farrukhabad were intended to serve, was to make clear to the people of means and influence, who could be brought to sympathize with his mission, the necessity of providing increased facilities for the acquisition, by promising vidyarthis, of sound and thorough ecucation in Sanskrit.

The words of such a Sanyasi could ot wholly fall ondeaf ears. Lala Panni Lal Seth, a Vaishya, who had from some time past been building a Shivalaya for the location therein of Shivalinga, was so impressed by the Swami's speeches that, bidding eternal farewell to idol-worship, had a Pathsahla opened in the newly-constructed building, undertaking further to pay Rs. 30 a month to the Pandit who was put in charge of the institution.

As to the expenses of food of students, some fifty in number, another generous man, Lala Durga Parshad, made himself responsible, for defraying these. The swami himself assisted in teaching the vidyarthis as well as the outsiders, and to many he gave the Yajnopavit. This Pathshala, in the interests of discipline and good management, was eventually removed to some other building. It remained in existence for about seven years.

The second Pathshala, which the Swami established, was one founded at Kasganj in Samvat 1927, Lala Girdhari Lal, Shopkeeper, undertaking to pay Rs. 1,700 towards it s expenses from his charity fund (dharma-khata). A Pandit on Rs. 15 a month was engaged to do the teaching work. This Pathshala remained in existence fro about four years, being partially supported by the people in gerneral who sent it donations from time to time on occasion of joy in their families.

The third Pathshala was established in Mirzapur, in the same year as the second. Thanks to the large-heartedness of the people, it had an income of one hundred rupees a month to defray its expenses. The Pathshala ceased to exist after three years. The fourth Pathshala was established at Chhalesar, at the request of Thakur Mukand Singh, who had gone to Benares to bring the Swami, so that the opening ceremony might be performed in his presence. After a feast given to the Brahmans, on a grand scale, the Pathshala was opened. It drew vidyarthis from distant places, and remained in existence for six years.

The fifth Pathshala was opened Benares, in Samvat 1930, and put in charge of a Pandit, engaged on a salary of Rs. 25 a month. It was soon discovered that the Pandit, afraid of his brethren and influenced by selfishness, was unwilling to work conscientiously and on the lines suggested by the Swami, and he was consequently replace by a better man. The Pathshala died out after three years.

The rules in force in these Pathshalas were generally these:-

1. No vidyarthi shall be admitted till he has first thoroughly learnt his sandhya.
2. All Viyarthis shall be instructed in the Vedic Granths only - Ashtadhyai, Mahabhashya, and so on.
3. Every vidyarthi shall rise early in the morning and do his sandhya.. the vidyarthi (teacher) who fails to observe this rule shall forfeit his day-meal, care being taken that he does not go into the village (or city), to get from there anything to appease his hunger with. He will get his supper only after he had one his evening sandhya.
4. No vidyarthi (from mofassil) shall be permitted to visit the village (or city) except for the purpose of having his meals in response to a causal or permanent invitation.
5. The vidyarthis from the mofassil alone shall have food at the expense of the Pathshala Funds, the local ones providing for themselves.
6. The intelligent and hardworking vidyarthis shall receive special consideration at the hands of the managers, as regards the quality of food supplies to them.
7. The students who acquit themselves well in the examinations shall be allowed an extra quantity of ghee (clarified butter).

8. All vidyarthis shall make a point of joining daily in the Agnihotra.

The above are excellent rules, and the Swami took care that the teachers working in the different Pathshalas did not connive at the infringement, by the students, of any rule having for its object the maintenance of discipline; he further did his best to have the right kind of instruction imparted to the students, and to make them eschew entirely the misleading writings of the latter-day Pandits: but for all that he found that the Pathshalas did not show any desirable results.

The vidyarthis sent out by the seminaries, after their course of education had been finished, for updesh-work, relapsed, with a few exceptions, into orthodoxy, and commenced the pope-lila of their forefathers. This was most disappointing, and under these circumstances, the Swami had no alternative but to close these schools, one after another. Whatever funds were yet in hand, to the credit of these schools, were merged into the fund raised for the publication of the "Veda-Bhashya."

AT GARHYA GHAT & SWARON

While the Pathshalas were being established and worked, Swami Dayanand's energies continued to fiind an outlet in preaching as before. His advocacy of he primeval Vedic Religion and his chastising of modern superstitions provoked, as it had don't already, the fiercest opposition and frequently so maddened an individual here and as to lead him to attempt the daring Sannyasi's life. The discussion which took place at Garhya Ghat, for instance, and which reduced the Pandits defending idolatry and other similar institutions to a state of utter helplessness, soon brought on the Swami the ire of the Thakur of Aheudesar, who would be satisfied with nothing less than with cutting short a career which was proving itself so fatal to the interests of orthodoxy. The Thakur, who had given a daughter to the Maharaja of Jeypur, was haughty in the extreme, and intolerant of everything which did not seem to fit in with the old order of things.

Accompanied by four retainers, two armed with the sword and two with clubs the nobleman came and sat by the Swami, and commence talking after the style of the person having some wicked purpose in view. The Swami, regardless of what he said, severely criticized the Bhagvat, and, on the termination of the speech, rose and entered a mausoleum. Thinking that he had been foiled, the enraged chief from the Etah District ordered his servants to go and seize the Sadhu and bring him into his presence.

'The other people had been listening to the Swami's criticism and counsels took objection to such a queer order and requested the Thakur to rescind it. The latter refusing to comply, rough hands were laid on his followers and they were completely disarmed. Livid with passion at the failure of his scheme, the big man retired, making a virtue of necessity and postponing his vengeance to a future date, which, alas for his hopes, never arrived.

From Garhya Ghat the Swami proceeded to the town of Swaron, at the earnest request of many. In this place lived hundreds of Brahmans, who never care to perform their sandhya and gayatri, and with whom self-interest was always the one thing to be consulted. Having reached his destination, the Swami took up his quarters at "Ambagare," and began his work.

A pandit, named Narayan, was so impressed with his teaching that, being thoroughly convinced that the Vedic Religion was the only true religion in the world, he renounced the Charkrankit Faith, of which he had hitherto, been a zealous follower. The incident produced a sensation in the town, and the sole topic of conversation everywhere was the arrival of a Sanyasi who denounced all modern creeds, whether based on the Purana, or Semetic in their origin.

On the third day after the conversion of Narayan Pandit, the wealthiest and most prominent inhabitants of the town, accompanied by several hundred men, waited upon the Swami, with a request that a shastrarth on "Idol-worshipping" might be held. The Swami cheerfully acceded to the request. Pandit Khamai represented the idolators. The pandit had, however, asked and answered but a few questions when he miserably broke down. The followers of the Chakrankit Faith raised a howl at this, to wipe out, no doubt, the disgrace that had been the portion of their spokesman. Upon this the leading men of the town interfered, saying that the meeting had been convened for holding a shastrarth and not for making a noise. "Argue the thing out with the Sanyasi, if you would," said they, "but do not create a disturbance." No one came forward, the effect of which was that another votary of the Chakrankit Faith, one Pandit Gobind Ram, accepted the Vedic religion.

Finding the shame of the defeat something too much for them (for the common people now began to look down upon them), the Pandits of Swaron appealed to Pandit Angad Ram Shastri, of Badrya, for assistance. This man had the reputation of being the most learned individual in the neighborhood, being specially well up in Nyaya and Vyakarna. The discussion, as before, was on "Idol-worship." After the Pandit had had his say, the Swami refuted idolatry on the authority of the Vedas and Shastras, concluding, his remarks by an exposure of the Bhagvat, which, as he proved, was childish in its teaching, and faulty as regards its grammar and composition.

The Pandit was a great admirer of the Bhagvat, but he was also open to truth. When he heard the criticism of the Swami, he could not but feel that it was just and reasonable, and taking hold of his shaligram, which he worshipped daily, he consigned it tc the waters of the Ganges, declaring, at the same time, that he should no longer do katha from the Bhagvat or any other Purana. His example was not lsot upon others. Gosain Baldevgiri and many of the relatives of the Pandit himself dealt by their images in the same fashion, installing, in their place, the only one Lord of the Universe, on the throne of their hearts. This was the second present of the images to the Ganges.

Pandit Jugal Kishore, a fellow-student of the Swami, happening to hear some of his lectures (while Swami Virjanand was yet alive), carried a most unfavorable report of his work of the great teacher. "He is spreading adharma," complained the Pandit, "for, among other things, he says that the worship of shaligram is false." Virjanand answered that the shaligrametymologically meant nothing but a heap of rice, and it was useless to worship such a thing. "But why does he run down the kanthi and tilak?" persisted the discomfited Pandit. Swami Virjanand, in reply, asked the Pandit to quote authority in support of his contention. No answer was forthcoming, and the Pandit after some hesitation exclaimed, "If the required authority does not exist, then here goes," and tearing his kanthi from his neck he threw it away!

The Swami stayed in the vicinity of Swaron for six months, teaching, preaching and reclaiming people from superstitions. There were readings from the Manu Smriti and the Mahabharta instead from the Puranas, and the Pandits breaking away from the Kaumidi commenced the study of Ashtadhyai, under the guidance fo the Sami.

The spurious stotras lost their charm, and the Gayatri became, in scores and hundreds of households, the vehicle of meditation and contemplation. The apostles of the Chakrankit and other creeds began to be scarce, Rangacharya, of Brindaban, the most famous member of his fraternity, purposely avoiding paying visits to villages and towns where there was danger of his being brought face to face with the man he dreaded. Kailasparvat Swami, with whose name the reader is already familiar, was so very angry at what fell form the Swami's lips that, in loyalty to his orthodoxy, he thought it his duty to write a pamphlet in new-fangled creed, and to, in no case, hear his lecture before they had carefully gone through his own production. A glorious testimony this to the sound, irresistible logic of Dayanand!

At Garhi, a village some twelve miles from Swaron, the effect of the Swami's preaching was that a certain Kshatrya, a person of considerable influence, tore off his kanthi, and giving up idolatry, became the worshipper of the one true God. This wealthy man had great faith in the Vairagis, and the latter were in such a passion over his desertion that they made up their minds to kill the Sanyasi who had so grievously injured them. Their plots, however, eventually came to nothing.

A great fair was held at Kakaora, and the Swami preached on the occasion as usual, shaking, in varying degrees, the belief of his ever-shifting audience in orthodoxy. A large number of men waited upon him and besought him not run down idolatry and the Puranas, but their prayers were in vain. His reply was: "The things of the world which yield pleasure to you, have no charm for me. To me there is pleasure in the contemplation and adoration of God alone, and in carrying out His commandments. I shall work with the one, sole object of disseminating the true Vedic Knowledge." The Swami challenged any one to come forward and prove that the ancient Aryan Religion was not the purest and noblest of all, but though the votaries of the Chakrant Faith came to hear him in hundreds, not one of them would take up the gauntlet. The Collector, who was present at the fair in connection with his official duties, would now and then come to see the Swami and treat him with marked respect.

THE SHASTRARTH AT FARRUKHABAD

The leaders of orthodoxy in Furrakhabad, seeing a Sanyasi establishing schools in their midst with avowed object of reviving the study of ancient Sanskrit literature, to the prejudice of the modern productions, and preaching doctrines subversive of Puranic teaching, lost no time in calling upon Pandit Siri Gopal, a native of the Meerut District, to take up the cause of idolatry against the new-comer.

A shastrarth (debate) came off in May 1869. The Pandit quoting a verse from the Manu Smriti, which says that puja is due to the devatas, etc., contended that the worship of idols was inculcated therein. The Swami replied hat the word 'puja,' meant honoring or showing reverence, and that in the verse quoted it signified nothing more than the doing of Agnihotra, or treating with respect men distinguished for their learning and virtue. the discussion was prolonged as to the meaning of the verse, and it became every moment clearer that the Pandit was unable to uphold his position, his adversary being unquestionably a man of superior learning and deeply read in the Shastras. The Pandit perceived the impression which the Sanyasi had produced, and dreading lest all should be lost, hurried off to Kashi (Benares), and succeeded in obtaining from them a Vyavasthapatra in Sanskrit, supporting idolatry. The document, signed, among others, by Swami Vishuddhanand, ran as follows:-

The Vyavasthapatra or the Authoritative Document

"The worship of the images of Shiva, Vishnu, etc., of Shivalinga, the Shaligram stone, and so on, which ought to be attended to by men of all the four varnas, is lawful on the authority of many averse in the Puranas. To those who, on the authority of the Shruti and the Manu Smriti, prove the worship in question as false, and who further do not believe in the eighteen Puranas, in Gaya, the Shraddhas, and similar other things, we reply that their contention, that the adoration of Shivalinga, etc., is not in accordance with the teaching of the Vedas, is a mere assertion.

In the Devi, the Atharvashirsh, the Gopal and other Upanishads of the Atharva Veda, the worship of idols is allowed, even as the worship of the Linga is allowed in the Villw Upanishad. And in the Devi and Atharvashirsh it is written that man who worships the Atharvashirsh, not knowing him, regains purity after ten million recitations! Recitations unite a deity with a new idol, and the chanting of mantras for endowing the idol with paranas (life), does establish, in the image, the pranas. And in the Gopaltapni it is written, the Narayan Dev said, 'Just as there are seven regions on the summit of the Meru Mountain, even so there are seven regions or cities in this resolving world, the true region among these latter being the Brahma Gopal Puri - Mathura.'

On the authority of this quotation there are, on this earth, twelve forests, such as the Pradhaban, and twelve images of the twelve Lingas - Bhadreshwar, etc. Here (i.e. in this world) whatsoever people worship the forms or figures, they cross the ocean of death and obtain salvation.

Again, it is written in the Adbhudhshanti of the Vinshiti Brahmana of the Sama Veda, that the temples of the gods tremble, and that the idols laugh, weep, sing and feel pain.

Similarly, it is written in the Kaushak Grah Parishishta of the Sama Veda that the images of gods dance, shine and move. It is also written there that eight months after the weeping and roaring of the idols in a Shivala, the king dies and the fact is undoubted. It is further written there that the king is destroyed when the falgas erected in honor of Devraj (chief deity) fall or are broken, or when the wild beast invade the temples, etc.

"And in the Ashvalayam Grah parishishta there is the injunction that in the Naugrah Yajna a copper image of the sun, a crystal image of the moon, and a ruby or sandal-wood image of Mangal (Mars), should be established, on a singhasan. Further after giving instructions as regards the establishment of particular idols, the book says that the householder should do havan daily and worship the deities, for by worshipping the deities alone does the householder obtain good desires. Again it is written there that the householder is at liberty to worship Hari-Har, Ganpati, Skandh, or any other deity he likes. Deities are summoned into the and dismissed from idols. One having established them in fire, in the sun, in one's own heart or on a raised platform, should worship them. The idols which do not possess the exact forms of the deities they represent, into or from them their respective deities cannot be summoned or dismissed.

The deities are near unto the idols which represent their exact forms. As regards movable idols, the presence or disappearance of deities in or from them is a matter of imagination one ay or the other, and with respect to the every-being, the deities can be made to come into or depart from them at pleasure. The worship is done by the worshipper standing before the idol facing the east, his won face being towards the west, and the temple in which the worship is done should be facing the east. And in the Villw Upanishad it is written that Shiva said to Sanka, 'Just as there are leaves on the tree, even such leaves should be offered unto me.'

"Now we shall speak of the worship of Mahadeva: 'The worshipper after having bathed and cleaned himself, and having made an idol of clay or some other thing, should take his seat on a spot plastered over with cow-dung, etc." These words clearly prove that Bodhayana was a believer in the worship of idols."

"And in the Manu Smirit the worship of deities, the bringing of fuel, etc., is enjoined. Kuluka, commenting on the verse containing the injunction, says that in the idol, etc., Hari-Har, etc., should be worshipped, and gain it is written therein - Mridangam daivtam, etc., which also refers to idol-worship. Hence Kuluka also speaks here of a stone-image, etc. It is, further, written therein (i.e. in Manu Smriti), - 'Jirna devayatan, etc.'

"The shadow of devas, raja, and guru, etc." Only images can have a shadow. 'The being near to the devas and the Brahmans." This too can hold good of images only (i.e., the presence of the word deva shows that idol-worship is sanctioned, for being near to an idol implies the worship of the idol). Again, it is written (in the Manu Smriti): 'Temples should be erected where the boundaries meet.' What do all these thins mean? Only, that the worship of idols is perfectly allowable.

"If it be asserted, in connection with the foregoing quotations in support of idolatry, that the method of doing the worship not having been described, the worship of idols cannot be attended to (for the injunction is as good as useless), then we reply that your objection is equally telling against Ashtika Agnihotra, etc., for the Manu Smriti is silent as to the method of construction or performing these also.

If it be asserted that the method of doing the Agnihotra is set forth in the Kalpa Sutras, then we say that the method of doing idol-worship has also been described in the Bodhayana Kalpa, and this is why the Manu Smriti says nothing on the point. Bodhayana's Sutra has already been quoted. Hence the worship of Shivalinga being a source of progress, has been enjoined in the Shruti, the Smiriti, and in other Shastras, and this is the reason why good men do idol-worship in all the four quarters of the world. This is known to all. To assert that the Puranas, Gaya, Shradhas, etc. have no authority to back them, is to give a proof of one's own stupidity. In the Taittireya, Aranyaka it is written: 'Brahmannanitihasan puranani, etc.,' which proves that the Purananas are authoritative. Similarly, the words in the Atharvashirsh are: 'Itihaspurananam.'

"Manu also has said: 'In the pitrikarm, he should read to his class-fellow.' In the Mahabharata too it is written: 'Let him know the Veda by means of the ithasas and the puranas.' In the Anushashan Parab it is written: 'That whatever reward is obtained by reading the eighteen Puranas, etc.' "On strength of the foregoing authorities, the Puranas are proved to be authoritative. Hence Gaya, Shradhas, etc., must be accepted an indisputably authoritative institutions. Similarly, idol-worship is also lawful on the authority of Shruti, Smriti, Kalpa Sutras, etc. This had been written briefly."

The foregoing document speaks for itself. It contains two authorities from the Vedas in support of idol-worship, and any passages that it may be said to embody in support of idol-worship from the Shastras, either do not, in point of fact, uphold idolatry, or, being at variance with the teaching of the Scripture, are spurious and unauthoritative, and must be rejected as such by all impartial minds. The document, however, was a rare acquisition to Pandit Siri Gopal, the more so, as it had been obtained without incurring much expense, and he could not make too much of it. A copy of the document was shown to the Swami, and he could not help laughing, observing at the same time, "Is that the learning of the Kashi Pandits?"

Siri Gopal had the Vyavasthapatra nailed to a bamboo near the place where the Swami was putting up, and the sight attracted thousands of ignorant men, who, at a word from the Pandit, began to drench it with water, being under the impression, no doubt, that the bamboo, for the time being, represented some deity, Shivalinga perhaps! When the Pandit was asked to repair to the Swami's quarters and have a shastrarth (debate), he replied: "If I go there, I shall be defeated, and if the Swami comes to me, he will be defeated. He has placed his abode under the influence of a charm!" As to the Swami, his answer to those who wasted a shastrarth to be held was: "What would be the good of my going and holding a shastrarth with a man who cannot so much as tell the masculine from the feminine gender!"

The excitement and enthusiasm of the illiterate mob, however, was tremendous, so much so that the authorities thought there was going to be a breach of the peace. One of the information furnished by Munshi Bakhtawar lal, Superintendent, the Collector was sent the Head Constable to the Swami, to inquire what the uproar meant. The Swami replied that he was not responsible for it, being in his own quarters, and that it was not fro him to bid the mob disperse. Upon this the Constable went to the Pandit and called upon him to clear the spot of the multitude. A few words from the Pandit, and as many from the Police official sternly bidding the gathering to be off, brought about the desired consummation. Two policemen were appointed to prevent over-zealous followers of idolatry from breaking into the Swami quarters and creating a disturbance.

The second shastrarth which Swami Dayanand held at Farrukhabad, was that with a Pandit named Haldar, who at the request of the orthodox Farrukhabadis, had come all the way from Kanpur for the purpose. The discussion came off on the 19th June, 1869, and was, as minght be expected, on "Idol-worship."

Ere the parties had spoken much, Haldar, who was a Tantrik (believer in the Tantras), and held that indulgence in flesh and intoxication liquors, the unlawful gratification of the lower passions, and other like things, were far from being objectionable perhaps positively essential to the attainment of salvation, leaving the subject under discussion commenced defending "drinking," contending that the use of alcoholic drinks was justifiable on the occasion of a Sautramani Yajna.

In reply the Swami pointed out the word sura, when employed in connection with such Yajnas, did not mean alcoholic liquors, but the juice of healthy and delicious fruits. It was samaras, he added, that was imbibed on the occasion of aSautranmani Yajna, and not an intoxicating liquor. The Swami's remarks on "drinking" certainly did not tend to advance idolatry in the affections of an audience!

Finding the ground slipping from under his feet, the Pandit Hladar asked the Swami the definition of "Sanyasi"." The Swami furnished the required definition, asking the Pandit, in his truth, the definition of "Brahman". No satisfactory answer was forthcoming, for, being aPuranic, the Pandit would not commit himself, and drifted into irrelevant maters. The Swami did his best to bring him to the point originally under discussion, but it would not do. Quoting a Sutra of the Mahabhashya, the spokesman for the orthodox commenced a discussion thereon, and the Swami had no, alternative but to send for the book and show to the people assembled how the Pandit was wrong here also. The discussion lasted till one O' clock in the night.

A VISIT TO KANPUR

Leaving Farrukhabad and visiting Kanauj, Bathora and Madarpur on his way, Swami Dayanand reached Kanpur with the commencement of the rainy season (Samvat, 1926 A.D. 1869), the local paper (Sho'la-i Toor of 27th July, 1869), noticed his arrival in the following words:-

"For some days past one Maharaj Swami Dayanand Saraswati Swami has been in our midst. He is putting up at the newly-constructed ghat of Lala Sargahi Lal, Pleader, Civil Courts, on the bank of the Ganges. He will not speak in any language other than Sahstri or Sanskrit - neither in 'Nagri' nor in any foreign tongue. He is a recluse, avoiding bustle and crowd.

His appearance is that of a true saint. He is wholly opposed to the worship of idols, and to the erection of temples for purposes of idolatry. He maintains that idol-worship is not inculcated in the Vedas. This Swami is a scholar among the Pnadits of India, a man of unique erudition. In the Vedic and Shastric grammar and in logic he is deeply versed, and one of the chose Pandits. He gives himself out to be a native of the Deccan. When he was five years old, his father commenced teaching him the Veda. At Mathura he perfected his knowledge of Sanskrit, For some time he stayed at Jeypor also, and there he had discussion on the Hindu Faith, after that he went to Gwalior and to Farrukhabad, and there also he had discussions with the Pandits.

Now ever since he has been at Kanpur, his fame has been going forth. We hear that a large meeting will be held at the Ghat referred to on 31st July, 1869. Maharaj Haldar Ojaha, a native of the village Hola, who has been staying for some days past in the newly-constructed temple of Maharaj Guru Parshad and who is perfect in the Sanskrit language, will attend the meeting and will hold a discussion with Swamiji."

Almost simultaneously with reaching Kanpur, the Swami had a manifesto put up in Sanskrit, in which speaking of the contents of the twenty-one Shastras, - the Vedas, the Upavedas, the Vedangas, the Upanishads, he acknowledged them as authoritative, adding that whatever in the Rishi Granths (the composition of the sages) too was opposite to the teaching of the Veda, to Vyajarana and to virtuous conduct, was also rejectable.

In illustration of his position he said: "There are eight gups (things that injure and debase), which ought to be rejected, and eight true things which ought to be done or accepted." These respectively, enumerated as follows:-

The Eight Gups

1. All the works published by common mortals - the puranas, such as Brahmavaivarta, etc.
2. The worship of stones, etc., in the belief that they represent devtas (gods).
3. Shaiva, Shaktik, Vaishnav, Ganpatya, and other orders and sects.
4. Vammargism, taught in the Tantras.
5. The use of intoxicating drugs and liquors, such as bhang, etc.
6. Adultery.
7. Fraud, conceit, lying, etc.
8. Theft.

The Eight True Things

1. The twenty-one Shastras, - The Rigveda, etc., of Divine origin, or works coming from the Rishis and Munis.
2. Serving the Guru from the commencement of the Brahmacharya Ashrama and the study of the Veda, in keeping with the behests of Dharma.
3. The performance, in keeping with the Vedic Varna and Ashrama, of the practical duties, sandhya, agni-hotra, etc.

4. Conjugal faith, base don't the teaching of the Shastras, the performance of the five daily maha-yajnas (great duties), sexual connection with the wife in proper season, regulation of conduct in conformity with the behests of Shruti and Smriti.
5. The practice of tapa (severe contemplation), etc.) of yama (self-control, etc.), rising gradually to the trance stage of upasna, and the obervance of the Vanprasth Ashrama, in the company of, and under instructions from, the righteous.
6. Meditation, introspection, indifference towards the temporary and transcient, the cultivation of spiritual knowledge, the non-desire of fruit of action on being initiated into Sanyas.
7. A constant effort to subdue and conquer by science, mundane and spiritual, birth and death, joy and grief, lust, anger, avarice, partiality, and the evils of bad company.
8. The destruction of all pain - resulting from ignorance, self-conceit, love and hate, fear of the dissolution of the body, from tamas, rajas, and satva and the realization, after shaking off the hold of the Five Elements (panch mahabhuta), of the nature of moksha (salvation) and the bliss attendant thereon.

THE KANPUR SHASTRARTH

The pasting up of the foregoing manifesto in different parts of Kanpur, and the presence of the author of the manifesto in the population of that town, produced the result that might naturally be expected. The entire Hindu community was in a ferment, and the representatives of orthodoxy, its leaders, were in a state of positive alarm.

A man named Brahmanand Saraswati was put forward to try conclusions with the 'heretic' Sanyasi, and duly waited upon the latter with a large following, but all his arguments taking the form of invective and anathema, the discussion proved nothing but a disgusting farce, and evidently extremely disappointinag to his admirers, as, without much delay, they appeared at the Swami's quarters with their favorite Pundit Haldar Ojha, perhaps the most astute and learned champion of the Puranic Faith in their city, at the time.

It was a tremendous gathering that was to hear the shastraarth, being composed of no less thatn twenty thousand persons, or thereabout. The official element was fully represented. Mr. W. Thaine, Joint Magistrate of Kanpur, and a tolerable Sanskrit Scholar, being nominated madhyastha. The discussion commenced at 2 P.M.. (31st July, 1869), and parties spoke in Sanskrit only.

At the unset Pandit Haldar Ojha, addressing the Swami, declared that the manifesto he had issued was grammatically faulty. To this the Swami replied that the Pandit was talking after the manner of school-boys and not after two serious and grave men of advanced years, who, in the hearing of thousands, were to speak on a subject of greatest importance. "If you think," he added, "my manifesto grammatically faulty, come to me to-morrow, when we are both at leisure, and I will make everything clear to you."

The rebuke had its effect and the Pandit came to the point without any longer beating about the bush.

Asking Swami Dayanand if he believed in the Mahabharata, and getting an answer in the affirmative, the Pandit quoted a verse from the book, saying that a "Bhil learnt archery by practicing in the presence of an image of Dronacharya," and the observed that idol-worship was justifiable on the authority of the great Epic.

To this the Swami replied: "I want you to quote a pssage which enjoins idol-worship. That which you have quoted contains no injunction whatever: all that it says is, that a certain Bhil did such a thing, as the ignorant and illieterate will always do. The Bhil was not a Rishi or a Muni, nor had he been taught to do what he did by an (saint or sage)."

To this no answer was forthcoming, and the next question, which the Pandit asked, ws: "If the Veda does not enjoin idol-worship, where does it condemn it? Let the Swami Show it."

The Swami made an exhaustive reply, and as soon as he had done speaking, Mr. Thaine, taking a piece of paper containing something from the Pandit's pen, handed it over to the Swami and asked him to decipher it. The Swami did as desired, thereby removing the Joint-Magistrate's doubt, as to whether the Sanyasi, though such an eloquent speaker, could actually read.

Next Mr. Thaine asked the Swami: "What do you believe in?" "In the one only God," was the reply. Upon this dropping a courtesy to the Swami, he rose and, taking up his hat and stick, left the assembly. This was a signal for dispersion, but the mob, inspired by the leaders, would not disperse quietly. "Hail, mother Ganges, hail!" they shouted out at the top of their voice, and an admirer of the Pandit went so far as to throw pice over his head, bawling out at the same time that the Swami had been defeated!

That the imaginary victory of the Pandit might have all the weight of a genuine fact, a man named Guru Parshad waited upon the Editor of the Shoal-ai-Toor on the following day, with an account of the discussion, for insertion in the Paper. The Editor declined to accede to his request, on the ground that the account was one-sided statement, and that, in the event of its appearance in the Shola-ai-Toor complications might arise, which might place the press in a serious position and cause it heavy loss. "The officials, you know, were present at the discussion," he observed, "and their testimony would have weight in a Court of law." Guru Parshad told him not to fear, adding that, if it came to the worst, he should be ready to spend as much as ten thousand rupees from his own pocket to shield the Paper. The assurance had its effect, and the following lines in connection with the shastrarth appeared in the Shola -i-Toor of 3rd August, 1869:--

"In our last issue we announced the arrival in this city of Dayanand Saraswati Sanyasi, and the fact that a shastrarth had been arranged between him and the Pandit Haldar Ojha, to come off on the 31st of July (1869). The discussion did take place on the date specified. From the very day, Dayanand Saraswati, in the disguise of a Sanyasi, came and took up his quarters at the newly-constructed ghat at Lala Dagahi Lal,

Pleader, near the Ganges, a stir has been created in the city and its neighborhood. The high and low have all come to see him, and he was warned every one against 'idol-worship,' saying that it is unjustifiable.

"Coming to hear of this teaching of the Swami, the reises of the city, as well as its learned Pandits, went to the Swami and gave him proofs of every description, on the authority of the Shastras, in support of 'Idol-worship.' Upon this the Swami declared that twenty-one Shastras alone were o9f Divine Origin, and the rest nothing but idle gossip and unworthy of being followed.

In as much as it is objectionable in all creeds and among all classes to speak harsh of a deity or God, the practice being nothing short of 'hellish' according to the Hindu creed, it was this unanimous opinion of Messrs. Guru Parshad Shukal and Prag Narain Tiwari that a shastrarth ought to be held, so that proofs in support of idolatry might be furnished.

With this object in view the name of an Englishman, who is thoroughly versed in Sanskrit, etc., was proposed as that of a person who could act as madhyastha. It was no other than Mr. Thaine, the Assistant Collector, Kanpur District, who possess a sound and perfect knowledge of Vyakarna, etc., on whom this responsibility devolved. Lachhman Shastri of atora was also summoned and appointed to act as madhyastha of the shastrarth between Halsdaree Ojha and Dayanand Saraswati.

"The discussion was take place at 2 p.m. on 30th July, 1869. at the hour fixed, the learned Pandits, the reises, the official of the city and others present at the ghat made up a huge crowd, and the people from the neighborhood had also thronged there. The shastrarth commenced between Haldar Ojha and Dayanad Saraswati on 'Idol-worship.' Whatever statements the Saraswati made in condemnation of idolatry, to the same the Ojha replied by quoting from the Shruti, Smriti, the Vedas, the Upanishads, the Bharta, the Manu Smriti and other works which, as the Swami in his printed manifesto says, constitute the 'Vedas.'. He further showed to the Englishman and the other madhyastha the pages on which the authorities quoted were to be found, and they read out the same. From these it was fully apparent that the worship of idols was absolutely necessary for the Hindus. After this the Sanyasi was asked to show, from the Shastras, authorities condemning idol-worship. The Saraswati observed, in reply, that these Shastras also contained many false things, upon which the Ojha (in continuation of his remarks) observed that 'the shadow of a devta (God) and of a guru (preceptor') should never be crossed. A devata having no shadow, the line in the Shastra should be taken as referring to the shadow of an idol.'

Lachhman Shastri, madhyastha quoted largely from the Vedas, the Vedanta, the Mimansa, from the Dharma Shastras, etc., and from these quotations it appeared that the worship of idols was right. All the madhyasthas accepted this verdict and praised the Ojha. The statements of the madhyastha Lachhman Shastri, as also statements and arguments of the Ojha, were acknowledged to be true and sound, and hence the European madhyastha gave it as his judgment that since the Sarwasti had failed to furnish proofs and to give answers according to the Shastras, it was perfectly allowable for the Hindus to do idol-worship, and further, that idolatry was inculcated in the Shastras.

As soon as the judgment was given, the reises, who were present there, burst into shouts of joy, declaring that the Ojha had won the field. At this time, Mr. Prag Narain Tiwari threw, as charity, rupees and pice over the head of Ojha, and then all returned to their homes. This shastrarth was due to the energy and high-mindedness of Messrs. Shukal Parshad and Prag Narain Tiwari. Both these gentlemen have constructed, in the city of Kanpur, grand and magnificent temples at an enormous cost, and have thus done themselves good in this and fore the next world. It was proper that a shastrarth should take place in this town, and one did take place, resulting in additional glory to 'idolatry.'

as soon as the Paper was in the hands of the people, they went to the Swami and read out the account to him. He observed that he was neither glad nor sorry at what had been written; none but the foolish would recognize victory or defeat as the end of a shastrarth. The reply was far from being satisfactory to the Swami's well-wishers, and, annoyed at the want of fairness which the writer in the Paper had displayed, they waited upon Mr. Thaine, and respectfully asked him what he thought of the account, Mr. Thaine having heard the statement from beginning to end, wrote, the following letter and handed it over to them:-

"Gentlemen,

"At the time in question I decided in favor of Dayanand Saraswati Faqir, and i believe his arguments are in accordance with the Vedas. I think he won the day, If you wish it, I will give you my reasons for my decision in a few days."

Yours obediently,

(Sd) W. THAINE.

The above letter was printed with a complete refutation of the assertions in the Sho'la-i-toor, and scattered broad-cast in the city. But valuable though Mr. Thaine's letter was, it was hardly indispensable. The worshippers of idols themselves furnished a stronger testimony to the truthful character of the Swami's doctrines. Snatching up their idols, they commenced throwing them in the bazaars or into the river - a procedure unquestionably annoying to the Ojha and his supporters. Unable to see the images treated with scant respect, the Ojha had a Notice printed and copies of it pasted in scores of places, requesting the people, in Sanskrit, Hindi, and Urdu, to cease from throwing idols in the bazaars or into the river, and to restore them to their places in the temples! The Notice ran as follows:-

"Many Brahmans, Kshatryas and Vaishyas, in accordance with the religion of Dayanand Saraswati, giving up their own family faith, are throwing the images of deities into the river Ganges, a practice which is most objectionable. This notice is issued in order to convey to the people, who have accepted or should come to accept the religion of the Swami, the request that they would get any idols they may have, taken into the temple belonging to Maharaj Guru Parshad Shukal, or into that belonging to Maharaj Prag Narain Tiwari. If they cannot find leisure to do it themselves, they should send us information, and we shall arrange to have removed. The sin of throwing away the images or flinging them into rivers is pointed out in Sanskrit." -- OJAHA HALDAR.

The editorial which appeared in the Sho'la-i-Toor of 3rd August 1869, in connection with the Ojha's Notice, might be given verbatim here:- "Through the wholesome influence of the Swami's company many people have commenced throwing their idols into the river. The Ojha has, therefore, issued a notice, declaring that the practice is objectionable according to the Hindu Shastras, and adding that whoever be disposed to throw idols into the river, the same should have them sent to the Pandit and not incur the penalty attending the sin of throwing them into the river."

Such is the might of truth. No amount of sophistry of underhand dealing or prejudice can suppress it: it must eventually vindicate its majesty and prevail in spite of them. As an illustration of the truth of this fact, we may give here the following story:-

"My younger brother," says a gentleman, "having bought some publications of the Swami, brought them home. I took him severely to task for having done such a thing. The books, however, having a winning look about them, I could not resist the temptation of looking into them. And once begun, I could not leave them unfinished. The inevitable result came - I renounced the worship of idols and became a humble follower of the Vedic religion"! The story is one of the many similar ones that might be told!

-

4

First Ceremon

Ever since the birth-hour of Jainism Kashi has been the stronghold of Puranism, and greater and more learned champions of idolatry and kindred institutions will be found nowhere. Swami Dayanand felt that if he was to deal Puranism a blow from which it would find it hard to recover, if he was to bring home to the orthodox world the truth (though it might never acknowledge it) that the worship of stocks and stones was absolutely false and degrading and opposed to the teaching of the Scripture and the ancient Shastras, he must assault the "citadel of myth and marvel itself."

With this conviction in his mind, he quietly lef t Kanpur in the Kartak of Samvat 1926 (22nd or 23rd October, 1869), and reaching Kashi took up his quarters in Anandbag, right on the road leading to Durgakund. His shastrarths at Farrukhabad and Kanpur had already made him widely known in the leading orthodox circle at Benares, and he news of his arrival spread like wild-fire in the city. Pandits and vidyarthis flocked to him from all sides, displaying their learning and their powers of argument, but invariably returned discomfited and crest-fallen.

The public at large heard the Sanyasi's arguments with wonder and astonishment, tried to say a word in favor of idolatry, but finding themselves compelled to be silent, returned home in doubt and despair. And as the Swami was, from the very first, bent upon being the aggressor, to bring matters to a crisis in this great city of idol-worshippers, he, one day, wrote down a question connected with in the Mahabhashya on a piece of paper, and sent the slip to the famous Pandit Raja Ram for an answer.

The Pandit sent back the reply: "Let a knife be placed between us before I answer your question. If I can satisfactorily answer the question, I will cut off your nose, but if I fail, you may cut off mine!" When the answer was conveyed to the Swami, he said: "By all means. Put two knives instead of one. If you are for a shastrarth (weapon-contest), instead of a shastrarth (Shastric contest), we might as well go in for it."

The place where the Swami had put up one of the most frequented ones. It was visited by thousands of vidyarthis daily, and Vairagis in huge crowds. A party of the latter one day waited upon the Swami, but perceiving that they were wholly unable to maintain their ground against their adversary, they took to abusing him. This was a species of argument which the Swami would not condescend to answer, and his opponents dinding themselves baffled (how they wished they had a member of their own order to relpy to!), retired, indulging in still more foul language.

Somebody carrying. The news of this most unbecoming behavior to the Maharaja of Benares, he administered a severe rebuke to the offenders, observing that every one was welcome to have a shastrarth with Dayanand, but that no one was to abuse him under any circumstances.

The Swami's fearless and thorough exposure of idolatry at last aroused the Maharaja of Kashi to a sense of the danger which menaces the dominance of orthodox belief under his very nose. He called together a meeting of his Pandits and emphasized the necessity of their holding a shastrarth with him without further delay.

After much deliberation the necessity of a discussion was admitted, but it was hinted that a discussion with Dayanand could not be held till it had been first ascertained what books he believed in. "He is in the habit of setting down this and that book as utter nonsense," complained the Pandits, " and who knows but hat he may try with su the same trick just when we are on the point of running him to earth!" Very modest this of the Pandits, but, for all that, the Maharaja could not but admit the justness of their contention, and authorized them to take the necessary steps towards finding out what constituted authoritative literature and Dayanand's opinion. Accordingly, five Pandits - Shalig Ram Shastri, Dhondi Raj Shastri, Damodar Shastri, Bharadwaj and Ram Krishn Shastri were deputed for the purposes. When these gentlemen put in an appearance, some one form among the numerous students, who surrounded the Swami at the time, gave out that vidyarthis from the opposite party wer approaching, and the result was, that when the Pandits disclosed their errand, the Swami indifferently replied that the discussion should come off in few days, and under the supervision of the City Kotwal. As to what Shastras he believed in as authoritative, he would give a written answer to the question as soon as the Pandits from the opposite party saw him.

The five Pandits not quite clear as to what the reply meant, returned to their chiefs, but soon discovering the mistake that had been committed in ignorance, they once more waited upon the Swami, and informing him of their status, begged for an answer to their question. This time the Swami, gave them the needed answer, telling them to put down, in writing that he believe in, as authoritative the four Vedas, the four Upavedas, the six Angas, the six Upangas and the Manu Smriti. The Pandits asked on what authority the Swami believed these books to be authoritative. "I will answer this question at the time of the shastrarth," replied the Swami, "if you Pandits desire to have its answer." Again the Pandits asked to be informed as to what particular verses in the Manu Smriti the Swami regarded as meaningless interpolations, and false. The answer of the Swami was the same as before.

The leaders of orthodoxy could not reasonably take exception to their opponent's reply, and consequently they set about making preparations for a "tussle." Monday, November 16, 1869, was fixed as the date of the shastrarth, by mutual consent. Knowing how much depended upon the issue of the struggle, the Pandits resolved that the learning of the city should be completely represented on the occasion. The news of the discussion was received in the various parts of the city, and in the neighborhood of Benares, with mixed feelings, profoundly stirring whatever side arrayed, that a crisis was at hand. The officials of the city, yielding to natural curiosity, sharpened by the intense prevailing excitement, suggested an alteration in the date fixed, but the Maharaja of Benares, for reasons of his own, expressed his inability to adopt their suggestion, and desired that the shastrarth should come off on the day specified instead of on - Sunday.

The specified day came, and at the hour appointed Anandbag presented a spectacle superbly grand and imposing. Some affirm that no less that fifty thousand persons were present on the occasion, while others put the number at a considerably lower figure, asserting that the gathering did not exceed ten thousand souls. Whatever the actual number, there is reason to believe that it made up the biggest assembly of its kind ever witnessed in Benares.

Besides many other famous Pandits there were many of the richest and most influential local men, many Thakurs from the villages around, and several ministers of the Gospel (Bible) who formed part of the surging mass of humanity assembled. The police arrangements were satisfactory, the Kotwal with fifty of his men being in attendance, but in spite of all that they could do, a large number of the rowdies of the town, notorious characters, out and out, found their way to the very spot where they were least wanted, - the spot reserved fro the controversialists and the pick of cream of the locality.

The well-wishers of the Swami, apprehending personal violence, made known their anxiety to him, adding that had the discussion taken place at Farrukhabad, there would have been not fear of a disturbance. At this the Swami burst out laughing, and replied. "It is always the firm conviction of genuine Yogis that the sun of truth is stronger than any forces which darkness can muster. He, who following the Will Divine, is above all partially and preaches the truth, what has he to fear? Men of truth hide not the truth through fear. They will risk their lives rather than be false to a Divine Commandment. I have nothing to be afraid of, for I live for the Ishwara (God) and the Dharma (duty). Let us wait and see what happens."

After uttering these words the Swami desired a barber to summoned, and having got himself thoroughly shaved, he had a bath and spent some moments in contemplation and meditation, and then taking his meal repaired to the meeting.

The Maharaja of Kashi and his son soon followed. As soon as His Highness entered the assembly, the orthodox Pandits rose and give him their blessing, and disregarding all discipline, followed at his heels and surrounded the Swami, thus largely usurping the place which, in all fairness, belonged to the Swami's supporters. They further had an order issued by the Maharaja that no more men should be allowed to come near the Swami or the Pandits, which meant nothing less than the exclusion of the Swami's admirers from where they had every right to be present! Of this move the Swami was duly informed, and he, in his turn informed the Kotwal of what had been done.

That good official perceived the justice of the complaint, and at once conducted Pandit Jyoti Saroop and other sympathizers and followers of the Swami to him. The latter received them with every mark of respect, and desired them to take a seats near himself. Nothing could be more distasteful to the orthodox Pandits, who made a significant sign to the Maharaja, as much as to say that the addition to Dayanand's ranks was wholly undesirable, as Dayanand alone was more than a match for them all! The chief understood the sign, desired that the Pandits should take the front places, and the Jyoti Saroop should retire to a distant seat. Similar shameful treatment was meted out to the other supporters of the Swami, but it was no time to grumble, for a shastrarth must be had at any cost, and so he kept quiet and let the Maharaja and his Pandits please themselves.

Before the Shastrarth began, Swami Dayanand asked the Maharaja of Benares if he had brought the Vedas with him. The reply was, that the Pandits present knew the Vedas by heart, and hence it had been deemed unnecessary that they or the Maharaja should come provided with the Books of question. Upon this the Swami observed that, in the absence of the Vedas, the import and drift of an authority could not be fully understood, as the passages preceding and following a quotation cited had often an important bearing on the quotation, and minimized the chances of its being twisted and distorted to suit a present purpose.

Presently after this remark from the Swami, the rule was laid down and proclaimed by the Kotwal, Pandit Raghu Nath Sahay, that only one Pandit Tara Charan Naiyayak came forward to open the discussion. On his admission that all who were faithful to the requirements of varna and ashrama believed in the Vedas as the final authority, the Swami desired him to cite, from the Scripture, a passage which enjoined the worship of Shaligram and other images, and to declare, if no such passage existed, the truth.

To this the Pandit making no satisfactory reply - indeed, he did little more than seek to evade the question, Swami Vishuddhanand cried out: "Vyas says in a Sutra that the Creator of the world is a conscious, intelligent Being and not inanimate; where is the authority for this in the Vedas?" The Swami answered that the question wash wholly irrelevant, adding that nothing should be said by either party that hand not something to do with the subject under discussion.

Vishuddhanand, compelled to come to the point, rejoined that since the worship of Brahma was allowable in the mind in and the sun, there could be nothing objectionable in worshipping the Shaligram also. To this the Swami replied that, although such expressions as - mano Brahm iti upasit and aditya Brahm iti upasit, were to be met with in the Brahmaans (which, in the opinion of the orthodox, were identical with the Vedas!), no such injunctions -pashan Brahmiti upasit, were to be found in these works, and under these circumstances, how could the worship of Shaligram be justifiable?

Swami Vishuddhanand made no answer to this, but another Pandit Madhvacharya came forward and, quoting a mantra asked what it dealt with. "With clouds, wells, tanks, etc." was the reply, and the Swami cited authorities from the Nirukta and Brahamanas in support of his reply. On being thus answered the Pandit turned his attention to the word 'Purana', asking of the words was to be found in the Vedas. The Swami replied in the affirmative, adding that although the world occurred in many places in the Vedas, yet nowhere had it any reference to the Bhagvat or any other so-called Purana.

Many minutes were spent in discussing this point, Swami Vishuddhanand, Pandit Bal Shastri and others, speakingone after another, and Swami Dayanand replying to each all alone. Once while the Swami was quoting apassage from the Upanishads, the orthodox Pandits in a body shouted out that the passage was nowhere to be found in the Upanishads, upon which their opponents observed that if what the Pandits asserted should be found to be true, he would acknowledge that he was defeated.

The Pandits readily signed the agreement, but it was on their part of a huge blunder, as they found out a minute later. The Swami opened the Upanishads and showed them the passage, covering them with shame and convincing those present that their knowledge of the Shastras was far from being perfect.

Finding themselves checkmated everywhere and displaying lamentable ignorance of the Shastric teaching (the great Swami Vishuddhanand could not tell so much as what dharma and adharma consisted in), and discovering further that their adversary could quote whole chapters of the Vedas and other works by heart, and could furnish lucid and comprehensive expositions of the same, the Pandits made haste to sound the Swami's knowledge of Vyakarna, and, upon their arrogating superiority in that branch of Science, the Swami asked "What is the Kalma Sangya (retained object?")

Vushuddhanand remained silent, but Bal Sahstri essayed to make an answer, only to fall back crest-fallen. Baffled at every point exasperated beyond measure, the Pandits now hit upon a plan, which was nothing but a foul trick, to circumvent Swami Dayanand.

It was now 7 P.M. and rapidly growing dark. Madhvacharya, seein his opportunity, took out two leaves from a manuscript, and placing them before the Pandits said: "This is the Veda (Samhita), and here it is written that on the tenth day after the termination of yajna, the yajman should hear the Purana read. What the word 'Purana' means here?" Swami Dayanand desired him to read out the passage, but before he could do it, Vishuddhanand (in accordance, no doubt with a pre-concerted plan) took the leaves and handed them to the Swami. The Swami desired him to read out the passage, but before he could do it, the famous man of Kashi excused himself from doing it, on the ground that had not his spectacles with him, and begged the Swami to take the duty upon himself. Suspecting no deceit, the Swami took up the leaves and silently began to go over them.

He had hardly been looking them two minutes, and was just going to reply, when Swami Vishuddhanand exclaiming that he was being unduly detained, the whole host of Pandits, with the Maharaja of Kashi at their head, stood up, and, clapping their hands, shouted out, at the top of their voice, that the dearly-earned victory might be celebrated in a becoming fashion, the notorious characters in attendance commenced raining dwon stones, old shoes and dung on the Swami. The life of the Swami was in jeopardy, but thanks to his own activity and the vigilance of the Police, the place was soon cleared of the scoundrels.

Thus ended the firest shastrarth at Kashi. Swami Dayanand did not leave the town at once. On the contrary, he stayed for three months longer, proclaiming the falseness of idolatry with the beat of drums, and preaching to all the true doctrine. Perhaps the Maharaja of Kashi and the Pandits were not prepared for this they sought vengeance in sending forth the flat that henceforth no true follower of orthodoxy should visit the Swami under pain of incurring the penalty that attends the omission of a great crime. Foul-play was also had recourse to.

Once the Swami narrowly escaped being poisoned. A Brahman bringing victuals for him, the Swami declined accepting the offering inasmuch as he had already had his meal; but not to disappoint the Brahman entirely, he took the betel-leaf from him and put it into his mouth to chew it. The taste was curious, and the Swami knew at once that it was poisoned. He spat out the deadly leaf, and, in order that the fact of its being poisoned might be fully authenticated, his well-wishers had it sent to the hospital and analyzed. The Swami's suspicions turned out to be well-founded.

THE PRESS ON KASHI SHASTRARTH

The shastrarth at Kashi was an event of the greatest importance, and created a profound sensation through out the country.

The utter incapacity of the most famous Benares Pandits to cope with Swami Dayanand in learning and argument, and the unrighteous course which they had finally adopted to overcome him and to wipe out their disgrace, were duly noticed by the Press in every part of India and freely commented upon.

THE HINDU COMMENTATOR

We shall have to content ourselves with quoting the remarks of only a few of the papers. The Hindu Commentator, a Sanskrit journal of Calcutta, whose editor was present at the discussion and took notes, wrote, as follows, in tis issue of December, 1869:

"Swami Dayanand is a Sadhu, who has girded up his loins to destroy falsehood by the dissemination of truth.

Swami Dayanand (S.D) : Do Indra and other devatas (Gods) exist in heaven (swarga)?

Swami Vishuddhanand (S.V.) : The very mantras of the Vedas are devtas.

(At this answer the Maharaja of Kashi frowned)

S.D. : How is worship to be done, then?

S.V. : Through the image of Shaligram, etc.

S.D. : Where is this written in the Vedas?

S.V. : The Sama Veda alone has a thousand shakhas. Have your read them all?

S.D. : Listen! Listen! The thousand shakhas mean nothing more than that the Veda can be interpreted in a thousand ways. The Samhita is one and one only.

S.V. : Yes, even that or space is God.

S.D. : (With a smile) - That is the Ishwara! But of that which is irrelevant, it is utterly useless to talk here. The discussion here is on idol-worship. In support of that you must cite authorities.

S.V. : (Placing his hand on the Swami's back) - Mendicant, thou has not finished thy education yet; study yet a while.

S.D. : (Removing his hand) - Has thou read everything?

S.V. :(With a sarcastic laugh) - Yes, I have read everything.

S.D. : (Looking him full in the face) - Vyakarna also?

S.V. : Yes, that also.

S.D. : (Sternly) - What is the Kalma Sangya (retained object)? (In a voice of thunder) - Answer, answer!

"When Vishuddhanand could make no reply to this, Bal Shastri, who could not but see that the honor of Kashi was at stake, and that utter disgrace would be the portion of the orthodox Pandits (if the question remained unanswered), came forward to save his great Pandit Vishuddanand and said: 'I shall reply to this.' The Swami replied: 'Do you explain what the Kalma sangya is'? Bal Shastri replied that the definition hand not been given, but that the commentator had, in a certain sutra, treated it as uphas (jest or something too insignificant to taken notice of.). Upon this the Swami said: 'In the commentary upon what Sutra has the definition not been given, and the uphas only been indulged in? Illustrate your answer by examples.' Upon this Bal Shastri and the other Pandits also said nothing and preserved silence.

"The Maharaja of Kashi heard the shastrarth from beginning to end, and was not at all satisfied. And upon this he thus spoke "Although Dayanand is stubborn and ignorant, yet no one Pandit can defeat him in any way. He is like Karna, who six warriors, joining together, felled to the ground. When no strength remained in him, he fell. Hear more. This discussion does not end by merely defeating Dayanand. Let all the Pandits join together and discuss, and having prepared a book containing the arguments for and against idolatry, publish it."

"Shri Hari Krishn Vyas, Shrie Jainarian Tarak Panchanan, Shri Krishn Vedant Saraswati, etc., who were present and were counted among the learned, observed that the shastrarth had not been satisfactory conducted, though it was true that Dayanand had been defeated!"

The Tattva Bodhni of Calcutta wrote in its issue for 1794 Shalvahan:-

"Thanks to the efforts of the Ruler of Kashi, the Pandits from different places held a shastrarth with the object of refuting the contention above specified, but from the perusal of the pamphlet (Sattya Dharma Vichar) it appears that no Pandit could defeat the Swami by proving idolatry justifiable. For this reason the Swami ought to be regarded as the greatest Pandits of the Vedas."

Again, in its issue for Aswaj, 1794, Shalvahan it wrote: "At this time Swami Dayanand Saraswati, a Veda-knowing Pandit, going into Kashi, etc., proclaimed that the Vedas did ot enjoin idolatry. Upon this a grand meeting of the Kashi Pandits and of Pandits from other places was held under the auspices of the Ruler of Kashi, but not a single Pandit could produce authority in support of idol-worship from the Vedas."

The Rohilkhand Akhbar wrote in November, 1869 :-

"Dayanand Saraswati Swami obtained a victory over the Benares Pandits, and the Benares Pandits falsely gave out that they had been victorious."

The Gyan Pradinst Patrika of Lahore wrote in April, 1870:-

"It is apparent from what both parties said that the shastrarth between the Kashi Pandits and the Sanyasi was mostly on subjects perfectly irrelevant, but there can be no doubt that, when discussing the subject of idolatry, the Pandits could not prove it on the authority of the Vedas."

THE "HINDU PATRIOT' ON THE SHASTRARTH

The Hindu Patriot of 17th January 1870, had the following in connection with the shastrarth :-

"The stronghold of Hindu idolatry and bigotry which, according to Hindu mythology, stands on the triend of Shiva, and is therefore not liable to the influence of earthquakes, has lately been shaken to its foundation by the appearance of a sage from Guzerat, the name of this great personage is Dayanand Sarawati. He has come with the vowed object of giving a death-blow to the system of Hindu worship. "He considers the Vedas to be the only religious books worthy of regard, and styles the Puranas as cunningly-devised fables - the inventions of some shrewd Brahmans in the later period for the subservience of their selfish motives.

"The Vedas, says he, entirely ignore idol-worship, and he challenges the Pandits and great men of Benares to meet him in argument. A curious and protracted logomachi took place between Dayanand Saraswati and the Pandits, but the latter, notwithstanding their boasted learning and deep insight into the Sahastras, met with a signal discomfiture. Finding it impossible to overcome the great man by a regular discussion, the Pandits resorted to the adoption of a sinister course to subserve their purspose. They made over to the sage an extract from the Puranas that savored of idolatry, and handed it over to the Saraswati, saying that it is a text from the Vedas. The latter was pondering over it, when the host of Pandits, headed by the Maharaja himself, clapped their hands, signifying the defeat of the great Pandit in the religious warfare. Though mortified greatly at the unmanly conduct and bad treatment of the Maharaja, Dayanand Swami has not lost courage. He is still waging the religious contest with more earnestness than ever. He has the shield of truth to protect him, and his banner of victory is waved in the air."

"The Pandit has lately published a pamphlet, entitled the Sattya Dharma Vichar, containing particulars of the religious contest above alluded to, had has issued a circular calling on the Pandits of Benares to show the part of the Vedas which sanctions idol-worship. No one has ventured to make his appearance."

"Hearing the great fame of the sage, we made up our minds to pay him a visit, and accordingly went to Anandbag, near Durga Vati in Benares, in which romantic garden he has taken up his temporary residence. The Rishi-like appearance of the venerable Pandit, his cheerful countenance and child-like simplicity, made on our minds an impression never to be effaced. When he began to speak, manna dropped from his lips, and the wise instructions he gave us forces us to the conviction that the golden age of India has not altogether disappeared."

"The great Pandit after 18 years of research into the Vedas has come to the conclusion that they do not savor of idolatry at all, and with the view of resuscitation the Vedic religion of the ancient sages of India, he has come out on his mission of religious reformation. He has bid adieu to all worldly enjoyments, he has assumed the austerities of an anchorite, and is buoyant with the hope of regenerating Hinduism and securing a lasting boon for his countrymen. With the view of promulgating correct theistic doctrines and dispelling h misunderstanding of the present Sanyasis and Pandits who hold pantheism to be the main doctrine of the Vedas, he is now appealing to his educated and enlightened brethren to establish a Vedic school, the teachership of which he will most gladly accept.

THE "CHRISTIAN INTELLIGENCER", BENARES, ON THE SHASTRATH

"The fame of the reformer, who lately put the whole city of Benares in commotion, seems to have gone abroad. Some account, therefore, of him and his views and the public disputation held with him, from one who was present oat the disputation, and met and conversed with the reformer several times before and after that event, will perhaps be not uninteresting to the reader of the Intelligencer.

"The name of the reformer is Dayanand Saraswati Swami. He is a native of some village in Guzerat. He is a fine-looking man, large and well-proportioned; his face, especially, expressive of much intelligence. His outward appearance is that of a Sanyasi or a religious beggar, almost entirely naked. He speaks Sanskrit fluently, never stopping wile speaking, though his Sanskrit is not of the polished kind and often not even correct. He is good reasoner, and pretty fair in a controversy, at least so far that he generally allows his opponent to state his case without interruption; but extremely authoritative in all his positions. His case and mind is made up, and believing his acquaintance with the Vedas to be superior to that of any of his adversaries, he will listen with a kind of contemptuous courtesy to anything that they may have to bring forward, and often, especially in the case of inferior Pandits, only answers, by authoritative assertions, to the contrary."

"He is well-versed in the Vedas. He is devoted himself entirely to the study of the Vedas from his eleventh year, and thus he is more practically conversant with them than most, if not all, of the great Pandits of Benares, who only know them second hand or even less. At any rate, and this is the most remarkable feature distinguishing from other Pandits, he is an independent student of the Vedas, and free from the trammels of traditional interpretation. The standard commentary of the famous Sayanacharya is held of little account by him. It can be no wonder, therefore, that his Vedic studies conducted in that spirit led him to the conviction that almost the whole of the comparatively modern Hinduism is inactive and irreconcilable contradiction with the Vedas.

"Being an active character, he determined not to keep his conviction to himself but to impart it to his country-men, and to try and effect an entire reform of the Hindu society. Briefly, his object is to place the Hindu society exactly in the state it was in two thousand years ago, that is, at the time when there existed none of the present Six schools of Philosophy, and not one of the eighteen Puranas, the source of modern Hinduism with its caste and idolatry, when the Vedas and the Vedic religion alone were in the ascendant, when one God onlywas adored, and the Vedas only were studied, and the sacrifice of homa only was, with all the attendant rites, performed by the Brahmans - for themselves, the Kshatryas and Vaishyas. At least is the fond ambition of this reformer.

"But history is a stranger to such changes. No community or nation, especially on like the Hindu, will attempt, or desire to attempt, to step back into the state in which it was two thousand years back. It is, however, not improbable that his efforts may pave the way of another reform, ân it's not impossible that he may succeed in convincing the Hindus that their existing religions is entirely at variance with the teachings of the Vedas.

"Of this fact, the generality of the Hindus are totally ignorant, and the few who are conscious of it, or who have come to suspect the reality, think it safest to preserve silence on the point. If they are once convinced of the fundamental error, there is not the slightest doubt that they will at once give up the Hindu Religion. For their faith in the prevailing Hindu Religion is the result of a conviction on their part that the religion has been so from ancient times - that it is the religion of their remote ancestors, who, it is believed, were directly inspired by God. The Vedic period cannot be brought back, it is dead and gone, it cannot be resuscitated. The conditions, which may now be brought about, must be different, more or less. We have hopes that the Christian Religion will now spread. At all events, the religion that will now spread will be identical with something superior to the present idolatry and the restrictions of caste. I must, however, declare that I am not sure whether this reformer's efforts in the interest of refore will be successful even so far. He travels up and down the banks of the Ganges, and stops here and there in the larger towns to disseminate his views; but, as far as I could ascertain, he seems to have met nowhere with much success except at Farrukhabad, near Kanpur, where, indeed, the report is to be trusted, his success has been complete.

"The Brahamans of that place in a body are said to have declared for him and to have cleared the temples of all idols. It is certain that a very rich Maharajan of that palce had become a convert to his views, and has established a school where reformed Hinduism is taught. It is not unlikely that, perceiving the extent of his influence, all those poor Brahmans should have become his followers, who get their living from him. This seems to be the fact and anything more we are told is probably exaggeration.

"His arrival at Benares was in reality a failure. The excitement which his arrival here produced at first was prodigious, but it has largely subsided, though it still prevails among many to a certain extent. If the people of our mission were to act wisely on the present occasion, and some secret help were given to the movement of this reformer, it is not improbable that what his previous attempts have been unable to achieve, may be accomplished now.

"The date of his arrival at Benares, I do not know. It must have been in the beginning of October, I was then absent. I first saw him after my return in November. I went to see him after my return in November. I went to see in company with the Prince of Bharatpur and one or two Pandits. The excitement was then at its height. The whole of the Brahmanic and educated population of Benares seemed to flock to him.

"In the verandah of small house at the end of a large garden near the monkey-tank, he was holding daily levees, for a continuous stream of people who came, eager toseee and listen to, or dispute with, the novel reformer. It does not appear, however, that the heads of the orthodox party or the Pandits for the greatest repute ever visited him, unless they did it secretly. The intensity of the excitement at last induced the Raja of Benares, in concert with his Court Pandits and other men of influence, to take some notice of the reformer, and to arrange a public disputation with him and the orthodox party, in order to allay the excitement by a defeat of the reformer. But I fear there was a determination from the beginning that they would win the day by any means, whether foul or fair.

"The disputation took place on the 17th of November, in the place where the reformer was putting up. It lasted from 3 to 7 P.M. The Raja himself was present and presided. The great Vedantist, the leader of the party of the Pandits, - I mean Vishuddhananda Gaur Swami, who is said never to have left his retreat before, came out from his place on the bank of the Ganges, to assist the Hindus with his erudition and to urge them on to victory. This shows how greatly the reformer was feared by these people. All the famous Pandits present, and other people, were on the spot in crowds. A posse of the Police was also in attendance, guarding the entrance and taking the necessary precautions against a rush inside. The Plice I have a suspicion, were also keeping any eye on the powerful opponents surrounding the Sadhu, to prevent their dealing with him in a high-handed fashion. But there was no disturbance, and the proceedings terminated peacefully, except that at the last, when the meeting broke up, the Hindu party gave a should indicative of their unfairly-acquired victory.

"This victory, gained by means, fair or foul, accomplished the object they had in view, the excitement subsided as rapidly as it had risen. The people who formerly flocked to Dayanand in crowds, now commenced to visit him in numbers which could easily be counted. The reformer came, as it were, to be outcasted, the orthodox Pandits threatening to excommunicate anyone who should dare to visit him henceforward. Shortly after the discussion in question, the reformer sent a written answer to his opponents, but nobody took any notice of it.

"A month after this he had a pamphlet, containing his teaching, published, and called upon his adversaries to furnish an immediate reply. The Hindus still declined to answer. Nevertheless, the reformer stayed where he was till the end of January, 1870. after that he left Benares for Allahabad, to be present there at the approaching fair and to preach to the people who might attend it. When, after that, I last saw him, he had not yet decided whether, on the termination of the fair, he would go to Benares or somewhere else. When the reformer had left the place, the Hindu party had an account of the discussion published, mentioning therein the points of dispute.

"The teachings of the reformer can be put under there heads:- " Those concerned with the Hindu Dharma Shastras;

1. Those, with the origin of idolatry;
2. Those, with the Puranas and the Caste-question.

   Connected with these there are many other minor points. His views as to the teaching of the Shastras are at the bottom of his entire scheme of reform. The following books only he believes in as authoritative:-

3. The four Vedas
4. The four Upavedas
5. The six Vedangas
6. The twelve Upanishads
7. TheSharirak Sutras
8. The Katyana Sutras
9. The Yoga Bhashya (Vakavak)
10. The Manu Smriti
11. The Mahabharata

Of these he believes in the Vedas because they are the word of God, and in the others because they are founded on the Vedas, or make a particular mention of the same. The remaining books, elevated to the position of "Shastras" by the Puran Hindus, as, for instance, the six Darshans and the eighteen Puranas, he regards as of minor importance, for their contents are either opposed to the teaching of the Vedas, or they are silent as regards their supreme authority. Taking his stand on this principle he refutes everything in the Hindu creed that is either clearly antagonistic to the Vedic teaching, or that does not find support in the Vedas. From this statement it will be evident that he does not differ with the Puranic Pandits as regards the dictum of the Shastras - that the Vedas are the supreme authority and that whatever is opposed to them is false. The point at issuer really is, what are the Vedas? Dayanand believes in the existing Vedas only, that is, in the Samhita or in whatever may be shown to be right on the authority of the same. The other Pandits, on the contrary, believe and maintain that originally there existed many other Vedic works, now no longer available, which supported every Hindu Shastra and everything Hindu not countenanced by the existing Vedas. But this very hard to prove, though certain English scholars of Sanskrit declare that the Pandits are in the right.

"Max Muller is one of these. What he says, stated briefly, is this: 'The lost Vedas were first mentioned in the discussions of the Buddhists, to prove some of the Brahmanas as parts of the Vedas. It is not easy to prove the theory. It may have been put forward (by the Brahmans) as something convenient to back up their contention with. It is dangerous argument, however, though it is though the Brahmans would never have advanced it, if they hand not regarded it as sound.'

"I am inclined to think, however, that Max Muller is not right in his argument. In as much as many things did not find support in the existing Vedas, the Brahmans (Pandits) had no alternative but either admit that such-and-such thing was not allowed by the Vedas, a suicidal admission on their part, or to assert that originally other Vedas existed, though the declaration may or may not have any foundation. The latter assertion might render their position still more critical, yet there could be no doubt as to which of the two alternatives they would prefer. Dayanand wholly denies that the Vedas were ever lost. What part may be there real fact, it will be evident to an import enquirer that if any other Vedas originally existed their general import would be the same as that of existing ones, and they could not be in any way favorable to the present Hindu Faith.

"Idolatry and the Puranas:- Dayanand utterly condemns idolatry not because it is the harmless error but because it is a positive sign. He is opposed to the worship of gods or polytheism. He believes in one only God, and in those attributes of His only which commonly begged in by theists. His God is primarily the creator of the Vedas and then of universe. Hence the Vedas, compared to the universe, are everlasting, though compared to God they are non-eternal.

In the Vedas God is spoken as Atma, Agni, etc. according to the different Divine attributes, God, though distinct from the world for Dayanand does not believe in the Vedantic doctrine, that everything is God, yet pervades and permeates it as the principle of life. To illustrate Dayanand's position: God is believed in as Agni because Agni means life, and consequently He is worshipped through Agni (fire). To avoid misapprehension it must be distinctly understood that when he says that God in the universe is Agni, by Agni he does not mean fire, but that something which stands for Spirit and Life. Again he does not mean that this ordinary fire represents the Divine form or is a Divine representative, but only this, that it pre-eminently reveals His glory presence, and that, being such a manifester of Divine glory, God can be very well worshipped through it. The Agni it self should not be worshipped but should be sued only as a medium of His worship. The worship of God consists primarily in these there things:-

1. Studying the Vedas, for the acquisition of Divine Knowledge.
2. Obeying Moral laws as the commandments of God.
3. Adoring the divinity through the Agnihotra, etc.

By doing these there things salvation may be attained. There never was an incarnation (of the Deity) for man's salvation, nor can there ever be one. Such a thing is opposed to the attributes of the Deity. Thus Dayanand condemns Hindu incarnations as thoroughly as he does the Christian incarnation. In other words, he has no faith whatever in Divine incarnation. And if there were ever any incarnations, these were those of the sages and saints (devtas) and not of God. Consequently, the reformer runs down nearly all the Puranic stories or legends, and especially the lila of Krishna.

THE CASTE SYSTEM

"Caste, etc. - This reformer looks upon caste as a merely political (civil) institution, established by the rulers of the times for the convenience and comfort of their subjects, and not as a natural or religious mark. It is not a natural mark or symbol, inasmuch, as God did not create the four castes as four distinct kinds of men; on the contrary, all human beings are the same in their general and species, and it is not a religious mark inasmuch as the salvation and the destiny of men in the world to come do not depend on caste.

"The castes are merely different professions or privileges, and were organized by those in power to prevent confusion, and for the better discharge of the duties of different kinds . Certain persons, specially fitted for the purpose, were chosen by Royalty for conducting worship and for the cultivation of moral science and philosophy, and these were named Brahmans. Others were constituted Kshatryas, to guard the empire against external danger and to preserve internal order; the Vaishya class was organized for trade and commerce and for agriculture, while the people that yet remained were put into the Shudra order, to serve all.

"Every caste was granted privileges of a distinct nature, and they were made hereditary. But inasmuch as all these divisions were made and fixed by Royalty. Royalty alone can elevate, to the position of a Vaishya or Kshatrya or a Brahman, any Shudra that may be deemed worthy of the promotion. Similarly, one who deserves to be degraded may be degraded to the position of a Shudra by Royalty. To be brief, every Brahman, who is incompetent to perform the duties of a Brahman, falls at once to the level of Shudra, and every Shudra that acquires worth and excellence may rise to be a Brahman. The individual concerned, however, has no power to make the change in his status; the Royalty alone will do it for him. The last named condition renders the reformer's theory impracticable. Government, in these days, has nothing to do with the regulation of privileges of this nature. In other words it should be the concern of the biradari itself to degrade an immoral Brahman to the level of a Shudra, and to exalt a good and intelligent Shudra to the position of a Brahman.

"The discussion commenced by Dayanand , asking Pandit Tara Charan, the Raja's Court Pandit, who had been appointed to defend the cause of orthodoxy, whether he admitted the Vedas as authority. When this had been agreed to, he requested Tara Charan to produce passages from the Vedas sanctioning idolatry, pashanadipujna (worship of stones, etc.). Instead of doing this, Tara Charan, fro some time, tried to substituee proofs from the Puranas.

"At last Dayanand happening to say that he only admitted Manu Smriti, Sharirak Sutras, etc. as authoritative, because founded on the Vedas. Vishuddhanand, the great Vedantist interferred, and quoting a Vedant Sutra from the Sharirak Sutras, asked Dayanand to show that it was founded on the Vedas. After some hesitation Dayanand replied that he could do this only after referring to the Vedas, as he did not remember the whole of them. Vishuddanand then tauntingly said that if he could not do that, he should not set himself up as a teacher in Benares. Dayanand replied that none of the Pandits had the whole of the Vedas in his memory. Thereupon Vishuddhanand and several others asserted that they knew the whole of the Vedas by heart.

" Then followed several questions, wholly irrelevant to the subject under discussion, but put by Dayanand to show that his opponents has asserted more than they could justify. They could not answer none of his questions. At last some Pandits took up the thread of the discussion again by asking Dayanand, whether the terms 'pratima'(likeness) and 'purti' (fullness), occurring in the Vedas, did not sanction idolatry. He answered that rightly interpreted they did not do so. As none of the opponents objected to his interpretation, it is plain that they either perceived the correctness of it, or were too little acquainted with the Vedas to venture to contradict it.

"Then Madhvacharya, a Pandit of not repute, produced two leaves of a Vedic manuscript, and reading a passage containing the word 'Puranas' asked to what this term referred. Dayanand replied: it was there simply an adjective, meaning ancient, and not the proper name. Vishuddhanand challenging this interpretation, some discussion followed as to its grammatical correctness; but at last al seemed to acquiesce in it. Then Madhvacharya again produced two other leaves of a Vedic manuscript, and read a passage with this purport that upon the completion of a yajna (sacrifice) the reading of the Puranas should be heard on the tenth day, and asked how the term Puranas could be there an adjective. Dayanand took the manuscript in his hand and began to meditate what answer he should give. His opponents wanted but two minutes, and as still no answer was forthcoming, they rose, jeering and calling out, that he was unable and was defeated, and went away. The answer he afterwards published in his pamphlet.

"Unquestionably, Dayanand should have had more time.

It is, however, apparent that there was some difficulty in replying, and Dayanand subsequently published his answer in the form of a pamphlet, declaring that word 'vidya' ought to be affixed to the word 'Purana', the compound meaning the ancient knowledge of the Veda.

This answer is not satisfactory. There cannot be much doubt in this, that the word 'Puranan' here stands for the eighteen Puranas. But as the passage is out of a Brahmana of the Samveda, which contains many modern additions, its value would not, after all, be much in the eyes of the non-Hindus, and, I suspect, even of Dayanand; for he onve admitted to me that the Brahmanas did contain modern interpolated portions, and that any passage sanctioning idolatry, was to be considered as such as a spurious portion.

"This reformer is not unacquainted with the Christian religion. He has read the Gospels, though, in my opinion, not very carefully. I had a talk with Dayanand on the subject. At present his own scheme of reform claims his special attention, and he cannot afford to devote much time to the investigation of a different faith".

A correspondent of the Pioneer, writing to the paper, said that Swami Dayanand had failed to make out his case against the Benares Pandits, and in consequence had lost his prestige. To quote his own words, "the Swami hung down his head, and the Pandits clapped their hands in triumph. An attempt was made by some turbulent spirits to hoot the Swami, and to inflict a personal chastisement on him for his audacity in questioning the propriety of the national mode of worship, but the presend of the Maharaja quenched the ebullition of their spirit." In answer to what the writer calls an "unvarnished account of the discussion." The following lines appeared in the leading Anglo-Indian paper of India:-

"I refrain from giving the details of the discussion, for they would hardly be intelligible to the majority of your readers. Those who take a special interest in the controversy may refer to a small pamphlet, entitle the Shastrarth, which can be had of Messrs. Brij Bhooshan Dass, of Benares. Suffice it to say that the question at issue was whether idolatry is sanctioned by the Vedas which, according to the orthodox Hindu, are Divine Revelation.

The Swami maintained that the Vedas do not inculcate idolatry, and the Pandits did not produce at the time, nor have they produced since, a single passage from the Vedas that could dislodge the Swami from his position. The answers of the Pandits were extremely evasive. The whole controversy was no better than a regular tamasha, for the Brahmans did not confine their arguments to the point at issue, but carried on altercations on various points of Hindu jurisprudence, logic, and Sanskrit grammar, which had not the least bearing on the main question. How can your correspondent, in the face of the above facts, boldly assert that the Swami got the 'worst of the fight,' I leave for your impartial readers to judge."

THE PRAYAG KHUMBA FAIR, ETC.

Hearing that the Kumbha Fair at Allahabad was approaching, Swami Dayanand left for that place, and having arrived there took up his quarters in the open air on the bank of the Ganges. The Pandits and Sadhus waited upon him in numbers, and vidyarthis also flocked to him from all sides. His lectures on idol-worship, on tilak and kanthi, etc., attracted large audiences and revolutionized the religious ideas of many. The Pandits resented his scathing criticism, and some of them even made bold to hold with him a shastrarth on idol-worship, but the attempt ended in a signal failure. They cited mantras from the Vedas, alleging that they were chanted to endow the images with life, but when, in response to a call form the Swami, they translated the same, they found that the passage had nothing to do with their contention.

The Swami further pointed out to them how the mantra - Natasy pratima asti, inculcated the very reverse of what the Pandits asserted it did; it was an empathic refuation of the worship of images and insisted upon the adoration of the one God only, in spirit. The Pandits grumbles and finally retired growling. Some of the orthodox here went so far as to tell the Swami that were he in their part of the country, they world have him buried alive. A heavy laugh from the Swami was the answer, and resuming shi seriousness, he spoke to them exhaustively on "Dharma and Adharma."

After staying for about a month at Alllahabad, the Swami proceeded to Mirzapur, where he remained for about two months, and-a-half, in a beautiful garden, belonging to Ram Rattan Ladha. The effect of his speeches here also was of the most salutary kind. Among the Pandits, who, on hearing the truth, gave up idol-worship, were Nagin and Bhagwati Charan, and many of the Pandits commenced doing the sandhya regularly. While at Mirzapur, the Swami rose daily at about 2 A.M. and remained, till break of day, absorbed in meditation and contemplation (pranayama)

In May, 1870, the Swami returned to Benares, and, taking up his quarters in the garden belonging to Lala Madho Das, Honorary Magistrate, near Durgakund, delivered lectures daily on the falseness of Neo-Vedantism. He repeatedly challenge the orthodox Pandits to a shastrarth by means of printed notices, but no one had the courage to come forward. One Baboo Harish Chandra having his objections thoroughly removed, became a follower of the Vedic religion.

The Maharajas of Bharatpur, Riwan, and Nairwa were among the great personages who visited the Swami during his stay at Benaries. A conversation on the "Existence of God" ensued. The arguments advanced by the Swami in support of Theism were so strong and convincing that the Chiefs were extremely pleased and thanked the Swami for the trouble he had taken on their account.

Wandering about for a whole year along the banks of the Ganges, the Swami was again back at Kashi, in March, 1872, and having spent some days here, running down superstitions and declaring sublimity of the Vedic Faith, he proceeded to Bengal. Passing through Dumraon, he reached Patna, in September, 1872, and having stayed here for about a month, during which period many discussions on a small scale took place and hundreds of people heard him exposing idolatry and other institutions, the Swami repaired to Monghyr, where he lectured for fifteen days. From Monghyr, he went to Bhagalpur, arriving at his destination on 20th October, 1872. Here several discussions took place with the Brahmans and the Christians.

One day a Bengali Christian gentleman, hearing the Swami's updesh, burst into tears, remarking, "Had I found any one like yourself, O most revered Sir, a score of years earlier to resolve my doubts, I would never have permitted myself to be torn from my brethren and my ancestral religion. In those days, I waited upon on Pandit after another with my questions, but not one of them would or could answer them to my satisfaction."

The Maharaja of Burdwan also came to hear him, and discussion with the Padris took place in His Highness's presence on "Invarnation." His Highness was alleged to have a decided leaning towards the Christian Faith, but he heard the discussion in silence, and then retired. He requested the Swami to stay in his palace, but the Swami begged to be excused from acceding to his wishes, saying that he preferred retirement.

The Bengali Headmaster of the local school also waited upon the Swami one day, in company with some twenty of his pupils, and began to speak upon the merits of his Faith. The Swami gave him an exhaustive reply, disabusing, in the course of the reply, his mind of the impression that all the four varnas were one and the same thing and that promiscuous eating was anything desirable. The conversation lasted until 10 P.M.

The following day, there was another discussion with the Brahmos, in the open air, under a grand shamiana. The Maharaja was present at the discussion, although, as formerly, he never said anything for or against the position of any party during the period the debate lasted. The Brahmo gentlemen finding themselves pressed hard finally said: "If our great one in Calcutta accept what you say, we shall accept it too."

After two months' stay at Bhagalpur, the Swami left for Calcutta, on December 15th, 1872.

AT CALCUTTA

Swami Dayanand now thought of visiting Calcutta, and, in pursuance of this resolve, he left Kashi and proceeded to the Capital of the Indian Empire via Dumraon. Mr. Chander Shighar Sen, Barrister-at-Law, in response to whose invitation the Swami had undertaken the journey, was, at the proper time, at the Howra Station to receive his distinguished guest, and drove with him to Baboo Surendra Mohan's garden, where the Swami was to put up. The Barrister, as well as the owner of the garden was unsparing in his attentions to the Swami, making him feel perfectly at home in every respect.

As soon as it was known that the great reformer was in Calcutta, educated people of every denomination flocked to him in numbers. The Indian Mirror, type, noticing his arrival, spoke of him as an iconoclast of a superior type, as a man of unbounded learning who had proved himself more than a match for the greatest Pandits of Benares, as a teacher who, by his other various achievements, had made himself a name in Northern India.

The Brahmo Samaj of Calcutta was in the zenith of its power in these days, and the leading Brahmos were constantly by the Swami's side, being under the impression, no doubt, that he would ultimately come round to their views. But the impression was not long in being dissipated. The Swami took his stand on the Vedas, and everything Vedic had his profoundest sympathy and his earnest advocacy, - a thing, more or less, distasteful to the members of the Brahmo Samaj.

Of course, there must be discussions between Dayanand and the believers in the Brahmo Faith, and the debates took place almost daily, "What do you understand by caste?" a gentleman asked the Swami. The reply was, that caste or varna want social status determined entirely by the individual's worth and actions, and that it was not at all identical with the present arbitrary and false differentiation, in social life, of one person from another from considerations of birth alone.

"Should or should not the Yajnopavit be worn?" The reply was, that the members of the "twice-born" classes should, one and all wear it, though it did not signify much if the ignorant individuals, miscalled Brahmans, went without it.

Is God corporeal or incorporeal?" The reply was absolutely without form and figure, being essentially Truth, Intelligence and Happiness.

"Was the author of the Sankhya Darshana an atheist? He wrote - Ishwarasiddhe, denying thereby the existence of God." The Swami replied that such misconceptions were entirely traceable to the scant regard in which the present-day Pandits held the commentaries by the sages of yore. The aphorism, affirmed as declaring the belief of the author of Sankhya, was really an objection from a non-believer (in the Vedic Religion), and that there was a reply to it in the next aphorism. Kapila, the Swami added, was a believer in the transmigration of souls, he was a believer in the Vedas, he was a believer in yoga, and he was a believer in the existence of the Soul, and as such he could not teach the non-existence of the Deity. In point of fact there was no discrepancy whatever between the teaching of one Darshana-Shastra and another. Each of the six dealt, separately and independently, with one of the six causes which had been instrumental in producing the world. The Nyaya spoke of the atoms, the Mimansa of action, the Sankhya of the combination of elements, Patanjali of thought and intelligence, Vaisheshak of time, and the Vedanta of a creative Deity.

"Was not Agnihotra a kind of idol-worship?" The Swami's answer was in the negative. A function which necessitated a contemplation of the Deity and which was fraught with good to the entire world, could not be identified with the worship of idols.

So markedly attractive was the personality of Swami Dayanad to all true inquirers that his company was sought after both by high and low. Baboo Gyani Indra lal Roy, M.A.B.L. (Editor of a Bengali paper) referring to this attraction, speaks of the Swami's argumentative power and his erudition in the most flattering terms. "His power of lecturing , his skill in discussion and his thorough acquaintance with the Shastras, " says he, "astonished every one. Crowds of men would approach him in the capacity of true enquirers, and obtaining satisfactory answers to their questions, go away to their homes. They had never heard before any of their countrymen, not conversant with the English language, declare to them, in connection with the Dharma and the Samaj (society), a Faith so utterly devoid of partiality."

With Baboo Keshuv Chandra Sen the Swami had a discussion on the doctrine of the "Transmigration of Souls." It must have been an interesting debate, and it were to be wished that we had an account of the same to notice here, but perhaps none has been preserved. There can be no question, however, that Baboo Keshav Chandra Sen, though his religious beliefs differed widely from those of Swami Dayanand, had a sincere regard for his opponent.

This is fully evident from the fact that the Swami delivered, on January 9, 1873, at the Baboo's house, and at the learned Baboo's own request, a lecture on the superiority of the "Vedic Religion." Many of the reises and learned men of the town formed part of the Swami's audience on the present occasion. Only a few days after this the anniversary-date of the Brahmo Samaj came round. The Swalmi was also invited, and Maharishi Devindra Nath Tagore sent his own carriage to bring him, and when he came, the Maharishi received him in person in the most cordial manner possible. The Maharishi, like Baboo Keshave Chandra Sen, invited the Swami to his private place of residence. This was during the anniversary-day. The Maharishi was one of the greatest admirers of the Upanishads, and the Vedas in his palace being profusely embellished with texts from the same and with quotations from the other Shastras, the sight was most edifying to the Swami, and he confessed as much to the Maharishi. The latter requested the Swami to put up with him, but the Swami begged to be excused from availing himself of the offer on the ground that as a Sanyasi he could not live with grihasthis.

On February 23, 1873, Swami Dayanand delivered a lecture at the house of Baboo Guru Charan Datta, in which he proved that the Vedas did not countenance idolatry. Pandit Mahesh Chandra Nyayaratna, who was present, rose at he conclusion of the lecture and gave a summary of the lecture to the audience in Bengali. But not proving himself a faithful interpreter and saying many things which the Swami had never said, the hearers were much displeased with him, especially the students of the local Sanskrit College.

On 2nd March, 1873, the Swami spoke in the Hall of the Bara-Nagar Borneo Company on "Havan," and some seven days after that he addressed a large and influential audience on the "Vedic Doctrines" in the Bara-Nagar Night School. The lecture lasted over three hours. The up-shot of the speech was that the Vedas inculcated absolute unity of Godhead, that they recognized no artificial system of caste, that child-marriage and other institutions of similar kind were utterly un-Vedic, and that the one only remedy for the evils which were, and had been undermining India's prosperity lay in India's returning to the pure Faith of the ancients - even that taught in the Scriptures. Noticing this speech, the Indian Mirror said that it proved the speaker not merely a learned man but one who was also deeply thoughtful - one whose arguments were strong and forcible, and whose manner of speaking was bold and fearless.

This lecture was followed by two or three others, all largely attended. The Swami never lost an opportunity of enlarging upon the importance of studying the ancient Aryan Shastras, and when he visited the Sanskrit college of Prasanno Kumar Tagore, he spoke so warmly for these that the good Baboo actually agreed to include the Vedas in the curriculum of studies for the College. It is also affirmed that he spoke to Dr. Mohindra Lal very strongly as to the necessity of reviving the study of the Ayurveda.

We are told that Pandit Tara Charan Tarak-Ratan Naiyyayak thrice essayed to face the Swami, but each time the attempt failed. He was well aware what it was to hold a discussion with a scholar like Dayanand, and he might well shrink from a contest with him.

The Swami visited the Asiatic Museum with a view to purchase copies of the Vedas and the Upanishads, and he did buy some works from here.

It was here at Calcutta that Swami Dayanand realized the necessity of discontinuing lecturing in Sanskrit for the future. He could not but see that he was not always interpreted faithfully, and that by speaking in Sanskrit he could directly reach but the minority. Baboo Keshav Chandra Sen is said to have hinted to him as such, and he resolved that henceforward his public lectures should be, if possible, invariably in Arya Bhasha (Hindi). And it was probably at Calcutta that the Swami took to wearing clothes. The whims of society, so long, as they were comparatively innocent and did not encroach upon the principle, might be tolerated in the interests of the great mission so dear to him and all true well-wishers of their mother-land.

One day, in the course of conversation, Baboo Keshav Chandra Sen is said to have expressed regret at the Swami's ignorance of English. "If the Vedic scholar like yourself were conversant with English," said he, "what a suitable companion you would make me in my contemplated visit to England?" The Swami in reply observed that he too was sorry at Baboo Keshav Chandra's ignorance of Sanskrit, considering that the pure and enlightened Faith of the Aryan nation lay enshrined in that language. Certainly nothing could be more pretentions, added he, than that the Baboo, the master of a foreign tongue, should claim to teach to his countrymen what he himself understood but little.

The lectures which Swami Dayanand delivered at Calcutta were considered, as might well be presumed that they were, worth preserving, and his admirers thought they would print them. The proposal had the heartiest approval of Babool Keshav Chandra Sen, but before it could be carried out, the Swami had left the town.

What had among other things, principally influenced the Swami to pay a visit to Calcutta, was to found there a Pathshala (school), on true Vedic lines. While he was yet at Benares, the following editorial had appeared in the Hindu Patriot (January, 1870);-

"Here is an opportunity for the Dharma Sabha to prove itself useful, which we trust and hope will not be thrown away. The Sabha is an anachronism, but its existence may be tolerated by enlightened public opinion, if it make its existence may be tolerated by enlightened public opinion, if it makes its objects to revive Vedic learning and Vedic religion, the glorious heritage of our proud ancestor.

"We wish our correspondent had given an estimate of the cost of the proposed Vedic School, which ought, of course, to be moderate, and we cannot believe that if the objects of the projected institution were properly explained and circulated, there would be lack of funds. A single Native Prince might give the money required. It would certainly redound to the credit of the Dharma Sabha if it should come forward liberally and second the laudable efforts of the New Reformer. Other wise we would recommend the Brahmo Samai, as the chief instrument of the revival of Vedic worship under the guidance of the late Raja Ramamohan Roy, to interest itself in this sacred cause, and lend its support and authority to the new Reformer."

Further on the paper said:-

"In conclusion, we would make a strong appeal to the heads of the orthodox class of Hindus to assist Dayananda Saraswati in establishing a Vedic School. Almost all the educated natives are theists at heart, and though some cling to idolatry for the sake of their parents and nearest relations, many have avowedly adopted Brahmoism. It is, therefore, meet that the Vedic religion should be revived, the tide of progress cannot be obstructed, and the members of the Sanatan Dharma Rakashini Sabha will ill-succeed in keeping upt he present system of Hinduism. They will secure the lasting gratitude of the Hindus if they try to purify Hinduism from the corruptions that have crept into it, and establish the Vedic religion of the educated."

On the appearance of the forgoing lines, the Benares correspondent of the Patriot wrote to its as follows:-

"Emboldened by your words of encouragement we repaired to Anand-Bag in Benares, and explained to the venerable Pandit the substance of your editorial remarks. The joy of the sage knew no bounds, and with a blooming countenance he thanked you most heartily. He then propounded the following plan in accordance with which the working of the pro0psed Vedic School is intended to be carried out. As a first step, the services of a good Pandit should be secured for teaching Sanskrit literature. As Saraswati has in contemplation the introduction of a system of training that will lead to a clear understanding of the Vedas, he intends selecting a Pandit from among a few best scholars he is acquainted with. "Though a native of Guzerat, he was brought up in a Vedic School at Mathura, under the tuition of the great sage, the late lamented Sura Dasa. There are a few scholars of this great man, who will gladly accept the teachership of the proposed School, if remunerated on a somewhat liberal scale. The salary should be from Rs. 75 to Rs 100 per month. After the pupils have been thoroughly initiated into Sanskrit literature, which will take two years to accomplish, the services of another Pandit should be secured at say Rs. 100 per month, for teaching the Vedas. As liberal education has inflamed the hearts of many a youth with the fire of religious zeal, advanced Scholars of the Sanskrit College and Pandits of the Vernacular schools might be induced to enter the Academy with a view to obtain an insight into the Vedic lore.

"In that case, a Night School ought to be organized; and not Eleemosynary aid will then be needed. But as there is every probability of pupils from Nabodeep or other Samajes joining the School, arrangements should be made for supplying all their necessaries, including purchase of books, etc. a At the outset, a monthly subscription should be raised sufficient to pay Rs. 100 per month to a Pandit, and to defray the necessary expenses for teaching 10 pupils. In addition to the monthly subscription there should of course be a reserve fund to meet contingent expenses.

"I do not say anything at present about School-building and boarding house, because I think any one of our wealthy countrymen might be induced to spare one of their supernumerary buildings for this noble purpose. As soon as arrangements have been made opening the proposed school, our venerable Pandit Dayanand Saraswati will start for Calcutta in company with a Sanskrit teacher, and will stay there as long as his assistance will be considered necessary to place the long as his assistance will be considered necessary to place the Pathshala on a firm footing. It is the intention of our Pandit to make Benares, which has an academic fame of no recent date, the center of his educational scheme, with Schools spread all over India; and if the liberal-minded gentry come forward to fulfill the desire of this great man, they will assuredly confer a great boon on India. The branches of the tree of corruption have overshadowed the whole of India, and it is his noble intention to apply the axe of truth to the very root of the tree, which has gone deeper at Benares than elsewhere. Yesterday, the Pandit left this station for Allahabad where he intends staying for a month."

The Swami's object of establishing a Pathshala at Calcutta, however, was never realized, for the people would do little more than showing "lip-sympathy."

AT DIFFERENT PLACES IN BIHAR, ETC.

Swami Dayanand left Calcutta on Ist April, 1873, and reaching Hughly put in the garden belonging to Bindraban Mandal Zimindar. The news of his arrival produced the usual stir in the town and brought numbers of people to see him. The well-known Professor Rev. Lal Behori Dey waited upon him and had a talk with him on "Caste" were perfectly reasonable and sound, and frankly acknowledged that his own ideas on the subject had been rather confused and erroneous.

At Hughly the Swami delivered several lectures, the one on the 7th April being given in the presence of the principal men of the town. Pandit Tara Charan was not far from the place where the meeting was held, but he would not venture near the Swami, though getting on the top of a neighbouring house he held forth to his admirers on the unorthodox character of the Sanyasi's teaching. When the Pandit's conduct was reported to the Swami, he regretted that he should have behaved in the manner he had done, for he was perfectly at liberty to give expression to his views at the meeting and to have the truth threshed out. The leading men of Hughly agreed with the Swami, and they besought Pandit Tara Charan to hold a shastrarth with him. The Pandit at last consented, and the discussion came of on the following day - 8th April - on "Idolatry."

The Pandit commenced by reciting an aphorism from, as he declared, the Yoga-Darshana of Pantanjali, and commenting upon it declared that the mind could not be concentrated without the help of material objects, and hence the necessity of idol-worship in upaasna, according to the aphorism of Vyasa! Swami Dayanand replied that no such aphorism was to be found in Patanjali, andif it was Pantanjali's, it could not possibly be Vyasa's.

He then recited the real Sutra and, repeating Vyasa's commentary thereon, said, that what the commentator meant was that the mind should be concentrated on the forepart of the nose. The discussion proceeded, and eventually Pandit Tara Charan, finding himself hard pressed, became reckless and exclaimed: "All worship is a lie." The audience was astounded, while the Swami smiled and said: "You confess then that idolatry is false?" The Pandit, it is asserted that Swami in private and he was an admirer of Classical Sanskrit Literature and an enemy of the modern productions in Sanskrit, and the he fully believed that idol-worship was false out-and-out; but he could not , he added openly avow what he believed in his heart, out of consideration for his worldly interests!

Departing from Hughly on the 16th of April, 1873, the Swami arrived at Bhagalpur, wehre he stayed for one month, and then left for Patna. At Patna he delivered several lectures, and it was towards the close of May that eh proceeded thence to Chhapra, where he became a guest of Rao Shiv Gulam Shah Bahadur, Zimindar, whos reception of him was markedly respectful and cordial. The interested portion of the Chhapra community taking their cue from their brethren of Patna, who had proclaimed the Swami to be a "German Christian," gave out that he was an infidel.

The sensible and enlightened residents of the place, however, could not be hoodwinked, and they called upon the local Pandits to hold a shastrarth with the new-comer. The Pandits declined to accede to their wishes, on the ground that the man was a nastik (infidel or athiest0, that they would have to undergo a prayashchit (expiation) in case they say his face.

The Swami coming to hear of this objection, observed that he difficulty was not insuperable, that a screen might be hung between himself and the Pandits, which would prevent his being see by them, and they hung back silent and sullen, till one of them, Pandit Jaggan Nath, took up the gaunlet and specified the day on which the discussion should take palce. The day came, and a screen was actually hung between the parties. The Swami put the Pandit some questions from the Smritis, in Sanskrit, and the Pandit replied; but so wretched were his answers that on the Swami's pointing out his bad grammar, he was wholly non-plussed and refused to proceed with the discussion.

The Swami had no alternative but to address the audience himself, and his lecture lasted for full four hours, convincing all thoughtful and impartial-disposed minds that idolatry-loving Pandits were completely in the wrong. The Pandits, however, were not going to take their defeat silently. The shouted out that the Swami was misinterpreting and disgracing the Vedas and hence one who was to be shunned and avoided by all true-believers. Some of the more zealous, in their disappointment, went so far as to openly assert that they would stone the atheist to death if they should get at him.

After about two weeks' stay at Chhapra, during which he visited the local school also, the Swami left for Danapur, whence he proceeded to Arrah, where he spent over a month, making known his mission to all who came to him. From Arrah he went to Dumraon, where he became a guest of the ruler of the principality, putting up in the state Bungalow near the Railway-station. The Maharaja, with his courtiers, met him and had friendly chat with him on various subjects. No shastrarth worth the name was held here - only a short discussion took place between him and the State Pandit, Durga Datta, on "Vedantism and idolatry," in the presence of the Chief and his grandees.

The Swami, when refuting the Neo-Vedantism, pointed out the true meaning of such expressions, as Ekamedvadvtiyam Brahm and giving the Niaruktak interpretation of the mantra - Brahmanaoasya etc., which Pandit Durga Datta had advanced in support of idolatry, showed that the Scriptural passage hand nothing to do with the worship of the creature in any form whatsoever. The Pandit then quoted from the Jabal Upanishad in defense of idol-worship, but the Swami's reply was: "This Upanishad is a spurious composition. Shankracharya, whom you profess to follow, does not, does not at all recognize it." To this no answer was forthcoming.

The Pandit, however, knew how to retrieve his defeat. In his own summary of the discussion, embodied in "the history of his triumphs" (Digvijai), published in Samvat 1941, after the Swami's death, he worte: "When Dayanand saw that he was unable to answer any further, he smiled and said: Pandit Druga Dattaji, you are a wonderful one. I am only aman, by you are omniscient and thoroughly conversant with all the Shastras. I, a mortal, cannot hold a discussion with you, the Brahm!" Very modest this of the pandit! And pray, why was not Dayanand as a good "Brahm" as the Pandit himself, according to the Pandit's own way of thinking?

Swami Dayanand set off from Dumraon on 8th January, 1873, and after making a day's halt at Mirzapur, where the affairs of the Pathshala received his attention, left for Allahabad, which had its due share of updesh, and it was not had well nigh gone that he reached Kanpur Here he stayed for about a month, living in a solitary hut on the bank of the Ganges, some two miles from the town, and delivering lectures at the various centers of the locality, in accordance with the suggestions of the leading men thereof.

lala Ghanya Lal, Alakhdhari, noticing on the authority of a correspondent, the Swmi's work at Kanpur, regretted that so true a reformer and teacher should be abused and hooted by the deluded, ignorant and priest-ridden kanpuris.

Leaving Kanpur towards the close of November he arrived at Farrukhabad, where he had interviews with the Director of Public Instruction, and Sir Charles Muir, Lieutenatn-Governor, N.W.P. He appealed to the Lieutenant Governor to protect, the cow , and His Honor replied the he would do what he could in that direction on entering the India Council, on his retirement from Service.

Taking leave of Farrukhabad and passing through Kashganj and Chhalesar, the Swami reached Aligarh on 26th December, 1873, in company with Thakur Mukand singh, and some other Rajpoots, and accepted the hospitality of Raja Jaikishen Dass, C.S.T. Enquirers from the town and the surrounding villages came in scores, and Dharma charcha (discussion on religions topics) was kept up till late in the night. On 27th December the Swami gave his first lecture at Aligarh, addressing a mixed audience of Hindus and Muhammadans and of Officers, Civil and Military. The lecture was followed by several others, all largely attended by representatives of every creed. As a matter of fact, the Swami had company all the day long, the Pandits and Moulvis and others having full permission to see him at any time and to have their doubts removed. The local celebrity, Pandit Mehr Chand, who, before the Swami's arrival at Aligrah, ahd been boasting that the Swami durst not face him, kept away from the Swami's meetings during the entire period of the teacher's stay at the station, calling his adversary a nastik and what not, and refusing to listen to the suggestion of his towns-men that he should go and have a shastrarth with the man whom he had so often worsted in his absence!

After about a month's stay at Aligarh, the Swami repaired to Hathras, , whence, in response to an invitation from Rao

Tikam Singh, he proceeded to Mursan, which, after a few day's halt, he left for Mathura (Vrindaban) via Hathras. Pandit Dev Parshad, Deputy collector, was aware of the Swami's approaching visit to Mathura, Raja Jaikishen Das having written to him about the same, and he selected Radhabagh for the Swami's residence. As to what had been instrumental in drawing the Swami to Mathura, was the refusal on the part of a class-fellow of his (Pandit Ganga Datta) to accept a teachership in the Farrukhabad pathshal till Mathura, the strong-hold of idotatry, had been visited and idol-worship there been given a death-blow. "Rangacharya he said, "goes about the city with flambeaux burning before him in the day-time, proclaiming that the worship of idols is right and good. If I am to accept the post in your gift and move from Mathura, I will do that only after you have been in our midst, and exposed the false teachers." The Swami was impressed by this communication from his class-fellow, and found himself erelong at Vrindaban.

When Swami Dayanand arrived at Vrindaban, he found it in a state of unusual excitement. The Raht Fair on the Brahma Utsav was bout to take place, and followers of Vaishnav creed had flocked to Krishna's birth-place in hundreds and thousands from the most distant parts of India. A more glorious opportunity the Swami could not look for to make known the Truth. Accordingly, a notice was issued in Hindi, under the signature of Bakshi Mahbu Masih, that Swami Dayananda's lectures would commence on the 5th of March, 1874, the very day on which the Fair was to begin.

At the same time a challenge was sent to Rangacharya to come forward and support idolatry on the authority of the Vedas, to show that the wearing of kanthi and tilak was, as the asserted, inculcated in the Scriptures. Rangacharya replied that he would answer the call on the termination of the Fair. The reply was significant and the Swami rating it at its proper worth, took to vigorously exposing the un-Vedic institutions and usages in the very thick of the Fair. The unanswerable arguments of the Swami were daily reported to Rangacharya, and the latter realizing, in the depths of his heart, the utter hopelessness of making good his position against such antagonist, had it given out that he was not feeling well. In proportion the day fixed for the shastrarth drew nearer, the illness of the learned Rangacharya increased, and at last when the day arrived, he would not leave his house and was self-denying enough to forego the pleasure of entering into a controversy, in spite of his promise to the contrary! The erudite Ranacharya is said to have confessed to an acquaintance of his in private that he had no desire to hold a shastrarth, for in the event of Dayanand's being defeatd, the "Sadhu" would lose nothing, but if he was worsted in the contest, all his reputation would be gone. Rangacharya caring for the world and it s opinion, had doubtless much at stake, and he was wise in his generation for avoiding Dayanand, for the latter was stronger in faith!

The admirers of Rangacharya took up cudgels in behalf of their master, not metaphorically but literally. Some four or five hundred Chovas (strudy, begging Brahmans) armed with clubs, surrounded the Swami's residence, abusing him and gnashing their teeth in rage, but the Deputy Collector was equal to the emergency and no disturbance took place. The effect of such conduct on the part of Rangacharya's followers was that many men gave up idolatry once and forever. Having done his work at Vrindaban, the Swami came at Mathura, where he stayed only four days, but something was accomplished even during this small period. Several enquirers were so impressed by his teaching that they threw their idols into river, and gave their allegiance to the one and only God of the Universe - even to Him whose glory the Vedas proclaim! Pandit Madan Datta, in particular, was so charmed by the Swami's truthful updesh that though he had started from home with the avowed object of defending and advocating idolatry, he commenced denouncing if before his very admirers and in the presence of hundreds of Vaishnavas and other non-believers in the Vedic religion.

From Mathura, Swami Dayanand accompanied Rao Tikam Singh once more to Mursan, which, after a few days's stay, he left for Chhalesar and thence for Allahabad, the Rao driving him to Medva Station in his own carriage. From Allahabad he proceeded to Kashi, arriving there towards the middle of June,

1874. he put up in the garden of Ram Parshad Udasi, and preached, for the first time,, in Hindi, in Benares. Through Sayyad Ahmad Khan, Sub-Judge, at whose residence he delivered tow or three lectures, had interviews with Mr. Shakespeare and the Maharaja of Benares.

His Highness's attitude towards the Swami had been anything but friendly on the occasion of the famous shastrarth with the Kashi Pandits - indeed, he had done all he could to have the Swami snubbed and discomfited, but now his behaviour was different. As soon as he saw the Swami, he came forward to receive him, embraced him and seated him on a golden chair. The Maharaja's action was little better than heaping live coals on the head of a favourite Pandit - Pandit Tara Charan, who happened to be by and who had taken prominent part in the Kashi Shastrarth; but that Maharaja had time to appreciate the Swami's sterling worth and unique erudition, and was now evidently desirous of atoning, iin some degree, for the past. He asked the Swami's pardon for his previous harshness, and assured him that he should no mind his criticisms any longer. When, after taking his leave, the Swami had arrived at his lodgings, His Highness sent him a present of a maund of sweets, which the Swami, as was his wont, distributed among the company.

In July, 1874, the Swami found himself at Allahabad gain, and he ahd notices put up, inviting all non-believers in the Vedic Religion to see him and have the truth sifted. A marhatta Christian waited upon him with Professor Max Muller's translation of the Rig Veda and asserted that the word "Agni" in the Vedas meant nothing but fire. The Swami gave the good Christian an insight into the motives which must sway a partial man like the Professor, and showed him how his translation for various reasons could not be accepted as authoritative.

While pointing out to him how "Agni" meant "God" as well as fire and so on, the Swami took occasion to make clear to the enquirer the immense superiority of the Vedic Religion over the Christian faith, which talked of the Tower of Babylon and what not! The Marhatta made no reply but one Pandit Kashi Nath Shastri shouted out: "What have you created this disturbance for through the length and breadth of the country? The reply was, that inasmuch as interested Pandits had been promulgating a system of trickery in the land, and as they were unable to distinguish between truth and falsehood any longer, in consequence of their intellects having become "petrified" through idol-worship, he had come forward to defend the eternal principles of right and justice and to offer the same of their acceptance.

His first speech on India's past glory began the fight for her independence. Swami Dayanand delivered several lectures at Allahabad- on the "Transmigration of Souls", "Dharma" and other kindred subjects. Their effect on the minds of the youthful community was particularly marked. It was the first man of the highest intellectual type and one profoundly verse in the ancient literature they had come across who gave the lie to the Native and European critics insinuating, orally or in books, that the primeval Vedic Religion was polytheistic or enjoined Nature-worship, and who held that patriotism was a virtue of the first order.

When these young men heard him prove, in the presence of thousands, incontestably and to the utter humiliation of those who would maintain the contrary, that the original Faith of the Aryas was the noblest and sublimest form of theism imaginable, and when they heard him speak of the glories of India in days gone-by, with the eloquence of a genuine, enlightened lover of his mother-land, their whole being was thrilled with emotions of the most agreeable kind, and they accepted his teaching and guidance, and registered a vow in the sight of Heaven, and often in the sight and hearing of man as well, that they would do all in their power to be worthy of the Bharatvarsha of yore and of the sages that once dwelt in it. Many of the students of the Muir college, who came in contact with the Swami at Allahabad, have turned out to be real patriots, and bulwarks of the Arya Samaj.

It was during his stay at Allahabad that the manuscript of the first edition of the Satyarth Prakash (Light of Truth) was made over to Raja Jaikishen Das, c.s.i.,to be printed under his supervision.

5

Journey to Bombay

Bidding farewell to Allahabad early in October, 1874, Swami Dyanand left for Bombay, which, after visiting Nasak and Jabalpur, he reached on 26th of the month. The motive which is said to have originally influenced those who invited him to Bombay would appear to be somewhat selfish in the character. These gentlemen, thinking, in their ignorance, that the great Teacher could be bent to their purposes, wanted to press his profound learning and his extraordinary intellectual powers into their service to secure a triumph for their own particular creed, being under the impression that once its superiority was indisputably established, they would get converts in any number.

But they never were more mistaken in their lives. And like them the members of the Prarthana Brahmo Samaj had also to undeceive themselves. They too discovered that the man whom they had joined in inviting was not the one after their own heart and that inflexibility of purpose and devotion to principle were his strongest characteristics.

A Seth was waiting at the Bombay Railway station with his carriage, and as soon s the Swami arrived, he drove him to the Mahadeva Balkeshar Hill, a place some two miles from Bombay, hwere he was put up.

Notices, in four different languages, were posted in different parts of the city, announcing the reformer's arrival and requesting all desirous of knowing the truth to visit him and have their difficulties explained. The orthodox Pandits spied danger and felt extremely ill at ease.

The Balbhacharies (Vaishnav sect) wields, as it were, an absolute sway in Bombay, and Swami Dayanand, having, by study and oral inquiry, gained a thorough insight into the character of this phase of Vaishnavism, delivered a series of lectures thereon, touching, in the course of his remarks, on some of the "dearly-loved" practices of its "acharyas," some of whom, among other things, see positively nothing to object to in a layman of their faith, who has just entered the life of a householder, taking his future partner in life to one among themselves fort he sanctifying and spiritualizing of the tie!

Another Failed Attempt on his Life

Revelations like these, whatever their effect on the outsiders, made the Balbhachari leaders frantic with rage, and one of these, Goswami Jiwanji, in his madness, determined to put the reformer out of the way. The services of four ruffians were hired, but these, though they dept dodging the steps of the Swami in season and out of season, could get no chance to carry out their fell purpose, as their intended victim was always well-attended. Foiled in this direction, the good Jiwanji sought to accomplish his object in another way. Having, somehow or other, entice Baldev Singh Brahman, the Swami's cook, into his dwelling he told him what he was after, promising him a reward of a thousand rupees if hw would destroy his master by administering to him poison food. To assure the cook that he meant business, Jiwanji gave him a note-of-hand confirming the reward, and Rs. 5 in cash and five seers of sweetmeats as an additional, preliminary gift for a speedy execution of the plot unfolded. It is impossible to say how far the cook allowed himself to be influenced by his tempter, but certain it is that the fact of his visit to the chief of the Gokalias did not remain a secret.

Some one who had seen the man in close conference with Jiwanji reported the matter to Swami Dayanand, who sharply interrogated his servant on the point. The latter confessed everything, and laid the note as well as the money and sweetmeats before the Swami. That true Brahman did no more than content himself with having the sweets thrown away, with tearing the note in fragments, and with giving a warning to the cook not to be led away by mischievous persons in future. All the reply that the Swami got to his challenges from the Bombay Pandits was at first no more than an anonymous hand-bill from one who styled himself P.E.N., containing twenty-four questions to be answered.

SERIATIM

The Swami was not bound to notice this hand-bill, but as an encouragement to and or the satisfaction of the Pandits he got Sadhu Poornanand to reply to the questions, seriatim, as follows:-

1. I accept proofs such as pratyaksha pramana occular demonstration or direct perception), and so on.
2. I believe in the Four Vedas as absolutely authoritative (infallible).
3. I don not look upon the Brahmans and other similar books as absolutely authoritative. I study them, because they are the compositions of Rishis, with the object of ascertaining as to what they day regarding the Vedas, to know how they interpret the Veda-mantras and what are their principles of belief.
4. The reply to the third question contains the reply to the fourth.
5. I study the Vedangas, such as Shiksha, etc. because, being the works of Munis. I want to find out what they day in respect of the Vedas. I do not accept them as my scriptures.
6. The commentaries of the Vedas and Vedangas and similar annotatory works, which are Arsha or are admittedly the compositions of Rishis - these I do not regard as absolutely authoritative, but I study them to know if they are correct. Even for this do I study them, and not thinking them absolutely authoritative.

   The Purva Mimanda by Jaimini, the Uttara Mimansa by Vyasa, etc., - these to I do not study regarding them as absolutely authoritative, but merely to see how far their teaching is nin accord with that of the Vedas.

7. I have no faith in the study and object of the Puranas and the Tantras; to look upon them, for me, as works of any authority, is out of the question.
8. Neither the entire Mahabharata nor the whole of the Ramayana of Valmiki is entirely authoritative, for the usages and customs of society vary with times. They are chiefly meant to be read as works of history, speaking of those that are no more.
9. The reply to the tenth question is contained in the reply to the ninth.
10. I do not study Manu Smrit, thinking it as primarily and absolutely authoritative, but merely to know what Manu teaches.
11. I do not regard Yajnavalka and Mitakshara Smriti as authoritative at all.
12. See reply to question of twelfth.
13. The systems of faith, such as that of Vishnu Swami, I do not regard as authoritative in the slightest degree. I refute and expose them, for these systems are repugnant to the Vedic Teachings.
14. See reply to question fourteenth.
15. I am not a free-thinker, but a believer in the Vedic religion. What the Veda says about the six essential or elementary Substances, even in that do I believe thoroughly.
16. What the Veda says about the creation of the universe, and in respect of the author thereof, even in that do I believe in all its entirety.
17. The time which has elapsed since the cycles of creation began, no one can compute. Even this should be known.
18. The yajnas and other rites enjoined by the Vedas, these should be performed by all, to the best of their power.
19. The system or usage sanctioned by the Vedas should alone be followed, and nothing to the contrary.

20. The rites or ceremonials, whose performance is enjoined in the Shakhas, these are to be performed if in accordance with the teaching of the Vedas, but not if they are opposed to that teaching.
21. Ishwara is not born, neither doth He die. He that is born or dies, is not Ishwara, because he is not almighty, nor omniscient, nor indivisible, nor all-pervading, nor absolutely just.
22. I belong to the Sanyas Ashrama.
23. The book called the "Satya-Dharma Vichar," printed in Yantrala - that embodies the beliefs of is author, and I have nothing to do with his beliefs.

"If we, the Aryas, talk on the Vedic Dharma in love, and without our minds entirely divested of prejudice, good will result from that. My wish is, that it should be so. If meetings were held for the purpose daily, I should regard it as something very desirable. Every one should so proceed that the various conflicting creeds be destroyed. The questions 13, 14, and 15 being mere re-iterations and the writer thereof being, consequently, guilty of repetition, I could not but ask myself, how a man who does not know how to put a question, cold, on closer acquaintance, carry on a discussion on approved lines. Thus did I reflect, thinking of the saying, that one who does not know how come by a meal, cannot possibly amass wealth. And the person who has put the above questions has not given his name, which is also very objectionable. So should all good men believe.

The Swami (Dayanand) too, is of this opinion. Whoever in future puts questions anonymously, he (says the Swami) shall have an answer through me (the under-signed). Also, whatsoever enquirer does not state, briefly, what creed he believes in, he too, shall have an answer to his questions through me (the undersigned) - Pooranand, 16th November, 1874."

Subsequently it was deemed necessary to issue a notice that anonymous enquires, whether made publicly by means of printed hand-bills or in private communications, would receive no attention whatever. Whoever wanted to ask anything, must come into the light of day and have his questions answered. The notice was followed by an exhaustive lecture on "Idol-worship," in a splendid building situate on the Dhobi Ghat. The audience is said to have numbered about ten thousand souls, the Superintendent of Police, with a strong posse of his men, being in attendance to keep order. The effect of the lecture was what might well have been expected. It threw the kanthi-wearing idol-worshippers into a state of consternation, and it was unanimously resolved that it should not go unanswered.

Accordingly, one Gattu Lal, a blind Pandit, delivered a lecture in Lal Bag in support of idolatry, the other Pandits, including Vaishnavites, helping him in citing authorities from the Shastras on the table. One of the audience calling upon the Pandits to cite from the Vedas a passage speaking of "Murti" (idols), they glibly read out a line or two from, as they falsely declared, the Sama Veda, interpreting it to mean, that idols (pratima) laugh.

At this the orthodox were delighted beyond measure, and the meeting broke up with shouts of triumph, each Brahman being given an eight-anna piece as dakshina (largesse) in commemoration of the victory! And we doubt not that it was Goswami Jiwanji who had principally influenced Pandit Gattu Lal to deliver his lecture; but however much he might make of the speech just for show, he did not appear to think very greatly of it in his heart of hearts. He cleared off to Madras, to be away from the 'heretic' who, in the meantime, did him the friendly turn of publishing a tract on the Balbhacharya System of Faith.

Pandit Gattu Lal's lecture seemed to have inspired his brother pandits with some degree of courage. They agreed to hold shastrarths with him, and accordingly two were held, - first, in the building of the Bombay Library on "Vyakarna and Idol-worship," and the other in the garden belonging to Seth Niladhar on "Vedantism." In the latter the Swami's antagonist was famous and learned Pandit, Jaikrishan Das. The result of this discussion, in a manner, is embodied in the small tract which Swami Dayanand published under the name of "Vedanta Bhranti Niwaran," a pamphlet which shows the falsity of the doctrines of "Non-duality," and establishes the distinctive existence of God and Soul.

It was the desire of many men at Bombay that an Arya Samaj should be established, and as many a sixty individuals actually put down their names for membership, but, though the proposal, in a way, was carried out, the establishment of the Samaj failed to become a matter of public cognizance, the want of moral courage on the part of the members being one of the causes. The Swami receiving a call from Gopal Rao Hari Deshmukh, a judge, left for Ahmedabad in company with the learned judge's son, a Barrister, who had been deputed for the purpose.

On alighting from the train at Ahmedabad, the Swami was received by an influential local Seth, a thorough believer in idols. On entering into a conversation with his guest, the Seth fell to praising his fine temple which he had but just built at a cost of two or three Lakhs. All the effect which this eulogy produced on the Swami's mind was his bringing his hand on the carriage-seat with some violence and crying out, in accents of sadness rather than anger,: "Alas! That you should have spent so much money on a stone. Had you laid it out in the establishment of a Pathshala, Veda-knowing Pandits would have come forth from the institution and benefited the world. To such a state have we been reduced, through our ignorance, that we have to look up to Germany to supply us with the Vedas, before we can read them. They are not to be had in our own country!"

This was a 'stunner' to the Seth, and, in his vexation, he said that he should have a shastrarth held between the Swami and the Pandits. The Shastrarth came off. It ea son "idol-worship," and lasted for some five or six hours. The other party finding that they could not prove idol-worship from the Vedas, lost their temper and took to abusing the Swami. At this moment Gopal Rao Hari Deshmukh, the Judge, arose and said, that it was fully evident from the shastrarth that the Vedas did not countenance idolatry. Of course, every one was at liberty to believe it or not, but he was of language, whatever their views might be.

After about a month's stay at Ahmedabad, the Swami repaired to Rajkot, where he delivered no less than twelve lectures. He visited the Raj Kumar College and gave an updesh to the students, all sons of princes. The Principal of the Institution put several questions to the Swami and got his answers, and, on the Swami's taking leave of him, made him a present, of two copies of the Rig Veda.

Leaving Rajkot on the 18th of January, 1875, Swami Dayanand arrived once more at Ahmedabad on 21st, and spent a week there, lecturing, his remarks being particularly directed against the "Swami Narain Creed." He also published a pamphlet here. On 29th of January he was at Bombay again.

THE SECOND VISIT TO BOMBAY

On Swami Dayanand's return to Bombay, the desire to make the establishment of an Arya Samaj a fait accompli, in a public sense; acquired additional strength, and it was finally settled that the predominant idea in the minds of the followers of the Veda should be given a practical shape in the right and proper way without further delay. Those competent for the task undertook to frame a set of principles for the guidance of the would-be organization, and the principles framed were discussed at several sittings. When they had been amended and altered and thoroughly approved by all, including the Swami himself, they were announced at a public meeting held on 10th of April, 1875, under the presidency of Mr. Girdhar Lal Dyal Das, Kothari, B.A., LL.B. in the garden belonging to Dr. Manakji, and the comtemplated Samaj was declared to have been established.

The principles res out the following:-

1. The establishment of Arya Samajes in the interests of Society is absolutely necessary.
2. The (Arya) Samaj shall regard the Vedas alone as independently and absolutely authoritative. For purposes of testimony and for the understanding of the Vedas, as also for historical purposes, all the four Brahmanas - Shathpatha, etc., the six Vedangas, the four Upa-vedas, the Six Darshanas, and 1,127 Shakhas

or exposition of the Vedas, shall, by virtue of their being ancient and recognized works of Rishis, be also regarded as secondarily authoritative, in so far only as their teaching is in accord with that of the Vedas.

3. There shall be a principal Arya Samaj in each province and the other Arya Samajes shall be its branches, all connected with one another.
4. The Branch Samajes shall conform to as model the Principal Samaj.
5. The Principal Samaj shall possess various Vedic works in Sanskrit and Aryabhasha (Hindi) for the dissemination of the true knowledge, and it shall issue a weekly paper under the name of "Arya Prakash," also an exponent of the Vedic teaching. The paper and the books shall be patronized by all Samajes.
6. Every Samaj shall have a President and a Secretary, other men and women shall be the members thereof.
7. The President shall be responsible for the maintenance of the integrity and for the promotion of the prosperity of the Samaj, while the Secretary shall reply to all letters, and shall keep a record of the names, state, etc., of all members fo the Samaj.
8. The members of the Samaj shall be men of truth, of upright policy and principles, of pure character, and of philanthropic impulse.
9. Whatever leisure a member gets from house-hold work, he shall devote the same to the good of the Samaj, with more than the earnestness displayed in the discharge of household duties. Those that have no family to care for, should, in particular, be always striving promote the well-being of the body. In no other way should they behave.
10. Every eight day the President, the Secretary and other members of the Samaj shall come together in the Samaj Mandir, giving precedence to punctual attendance over everything else.

11. Having assembled together, they should be calm and composed in their minds, and in spirit of love, and free from bias, they may ask questions and obtain answers from each other. This done, they shall sing the hymns of the Sama Veda in praise of God, and songs bearing on the true Dharma, the right principles and the right teaching, to the accompaniment of musical instruments. And the mantras shall be commented upon and explained and the lectures delivered on similar (Vedic) themes. After this there shall be music again, to be followed by interpretation of mantras and speeches as before, and so on in succession.

12. Every member shall cheerfully contribute a hundredth part of the money he has earned honestly and with the sweat of his brow, towards the funds of the Samaj, the Arya Vidyala and the Arya Prakash paper. If he contributes more, the greater shall be his reward. The more thus contributed shall be used for the purposes specified and in no other way.

13. The more an individual bestirs himself in bringing income to the Samaj for the purpose specified, and for the diffusion of a knowledge of the teachings of the Arya Samaj, the more honour shall he receive for his energy and zeal.

    The Samaj shall do, stuti, prarthana,and upasana (i.e. shall glorify, pray to and hold communion with the one only God), in the manner commended by the Vedas. To speak of God as the Being who is formless, almighty, just, infinite, immutable, eternal, incomparable, merciful, the father of all, the mother of the entire universe, all-supporting, the Lord of all, possessing the attributes of truth, intelligence, happiness, and so on: as all-pervading and the knower of all hearts, indestructible, deathless, everlasting, pure, and conscious; as inherently in a state of salvation, endless, the bestower of happiness, the giver of righteousness, wealth, comfort and salvation;- to speak of Him as endowed with such and similar other qualities and attributes, is to do His stuti (i.e., praying to Him), and to become absorbed in the contemplation of His essence, which is absolute Happiness, is termed upasana (i.e., holding communion with Him). The aforesaid Being, possessing the attribute of incorporeity etc., shall alone be adored, and naught besides.

14. The Samaj shall perform Vedic sanskars, such as Anteshti, etc.

15. The Vedas and the ancient Arsha Granths shall be studied and taught in the Arya Vidyala, and true and right training, calculated to improve males and females, alone shall be imparted, on Vedic lines.

16. In the interest of the country, two kinds of reform shall receive thorough attention to the Samaj, spiritual and worldly. There shall be uplifting in these two directions, for the promotion of purity; indeed, reform conducive to the welfare of entire mankind shall be undertaken by the Samaj.

17. The Samaj shall believe in what is right and just only, i.e., in the true Vedic Dharma, destitute of all element, of partiality and standing the crucial test of all the pramanas - ocular demonstration and so forth. It shall never have faith in anything else, if it can help it.

18. The Samaj shall send learned men, of approved character, everywhere to preach truth.

19. In the interests of the education of both males and females, separate schools shall be established, if possible, in all places. In the seminaries for females the work of teaching and that of serving the students shall be carried on by females only, and in the schools for males, the responsibility of doing the same shall lie with males. Never shall this rules be infringed.

20. The schools shall be looked after and maintained as the President of the Samaj shall direct.

The President and the other members of the Samaj shall, for the maintenance of mutual good-will, keep their minds wholly divested of all feelings of pride, of willfulness, hate, anger, etc., and, with such vices shut out, they shall, being free of enmity and pure of heart, love one anther, even as each loves his/her ownself.

21. When deliberating on a subject, that which has been, as the fruit of this deliberation, been ascertained to be in thorough accord with the principles of justice and universal benevolence, and absolutely true, the same shall be made known to the members and believed in by them. Acting thus in termed rising above bias or prejudice.

22. He who conforms his conduct to the principles specified, and is righteous and endowed with true virtues, the same shall be admitted to the superior portion of the Samaj, while he who is otherwise than this, shall belong to the ordinary portion of the Samaj. But the individual who openly appears to be utterly depraved and debased, he shall be expelled from the Samaj. Such a step, however, shall not be dictated by prejudice; on the contrary, both the things specified shall be done after due deliberation by the exalted members of the Samaj, and not otherwise.

23. The President and other Sabhasads of the Samaj shall ever strive, to the utmost of their power, to look after and improve the Arya Samaj, the Arya Vidyala, the Arya Prakash paper, and the finances of the Samaj.

24. So long as an Arya Samajist can get a brother Arya Samajist to employ or to serve him, so long he should not employ or get anyone else to serve him. The relations in existence between these two should be the relations that ought to subsist between master and servant.

25. Whenever an occasion for making a donation arises, as, for instance, in connection with a marriage, the birth of a son, the realization of a fortune, or a death in the family, and so on, the Arya Samajist concerned shall be expected to make a donation on such an occasion. No act is more meritorious, and the members shall always bear this fact in mind.

26. Whenever an addition is made to the principles or rules above laid down, or whenever any of these is altered or amended, such an addition, alteration or amendment, shall invariably be the result of thorough deliberation on the subject by the exalted Sabhasads of the Samaj, and the nature of the same shall be previously made known to al the members.

In accordance with the above principles, many of which, it will be evident, are nothing but By-laws, the election of office-bearers took place, and it was settled that the Weekly Meeting of the Samaj should be held every Saturday evening. A short time after, however. Saturday was for, obvious reasons, found to be an inconvenient day, and Sunday was fixed upon as the Weekly Meeting day. The latter arrangement remains in force down to the present time, in almost all the Samajes in India.

After establishing a Samaj at Bombay, the Swami for the third time left for Ahmedabad. The "Swami Narain Creed," so popular in the city and its suburbs, required a further exposure, and the reformer set about his task with his wonted energy, not leaving the station till the end of May, 1875.

RECALLED TO BOMBAY

On the Swami's departure from Bombay the impression gained ground in the orthodox circles that he had left the place for good, and that there was nothing to fear from him any longer. The Bombay Samaj being yet in its infancy and busy evolving system and order, as it were, out of chaos, the leading orthodox Pandits took in the situation at a glance, and thought they could afford to look 'big' now, without putting their head into the noose. Accordingly they gave out that they had been all along only too willing to hold a shastrarth with the Swami and that they have held one but for his leaving the town abruptly. This boldness went so far that notices were actually printed and circulated among the people. The Samaj could appreciate the move on the part of its antagonists, and resolved to please them.

A telegram was sent to the Swami informing him of the state of affairs, and requesting him to come back to Bombay.

The Swami came, to the utter dismay or the Pandits, and called upon them to come forward for a discussion. But they shrank from the contest, as they had done before, and refused to come forward. They were not, however, to escape so easily this time. A notice was served upon the famous local Pandit, Kanwal Nain Acharya, through a Pleader, and this brought them to their senses. The 12th June, 1875, was fixed upon for the discussion, and it duly came off on that day.

The Bombay Samachar, for June 17 and 18, (1875) describes the shastrarth as follows:-

As already announced by means of a public notice, the people began to pour into the Framjee Cowasjee Institute at 3 p.m. on Sunday last. Swami Dayanand Saraswati came exactly 3. He was provided with the ancient Shastras of the Aryas, - such as the Veda Samhita, the Brahmanas, the Aranyaks, the Upanishads, the Sutras, the Shikshas, the Kalpas, the Nighantu, the Vayakarna, and so on, all numbering over 150. these were arranged on a table placed in the center of the 'stage.' Two chairs were placed one on either side of the table for the principal parties, while a little below there were set eight more chairs for the Shastris, who were to take notes of the discussion. There were present at the meeting, among many other learned men, Sethsand Pandits, Rao Bahadur Bechar Das Albai Das, Seth Lakshmi Das Khemji, Seth Mathrua Dasy Loji, Rao Bahadur Daudabhai Pandurang , Mirasbhai, Shankar nanabhai, Gonga Das Kishore Das, Hargobin Das Nana, Mansukh Ram Suraj Ram, Ranchhorbhai Oodey Ram, Shastri Vishnu Parsram. The place was full to overflowing. "Swami Dayanand, who was the first to arrive, was, by those with whom the management rested, seated on the chair placed on the left-hand side of the table, the managers reminding one, by their action, of the proverb. - A bad workman quarrels with his tools. Why did not they choose the left side for their party? The chair on the right-hand side of the table ws thus reserved for Kanwal Nain, the leader of the Ramanuj System of Faith, and the people began to eagerly wait for the arrival of the Acharya.

The report presently spread that kanwal Nain Acharya had refused to come into the presence of an infidel (yavana) and that, bringing forward the question of Madhyastha, he would prevent the shastrarth from taking place, so that disgrace might not fall upon him (the guru). But while the audience was busy over these and similar other reports, the news arrived that Kanwal Nain Acharya would be at the meeting immediately (3 p.m.). He arrived accompanied by some twenty-five or thirty followers, and, over and above these, by many Marwari Seths and Sahukars. The managers of the Sabha descended some steps to receive him, and having conducted him with the greatest respect, seated him on the chair to the right-hand side of the Swami. Seth Bechar Das Albai Das was nominate to the chair.

The Seth made a brief speech, to the following effect: 'Brethren we are all idol-worshippers, including myself. Swami Dayanand, however, undertakes to prove that idol-worship is not countenanced by the Vedas. No one need take offence at this; on the contrary, it behoves all to hear the discussion patiently and attentively and to understand it, so that we may derive inestimable benefit from it, and know which is the right path in connection with Dharma. This will further the country's good, and will be conducive to our happiness and peace in the highest degree. Similarly, Kanwal Nain Acharya, of the Ramanuj Faith, beng present here and undertaking to prove that idol-worship is in accord with the teachings of the Vedas, we should all hear his speeches, and find out therefrom what is the truth.' After saying this, the Seth observed that he had but just come to know that a document had been executed between two laymen, and that it was this document that had called the meeting into existence, adding that the document in question should be read out to the audience by Mr. Bahi Sahnkar Nanabhai without further delay, which would make every thing clear to them.

On this Mr. Bhai Shankar nanabhai read out the following document:-

'We, the two undersigned, have gladly read the following document and signed it, and we shall abide by our judge:-

- The Sabha (shastrarth) to be held next Saturday in Framjee Cowasjee Institute, between Swami Dayanand and Kanwal Nain Acharya, - of that, we, the undersigned, shall defray the expenses, and we shall be responsible for police arrangements as well.

- If Swami Dayanand comes off, by means of the Veda, victorious and proves idolatry false, the marwari Shiv Narain Beni Chand, who always issues notices unde his signature on behalf of kanwal Nain Acharya, shall become a disciple (follower) of Swami Dayanand;; but if, on the contrary, kanwal Nain is victorious, then Thakur Jiwan Dayal shall become his dicidple, and put on the Ramanandi mark on the forehead. In the vent of Kanwal Nain's sustaining a defeat, Shiv Narain shall cease to put on the mark.
- Laying aside all sectarian differences, Sanskrit scholars of all denominations shall, without any invidious distinction, be invite to this meeting, and the summary of the Shastrarth which they furnish, the same shall be published, under the signatures of both the undersigned. Whichsoever of the two does not act up to the contents of the document, the same shall be known as having lost his dharma.'

Signed: - Thakur Jiwan Dayal ; Shiv Narain Beni Chand.

"The document read out, the meeting was formally informed that it was private in its character, but for all that, added the speaker, 'What an excellent opportunity it ahs afforded us! Swami Dayanand, who is present here today, will prove that idol-worship in is not indicated in the Vedas, while Kanwal Nain Acharya will prove that the Vedas do enjoin the worship of idols. I venture to express the hope that kanwal nain Acharya will forthwith commence his lecture, for the mere assertion that such a thing is not countenanced in such-and-such a book, will not have weight with those we want to convince till it is substantiated by proof.'

"upon this, one of the signers of the document, Marwari Shiv Narain Beni Chand, said that, according to the document, idol-worship was to be proved true on the strength of authorities form both Shruti and Smriti, and he wanted to know why, in reading the document, the word 'Smriti' had been left out. In reply to this Mr. Bhai Shankar Nanabhai read out the document over again, observing, in conclusion, that according to the paper, idol-worship was to be proved from the Vedas alone, there being absolutely no mention of 'Smriti' therein. Again, Shiv Narain spoke, saying that the names of the Pandits had not been read out, to which Mr. Bhai Shankar replied, that the number of names of the Pandits (to be present) had not been specified. Shiv Narain the asked to see the document, which was duly handed over to him by the President. The inspection satisfied him had his friends that he document said nothing on the points in question.

"After this , kanwal Nain spoke:-

"These Pandits who are sitting here, of what sect are they? For, sectarian Pandits should not be here."

Hearing these words of Kanwal Nain, the educated and enlightened laymen, composing the meeting, were greatly surprised, knowing that it was generally understood that Pandits professing to believe in the Vedic Dharma were of four different sects, the Shaivites, the Shaktaks, the Samarts, and the Vaishnav. A Pandit not belonging to any of these four sects was difficult to come across. In the face of this fact, the words of Kanwal Nain did not appear to be reasonable.

"Presently Kanwal Nain Acharya resumed, saying that no one who was a representative of a sect should be given the position of Madhyastha and that not till he had examined the would-be Madhyastha should the latter be nominated as such, - words which ostensibly had no other object than that the time of the meeting should be wasted and the discussion be avoided.

"One of the Pandits, addressed by Kanwal Nain, replied that he was a Vaishnav, and the Acharya requesting him to approach, made him sit near himself, and then addressing the other Pandits said: 'Will you swear by Shaligram and theGita to report the truth? Shastri Kalii Das Gobin Das answered that he should report nothing but what appeared to him to be the truth. Vishnu Parsram Shastri, who was questioned next, similarly answered that he should declare only what he knew was the truth, that his brother-Shastris and himself would write down, word for word, whatever the Acharya and the Swami said, and that they would subsequently give their impartial opinion as to the merits of what had been by each party.

Upon this Kanwal Nain asked Parsram what Shastra he had studied. The Shastri replied that the question was wholly irrelevant, and that if the Acharya was to ask the Pandits such questions, he might as well first tell them what he himself knew. The Acharya attempted a reply, but completely broke down in the attempt. The Vaishnav Shastri stood up and, commenting upon the words of Kanwal Nain, observed, that it was wholly undesirable that time should be wasted in useless talk. What was incumbent upon the great Acharya was, that he should prove idolatry from the Vedas. Wasting time is useless talk instead of proving his contention was not at all commendable.

On the Subject of Ldol-worship

"After this Swami Dayanand, most humbly addressing Kanwal Nain, said: 'I look upon to-day as a very happy day, inasmuch as it has given me an opportunity to meet you. I assert that idol-worship is not inculcated in the Vedas, and I am ready to prove it. I have delivered lectures and held discussions on this subject in various places. Of which fact you must also be aware. Hence I shall feel obliged if you will be good enough to inform me as to in which Veda the endowing with life, the invoking, the destroying and the worship of idols are spoken of, and what particular portion of the Veda in question. Let us know, further, how the commentators have commented upon and interpreted the passages dealing with these, and what interpretations of the passages the Brahmana of the Veda has adopted as pre-eminently satisfactory and reasonable. This will allay the restlessness of the audience and will be of great benefit to us. As to Madhyastha, there is no need of one between us. If you would have your way, then let the Vedas, the Brahmanas of the Vedas, and similar other works, be nominated as such. They are superior to all, and will be partial to none. They are all lying before you on the table. Whatever there be in the Veda favorable to your contention, bring the same out, and having translated it, make its purport clear to the audience, so that truth may soon come to be known from untruth. And whatever is spoken by yourself or by me, the Pandits will write that down word for word, and the same shall be subsequently published under the signatures of the two gentlemen who got aforementioned document executed between them. The Pandits of the whole country will then be in a position to judge of the merits of the publication, and the entire Arya world will know what is genuine and what is false in the discussion between you and myself."

"Kanwal Nain Acharya would not listen to this most reasonable prayer of Pandit Dayanand, and began to talk evasively. Seeing this Seth Mathura Das Logi stood up and thus addressed the audience: 'In company with several laymen I, with the permission of Swami Dayanand, waited upon Kanwal Nain Acharya of 6th June, 1875, and informed him that the knowledge of the fact that the Acharya was in Bombay and was strongly resolved to prove that idol-worship was inculcated in the Vedas, had created in the Swami a desire to meet him.

This being the case, it was desirable (I said) that a public meeting should be held in the house of some layman, or in a garden, or in Framjee Cowasjee Institute, or in a open place, just as it should please the Acharya to direct.

The Acharya, when face to face with the Swami, should prove idolatry from the Vedas. It was his duty to do so, millions of people (Hindus) having faith in idol-worship, and the Swami, on the contrary, having openly and boldly announced that the Vedas did not sanction the worship of idols and images. The Swami maintained that Vedas contained no mantras having to do with endowing the images with life, and that the mantras employed for the purpose did at all mean what they were made to. He maintained that the same thing held good in the case of mantras pressed into service for invocations, and in connection with the destroying and worshipping of idols. Similarly, he held that no Sankalpa mantras were to be found in the Vedas, and those made use of for the purpose did not at all bear the interpretation they were given. The mischief had been wrought by the so-called Acharyas, who, influenced by selfish motives, had created myths. Dayanand believed that no Acharya or Pandit could have the boldness to come forward and prove the reverse of what he maintained was the truth. It was, under these circumstances, clearly the duty of Kanwal Nain and the other idolatrous Acharyas, I declared, to meet the Swami and to prove that idol-worship was enjoined in the Vedas; as, in case of their failing to do so, the Vaishnav Dharma - our own Dharma - would sustain a great blow.

Kanwal Nain Acharya was aware he had a large following. Knowing that and asserting that he was well-versed in the Vedic Religion, he was, in duty bound, to come forward and to prove idolatry to be in accord with the Vedic teaching. If he did not do it, no other Pandit could be expected to. Consequently (said I he must take up the challenge. If he acceded to my request, all necessary arrangements should be made. The problem that faced the Acharya he should solve, he should give an answer to the question, as to in which particular Veda Samhita the mantras employed in connection with the endowing with life, the invoking, the destroying and the worship of idols were to be found.

They must be met with in the books of the Acharya's sect, and, if so, he could tell how the commentators had commented upon and interpreted them, and what particular interpretations of the same had been adopted by the Brahmanas of the Vedas as pre-eminently satisfactory.

The answer to the question under reference would end all altercation and would enable everybody to know the truth from falsehood. I assured Kanwal Nain Acharya that in the meeting the might be held, we should so arrange that whatever the Acharya or the Swami should say, the same should be written down at once, and they should run no risk that mere oral speaking is liable to involve one in. unquestionably the Acharya should be expected to point out, without delay, in the Vedas and other Granths, whatever passage he might quote professedly from them in support of his faith, and so should the Swami point out, at once, in the Vedas and other books, whatever he might professedly quote from them in support of his faith or against the faith of the Acharya.

All that was spoken by either party should be faithfully reproduced on paper, should be signed by both the parties, should be attested by the Pandits, and then the manuscript, a copy of which should remain separately in the possession of each speaker, should be published, daily, piece-meal, the printed matter, as the public should be daily informed, representing one day's work. The procedure would continue till the discussion was finished, and, on the termination of the discussion, the entire manuscript should be signed by the Acharya and Swami Dayanand, and attested by the Pandits, and, having been published, should be sent to all those principal parts of India, where our brethren in faith were to be found in large numbers. The cost of publishing should be met half- and-half by the two parties.

"Kanwal Nain Acharya's reply to all this was that four Pandits, verse in four different branches of knowledge, were wanted, and that these should be examined by him (previous to their attending the would-be meeting). I said that there was no need of such Pandits, fork when the proceedings of the meetings were published, they would be before the Pandits of whole of India, and the Pandits would pass their opinion on the same. And in the publication 9report of the proceedings) it should be stated that whatever Pandits felt disposed to express their opinion on the same. And in the publication (report of the proceedings) it should be stated that whatever Pandits felt disposed to express their opinion as regards the merits of the Shastrarth, the same should kindly forward their remarks, within three months, to such-and-such a person. Such testimony (I presented) would be more useful. And as to the kind of Pandits, of whom the Acharya want those that were well up in Nyaya Shastra, or those who were well up in Vyakarna, or hose who knew the uttara Mimansa, or htose who were well-versed in Sankya, or those who were masters of the Dharma Shastra? The Acharya answered that those who were well-versed in the Vedangas were wanted. I said that such Pandit were difficult to be had.

To wish to have such was (under the circumstances) very much like expressing a wish to possess a horned hare, no matter if such a creature was to be had nowhere. The number of books which the Vedas, the Vedangas, the Upanga and the Upavedas made up, was something tremendous, and so was their weight. Where could Pandis well-versed in these be had from?

However, if the Acharya aware of the existence one such, he would kindly say where the man was to be found. The Acharya replied that Rang Jeet Totawari was such a one, and that he was to be found in Nadia Shanti (a place, by the by, where the Acharya's faith has an unusually large following)!

I said that I knew none in Nadia Shanti, but that if he would name any Pandit thoroughly verse in the Vedas and the Vedangas in Benares, which unquesrionably was the seat of our Dharma par excellence, and rich in Pandits, I would wire to our agent in that city and find out all about the Pandit, though I was convinced that such a learned man could be had nowhere, yea, even one of an inferior type. Indeed, it was a question whether such Pandits were plentiful evening former times.

The Acharya decline to name any Pandits in Benares, adding that he would hold a discussion only if the kind of Pandits mentioned in the public notice, issued 4th June, 1875, were forthcoming at the meeting.

Upon this I read out the notice to the Acharya saying that the notice mentioned Friday as the day of the meeting, but that his disciple had signed the notice for Saturday and had further entered into a written agreement with a layman, fixing Saturday, as the day of the meeting. Would the Acharya abide by his disciple's announcement, according to which, as the notice said, the shastrarth-meeting should be held in Framjee Institute?

The Acharya answered, he was not aware of this, and he would not abide by the announcement. I remarked that I was sorry that the Acharya shirked a duty whose performance was incumbent upon him - a thing that did not at all reflect credit upon him. There could under certain circumstances, be no doubt atht what Swami Dayanand affirmed was true, and indisputable even in slightest degree and were now convinced that the charges which Swami Dayanand has laid at the door of the Acharyas were perfectly well founded.

If Kanwal Nain Acharya would free himself form those charges, he should make shi word good and prove that the Vedas inculcated idolatry, so that his reputation might be preserved. If he refused to attach any weight to my representations, well, not make Kanwal Nain Acharya pluck up courage to free himself from the charges brought against him.

'Now you all see on what absurd ground the Acharya is trying to back out of discussion. This must convince you that the Acharya is utterly powerless to prove the worship of idols to be in accord with the teaching of the Vedas.'

"When Thakur Mathura Das Loji had done speaking, Kanwal Nain Acharya, without, in the least, furnishing proofs in support of idolatry, rose and prepared to depart in silence. The Chairman, Mr. Bechar Das, turning to the Acharya, said; 'Sir, it is not right that you should leave meeting in silence, without having said anything.

All the people that are sitting here, are eagerly expecting you to prove that idol-worship is sanctioned by the Vedas. It does not behove you to depart, all of a sudden, without saying for their conviction that the Vedas do not sanction idolatry.

"No reply was forthcoming. For the last time Swami Dayanand addressed him in these words: 'You maintain that idol-worship is allowed in the Vedas, and it was incumbent upon you to prove your assertion. If you are determined not to do this, I must perforce expose idolatry and prove that it is opposed to the teaching of the Veda. You should least hear me.' Kanwal Nain Acharya took his departure. Many idol-worshippers who had flocked to the meeting, eagerly hoping that idol-worship would be proved form the Vedas, were disappointed.

Many householders, who had faith in idol-worship, lost all faith in the same, saying to themselves: Our Dharma is so weak and false! That which is the principal article of our faith, even that cannot be proved. How well the proverb applies to it (Hinduism) - Sufficiently capacious throated even to engulf an elephant, but occasionally unable even to swallow an ant.'

Exactly such has been the case with our Dharma this time. Kanwal Nain Acharya understood his interests too well when he declined to stop to listen to the Swami's speech, being well aware that to hear the exposure in the words of a man like Dayanand, and then to go away without replying to the denunciation, would expose him to the ridicule and contempt of the Believers in the Veda.

The meeting was thoroughly satisfied that the Acharya was utterly unable to prove idolatry from the Veda. It was indeed a marvel that he had even gone so far as to put in an appearance at the meeting.

"Subsequently, Seth hargobin Das Baba asked the Swami, whether idol-worship existed in Satyuga, or whether it had come into existence only recently.

In reply the Swami observed that I had no existence in Sat or any other (of the first three) Yugas: it had been fathered upon the believers in the Vedas by the selfish only in the present Kaliyuga, after the birth of the Jain and the Buddhistic creeds. When Shankarcharya exposed the Jain faith, many Jainis put their idols under ground, and it was these that were now and then found in many places where work of excavation was in progress.

The worship of idols, the Swami added, was wholly unknown to our sages, and it had no place in the Vedic teachings. After this reply, Seth Chhabil Das Lallobhai commented freely on the unfair move of Kanwal Nain Acharya and Mr. Moolji Thakarshi also expressed his opinion on the subject.

"At last Pandit Dayanand, speaking on the want of erudition on the part of Acharya, expressed his regret that so many works should have been brought together for a noble purpose but that not a single page of any one of them should have been turned.

To be brief, he commenced his speech, condemnatory of idolatry, by taking, s his text, the mantra - Na Tasya pratima asti yasya anma mahadyasha, and in support of the truth embodied in the mantra he read out many passages from the Vedas, alleged to be concerned with the avahan, pujan, visarjan and pranpratishtha of idols, and explained what these terms severally meant.

The Mantras in question, he made clear, had nothing to do with avahan or any other similar function, and the Vedas said nowhere that they should be applies in connection with such functions. Idol-worship had not originated with the followers of the Vedas, he maintained; and he read out passages from the Vedas in support of his position, translating them for his hearers.

He demonstrated the fact that idolatry had never been the faith of the followers of the Veda at any time, and that it would never be proved, and ended by exhorting one and all to renounce it without delay."

AT POONA AND BACK TO BOMBAY

The nominal shastrarth being over, Swami Dayanand left for Poona, where he stayed for about two months.

Poona is nothing if not a stronghold of idolatry in Southern India, and the Swami's presence there was deeply resented by some of the idol-worshippers who, in the heat of excitement, went so far as to put up hirelings to create breach of the public peace and to make themselves a positive nuisance to the reformer nd his admirers, to the disgust of the really brave and refined portion of the Poona Community.

It was inevitable that they should suffer for their misdeeds and two of the miscreants were sentenced to six and nine months imprisonment, respectively.

This had a very whole-some effect upon their fellows, making them behave peaceably in future. The Swami delivered fifteen lectures in all at Poona, five of these more or less historical in their character, one biographical, and the rest dealing with moral and religious subjects, such as God, the Veda , Revelation, the Transmigration of Souls, etc. These lectures were, in substance, published in the Marhatti language, in the form of a book. In a journal (Loka Hitavadi, February 1883) conducted by a Marhatta gentleman a complete account of the Swami's visit to Poona was published. The following passage occurs in the account:-

"In response to an invitation from the influential and learned portion of the Poona community, Swami Dayanand arrived here, staying during the monts of June and July (1875). We had occasion to hear some fifteen lectures in the local Hindu Club building.

These meetings were always full, and fascinated with the style of speaking of the unique orator and moved by the updesh which his speeches contained, the truth-loving people of the town received him in a manner at once cordial and respectful. One day the seated him on an elephant and took him through the various parts of the city.

The greedy, mischievous, hair-brained, thoughtless, selfish and vindictive individuals, in the Poona community, however, could not bear to see this honor shown to him, and they did what the should have abstained from doing. Under these circumstances, the availing of the assistance of the Police became a matter of necessity."

From the journal it appears that Gopal Krishna Bhandarkar, who enjoyed the reputation of being a distinguished Sanskrit scholar, had come to fall out with the Swami on some point, and was ever writing against him and helping the opponents of the Vedic Faith.

Towards the close of August, 1875, Swami Dayanand returned to Bombay to consolidate, by his presence and co-operation, the good work begun. This time, as was perhaps only natural, he put up in the Samaj Mandir. The Samajists and other gentlemen had all the benefit of Dharmacharcha (religious conversation and discussion) they could expect to enjoy by associating with the foremost Sanskrit scholar of his time, of a true thinker and genuine reformer.

The Swami told them to be perfectly free with him, and he was never tired removing their doubts regarding the Divine origin of the Vedas and on other points.

The Brahmo gentlemen, with their minds surcharged with ideas embodied in the works of Western Sanskrit scholars, would, again and again, bring forward objections, on one thing and another, connected with the Vedas.

One of these concerned the interpretation given to the word 'Agni'. They said they could not understand how it could be taken in the sense of 'God.' The Swami's reply was that the word was taken in that sense as well as in the sense of 'fire,' etcs., in the Brahmana Granths, and he quoted the passages bearing on the subject.

The internal evidenc of the Vedas also on the point was condencing. The word occurred in the eighteenth mantra of the Ishavasya Upanishad, the fortieth chapter of the Yajur Veda, and all the commentators, whether ancient or modern, had interpreted it there as God. Further, in the commentary on the Nirukta, the learned Pt. Satyavrat Samasrmi of the Asiatic Society, had clearly stated that the word 'Agni' meant also 'God.' And so on.

It was absurd to suppose that the Vedas taught 'element-worship.' Mantras like - Indram mitram varunam agni, etc. the eight mantra of the fortieth chapter of the Yajur Veda, and others, too numerous to detail, rendered such a supposition utterly groundless, and left no doubt as to the truth of the fact that the adoration of the one only God was taught in the Vedas, and of naught else.

After some eight months' stay at Bombay, Swami Dayanand resolved to visit the N.W.P. again, but just as he was about to depart, a learned of Nadiea Shanti came forward for a shastrarth on - "Idol-worship." The meeting was duly held, a still more learned Pandit, name Bhojaji Shastri, occupying the chair of Madhyastha.

Bhojaji's verdict, before the breaking up of ht assembly, was that Pandit Ram Lal had failed to prove idol-worship from the Vedas.

The Pandit himself acknowledged as such. His own words were: "The Swami is a Sanyasi, he cares for none. He has studied the Vedas and other Shastras thoroughly, and he is very wise and wields great powers. Whatever he says, is in accord with the Shastras.

We have not the strength to oppose him, for we are householders. We have to consult our interests in many things. If we were to say anything against "idol-worship," our living would be gone, and then how would things get on?"

The effect of this shastrarth was of a very wholesome character. On the 14th April, 1876, a notice appeared from Bhai Jiwan nothing to do with "idol-worship."

For, as the effect of Swmi Dayanand's updesh, he had renounced it for good. The notice promised a reward of Rs. 125 to any one who prove idolatry from the Vedas and convince the convert to the Vedic Religion that, is giving up idolatry, he had made a mistake. Who would attempt such a hopeless task?

6

Return to Lucknow

Leaving Bombay on 1st May, 1876, and visiting Farrukhabad for the fifth time, Swami Dayanand arrive at Benares and put up in the Atamgiri garden. He stayed here for over two months, but no shastrarth was held with the Pandits. It was Benares that the Swami came to make up his mind to engaged to write from dictation, and giving the usual details connected with the work. The book was to be brought out by the well-known local printers, E.J. Lazarus and Company, in monthly parts.

From Kashi and the Swami went to Jaunpur and thence to Ayudhia, which he left for Lucknow towards the close of September, preaching and holding discussions. The conversation which took place between him and Lala Brij Lal, Reis, is worth reproducing:-

EXPLAINING THE CASTE SYSTEM

Q. What are Brahmans, Kshatryas, Vaishyas, and Shudras? When did they come to be classified, and who was it that parceled out mankind into four classes or Castes?

A. ~ The four classes came to exist by reason of the diversity of men's occupations or professions. For example, the teachers of science of divinity came to be called "Brahmans;" the conductors of military affairs, "Kshatryas;" the traders in commodities, "Vaishyas;" and menial servants, "Shudras."

He is not a Brahman, who follows the profession of arms, and so forth, with the rest. Thus the classification of men into castes is based upon their callings and not, as is now regarded, upon birth. Hereditary castes, irrespective of professions, came into existence after the Great War.

Q. Were not Brahmans born from God's mouth, and Kshatryas from His arms?

A.The true meaning of the Vedic text, divested of the metaphor which has given rise to such absurd notions is, that men versed in Divine Knowledge and in Sciences hold the same position in the society of God's creatures as the head does in the structure of the body, - that is to say, they are the foremost of men by virtue of their superiority in knowledge. In like manner, the origin of the other Classes may be explained away.

Q. Why do the Brahmans wear the "sacred thread?"

A. ~It is the outward mark of their proficiency in knowledge.

Q. What kind of deeds should be done?

A. ~ Virtuous deeds alone should be done?

Q. What are these?

A. ~ Veracity, benefiting others, and other similar acts having for their object - the promotion of general good.

Q. What is veracity?

A. ~ It is telling the truth, and avoiding giving expression to what is untrue. The tongue should express what is in the heart.

ANSWERING THE PRACTICE OF IDOLATRY

Q. What do you think of idolatry?

A. ~ It is a thing, wicked and sinful. People should never worship images. Th spread of mental darkness is due to the prevalence of idolatry.

Q. How can we contemplate God without an object or idol?

A. ~ We should think of God just in the same way as we think or form a notion of pleasure and pain. Thus images are not required for contemplation.

Q. What actions are most praiseworthy, and should be performed?

A. ~ The doing of Sandhya morning and evening, the practice of truth, the exercise of benevolence, and so on.

Q. Should not Sandhya be performed thrice a day?

A. ~ No. The morning and evening are the only times for devotion.

Q. Is the act of repeating God's name or mantras, the performance of a tedious ceremonial, as done by the modern Brahmans, proper?

A. ~ People should try to know God, and imitate Him in their works. Mechanical repetitions and ceremonials are of no use.

Q. Has God any form or color?

A. ~ God has neither form nor color. He is incorporeal and infinite. Whatever is seen in the world, shadows forth His greatness. The universe being made by Him may be allegorically regarded as a means for allaying the mental thirst for a sight of Him.

Q. Why is God

A. ~ Were God to make His appearance in the world, every one would turn up to Him and importune Him to decree a gratification of his desires, and thus disorder and confusion would spread everywhere. At the same time, by means of the elements of which the human body is composed, the vision of God is impossible. How indeed can man see Him who has created him?

Q. How can God be known when He is not seen?

A. ~ Seen He is. All these things, men, animals, trees, etc., seen upon the face of the earth, point to their Maker. In this way He is seen through all His works. And he can be recognized even as we recognize pleasure and pain.

Q. Is or is not Brahma (God) in all of us?

A. ~ He is in all of us. He is known to us just in the same way as we know pleasure and pain.

Q. Is he uniform everywhere, or is He more in some and less in other objects?

A. ~ He is everywhere alike, only that He is manifested in us in proportion to the glory of the divine intelligence in our mind, i.e. wisdom.

Q. What are devatas (gods)?

A. ~ The are called devatas (gods) who are learned and intelligent, i.e., who are true pandits.

Q. Is it a sin to see the Ramleela or Rasleela?

A. ~ Yes it is a sin, equal to commission of a thousand crimes. Similarly, the worship of idols is sinful; for not likeness can be taken when there is no form, and where there is no form, there can be no image. It is allowable to take photos or execute other kind of pictures of persons to have them before us for being looked at or for remembrance. But it is improper to make pictures of images of God and thus caricature Him.

On Origin of Language

Q. How long as Sanskrit been in the world and why is called 'good'?

A.~ Sanskrit is from eternity, it is pure and correct, it has no match. For example, ba in Persian is expressed or represented as Bay, and in English as Bee; but ba (unencumbered with ay or ee) is only represented truly in Sanskrit.

Q. The Vedas contain praise of God. Has He written His own praise?

A. ~ As parents instruct their children to serve their parents and teachers and obey their elders, even so has God, by way of instruction, given us the Vedas.

Q. When God has neither form nor body, how can He have mouth to utter the Vedas with?

A. ~ God inspired them in the hearts of the four sages, - Agni, Vayu, Aditya and Angira.

Q. It is clear that these sages wrote the Vedas, is it not?

A. ~ No, they are from God; for the sages then had no knowledge whatever.

Q. How did God communicate to them the Vedas?

A. ~ Out of His mercy and power He inspired the 'supreme knowledge' in their hearts. As they were first at creation, they had no means of gaining knowledge, so god inspired them with it and thus it si God/s knowledge.

Q. Is the soul one or many?

A. ~ The soul is uniform in its nature, but its entities are many.

The Swami took his departure from Lucknow on 1st November, 1876, and, passing through Shahjahanpur, arrived at Bans Bareilly, where he stayed for about a month, and whence, on the expiration of this period, he proceeded to Karnvas. Here Thakur Muksand Singh received him with his usual hospitality, and took care that he had every facility to make known is mission to all around. As he result of a debate with the missionaries, a Samaj was established at Muradabaad, but lack of moral courage and energy in those who had accepted its membership soon made it a thing of the past.

THE IMPERIAL DURBAR

While the Swami was busy with this Bhumika and with his updesh, he heard of the importance of the coming Imperial Durbar at Delhi, and, wishing to be present on the occasion, if he could help it, he left for the scene of the approaching function in company with Thakur Mukand Singh and other Thakurs. Reaching Delhi, he took up his quarters in Sher Mal's Anar Bag, which had already been put in a fitting condition to receive him. Anar Bag was close to the plot of land on which the tents of the Rajas and Reises of Oudh stood, and over the gate of the garden hung a placard with the words - Residence of Swami Dayanand Saraswati.

The Swami had notices pasted in front of the tents of the Rajas and Maharajas, and to draw the attention of these magnates all the better to the contents of his manifesto had a copy of the same sent to each of them, with a request that they would bestir themselves to arrange for a shastrarth between him and the Pandits, so that truth might be known from what was false, and the great land of the Rishis should once more return to the primeval Vedic Faith.

It could be expected that the Rulers and Chiefs would think much of a shastrarth at such a time;: they were thinking of other things and were other wise occupied. The Maharaja of Indore was the only one who did make an effort to convene a meeting of his brother-Rulers and of the Pandits, but the effort was signal failure. For all that however, the work of updesh vigorously went on, and Hindus and Muhammadans and Padris thronged under his Shamianas all day long.

Occasionally, the Reises and Rajas of Oudh also would stop to hear him and would have conversations with him. Of the great ones of the Punjab, Maharaja Ranbir Singh of Jammu and Kashmir sent his Vizier, Anant Ram Diwan, and his Musahib, Babu Nilambar, to wait upon the Swami, with a request that he would see His Highness; but before the Swami could comply with His Highness's request, the State Pandits had changed his mind, and the interview never came off.

On the occasion of the Durbar, the Swami, failing to get the Rajas and Maharaja to come together and to hear his lectures, convened a meeting of some enlightened well-wishers and reformers of India, with the object of finding out, by discussion and deliberation, if co-operation in the work of reform was possible among them. The Sabha was composed of the following gentlemen:-

Baboo Ghanaya Lall Alakkhadahri, Baboo Navin Chandra Roy, Baboo Keshva Xhandra Sen, Munshi Indramani of Muradabad, Sir Sayyad Ahamad Khan, Baboo Harish Chandra Chintamani and Swami Dayanand Saraswati. The Swami's own solution of the problem before the Sabha was in these words: "If we have the same set of principles to believe in, and work on the same lines, I have hope that the country can be soon reformed." This solution could not be appreciated by the others, for there were differences in religious belief which could not be got over, and thus nothing was practically accomplished. Baboo Navin Chandra Roy speaking of the meeting in his Journal Gyan Darpan (1885) wrote: Inasmuch as we differed with him on fundamental principles of belief, the sort of union he sought to bring about could not be effected.

THE CHANDAPUR FAIR

Munshi Pyare Lal kayastha, Reis Chandapur, District Shahjanhanpur (N.W.P.), with a view to ascertaining which was true Dharma (faith), obtained permission from the Collector of his district to hold a religious fair at his native place, and having fixed upon 19th march 1877, as the day of the first meeting, had, printed notices circulated, inviting the most learned and distinguished followers of Hinduism, Islam and Christianity to come and have, by friendly conversation and discussion, truth sifted from falsehood.

In response to these notices, leaders of every religion, of profound scholarship, and well-known throughout India, came. First of all came the famous Vedic Scholar and Founder of the Arya Samaj Swami Dayanand Saraswati, accompanied by the well-known opponent of the Muslim Faith, Munshi Indramani of Muradabad a man who was a complete master of Arabic and Persian, and a critical student of both the Quran and the Traditions. These two gentlemen, deeply interested in religious matters, arrived at Chandapur on 15th March, 1877.

On behalf of the Christian religion came, on 19th March, 1877, the famous logician and profound scholar, author of many learned pamphlets and of commentary on the Bible - the Rev. T.G. Scott, accompanied by Rev. Mr. Noble, the Rev. Mr. Parker, and the Rev. Mr. John Thompson, and several other Missionaries of knowledge. And on behalf of the Muhammadans came, on the same day and at the same time, Moulvi Muhammad Qasim, the Principal of Devaband School, the most distinguished Arabic Seminary in India, the author of a delightful treatise or rhetoric, and the awarder of diplaomas to Moulvis, accompanied by Sayyad Abul Mansoor of Delhi, the foremost man in litetary discussions, the author of works like the Zinda Javais, written against Christianity, and the holder of a diploma from His Imperial Highness, the Sultan of Turkey, as a recognition of his scholarship, and by many other gentlemen.

Debate Preparation on Major World Religions

It was suggested to the Swami that if the Hindus and the Muslims formed a coalition and unitedly exposed the Christian Religion, it would be most commendable. But the Swami replied that he was sorry he could not agree to the proposal.

"It appears to me just and proper that no one in this fair should do anything savoring of partiality. To me it seems best that the Moulvis, the Missionaries and ourselves should meet in love and peace and investigate the truth. No one should be hostile to the others."

After this it was proposed that all the parties concerned should repair to the place where the jalsa (grand meeting) was to come off, and settle the conditions of the shastrarth; but I being pointed out that the crowd there would be in the way, two gentlemen from each repaired to the tents of the Missionaries, and there, assisted by Mr. Moti Mian and Lala Ram Parshad, Reises and Honorary Magistrates, Shahjahanpur, and Mukta Pershad, Reis, Chandapur, commenced their deliberations. But though hours were spent in these deliberations, no unanimity of opinion could be secured as to the conditions of the shastrarth.

The only point settled was the formal recognition of the necessity of holding a jalsa for the discussion. Seeing what little had been achieved and that the Padris were for not staying for over two days, Swami Dayanand observed that he and his companion had come to Chandapur on the distinct understanding that the Conference would last for a full week, and in no case for less than five days, and this period, he said, would have sufficed for determining the worth of every religion. To this the Munshi Indramani replied "Swamiji, be sure that the true religion will be found out even in a single day."

After 10 O'clock, it was unanimously resolved that the first spokesman, on behalf of each party, should speak on the question taken up for discussion for half an hour, and that the after-speakers replying to or expressing doubts and objections, should each speak for 10 minutes. The fact was made know to all would-be speakers that every one of them was to be perfectly master of his time, to enjoy, while speaking during the time allotted, complete immunity from interruption.

Opening Address

Mushi Pyare Lal rose and addressed the meeting in some thing like the following:-

"We should, first of all, be thankful to God, the omnipresent and all-pervading Lord. We are all fortunate in that this Supreme

Sovereign of the universe has placed us under a Ruler who permits us to talk freely on religious subjects. At the same time we ought to express our thanks to our Collector and District Magistrate, who, influenced by his sympathetic, appretiative and benevolent disposition, had been pleased to allow us to hold a discussion on an occasion like the present on 'god' and other kindred subjects. Language cannot describe the pleasure I feel today. It is a blessed day indeed, and happy is the land which finds so many influential and learned men, representing different faiths, assembled in it.

"Sirs, the world is a Caravansera, and life is not a thing to be depended upon. The mercy of God has been specially manifested today, in that so many gentlemen, in pursuance of a lofty resolve, have graced this meeting with their presence. I am confident that they will each speak of the beauties of his sacred Faith in words at once gentle and sweet, and will thus enable the audience to acquire, by his expositions, the fruit of salvation. I, Pyare Lal, a Kabirpanthi, pray to God for the preservation (success) of the Jalsa."

Appointing Representatives

On the termination of the speech, the discussion commenced as to how many persons should be appointed as 'representatives,' out of the professors of each creed present. Ultimately, five individuals were put forward by the Mussalmans as their representatives, as many by the Christians, and only two by the Aryas, namely, Swami Dayanand Saraswati and Munshi Indramani. The Moulvis and Padris insisted upon the full number (five) of representatives being appointed by the Aryas as well, but the Swami assured them that two were enough.

The Christians, not satisfied with the answer, made an attempt to add the name of Lakshman Shastri to the list of 'Arya representatives.' Swami Dayanand protested against such a conduct, observing that, though the Christians were perfectly free to choose representatives for themselves, they had no right to do so for others. And addressing the Pandit, the Swami said:

"Don't you see their game? These people want to create ill-feeling between us, in order to enjoy the fun!

The Mussalmans, however, would not listen to the Swami's protest, and the instant he had ceased speaking, a Moulvi came forward, and, cathching hold of the Pandit, urge him to have his name enlisted. Upon this the Swami observed that in the event of the Aryas agreeing unanimously to appoint the Pandit as their representative, his name might be put down as such, but it was no concern of the Mussalmans to select him.

A Mussalman critic, commenting upon the Swami's words, remarked that if such was to be the case, all the Hindus present should also be asked if the were willing to appoint Swami Dayanand and Munshi Indramani as their representatives. To this the Swami made answer:-

"When you have not been elected by the Shias and the Sunnis unanimously, when the Christians have not been assigned the position of 'representatives' by the Roman Catholics as well, where is the necessity for you to raise such objections with regard to us? There are many who would be willing to accept us as their representatives, but many there may be who would be unwilling to do so but for all that you have no right to create ill-feeling between us."

Munshi Indramani added: "We are believers in the Vedas and the Shastras, and so are these people; if there are any that do not, they may be constituted into a fourth party in the discussion."

The object aimed at by the Moulvis, by bringing forward the objections they did, was to stir up quarrels between the Aryas and the Hindus, and, keeping aloof from the wrangling that must ensue, to enjoy the 'fund' thereof. The Aryas, however, did not think it advisable to add the name of Pandit Lakshman to the list of their representatives, and the Moulvis (perceiving as much) retired, at this stage, to say their prayers.

On their return Moulvi Muhammad Qasin said, that he would address themeeting, for a whole hour, on his religion, independent of what he might to say directly on the questions to be propose for the discussion, later on, and that he would remove any doubts that might arise in any one's mind by his speech. To this all agreed.

The Debate begins between Islam and Christianity

The Moulvi, after praising God (in substance) said - "The ruler of the time ought to be obeyed by all. As all serve and obey the orders of the present ruler, and not those of him whose tenure of office has expired, and, further, as a law, which had been rescinded, is no longer obeyed, but that only which has been substituted for it, even so the Bible, which 'descended' in the time of the ancient prophets, cannot be conformed to and obeyed.

Muahmmad was the last of the prophets, and consequently, the Divine Word, Quran, which 'descended on him,' should be obeyed instead. We do not speak ill of Sri Rama and Sri Krishna since they were prophets of their respective times, but we maintain that Muhammad alone rules preset. Whoever traduces Muhammad, our Religion and the Quran, deserves death."

Rev. Mr. Noble (commenting upon the Moulvi's speech) - "There is considerable doubt as to Muhammad being a prophet, and the Quran being the word of God. The Quran has been borrowed from the Bible, and hence it cannot be a revealed book. The fact of Christ being an incarnation, however, is indisputable. It is perfectly clear from his teaching that he led the people towards righteousness. Men can get salvation only through his 'word'. He worked miracles."

Moulvi Muhammad Qasim (replying) - "We believe in the apostleship of Christ and also look upon the Bible as 'revealed', though the Christians have introduced into it many interpolations. It is no longer genuine. Besides, the Quran has refuted and replaced it. It is, therefore, not worthy of being believed in, our prophet being the last, our religion is true."

After this, the other Moulvis showed the Rev. gentleman a verse from the Bible, telling him, at the same time, that it was the Christians themselves who confessed that the verse was unauthenticated.

Rev. Mr. Noble - "He who said this was truthful, he is not to blame if he has corrected a verbal mistake. We love truth, and our religion is consequently true."

Moulvi Muhammad Qasim - "Of course, it was very good on his part to do so! But the book or document in which a mistake is discovered, cannot be authoritative. The document in question could never be valid in court of law."

Rev. Mr. Noble - "Are there no verbal mistakes in the Quran? It is not proper to ring changes on such things. We believe only in truth, and we strive only for the attainment of truth. We acknowledge therefore, the verbal mistake in the Bible. Your Quran, on which you have said so much, abounds, with interpolations, etc."

Moulvi Muhammad Qasim - "You are an inquirer after truth indeed! If you really believe what you advance, then how can you believe in three Gods?"

Rev. Mr. Noble - "We do not believe in three Gods, but only in One. Jesus was both man and God, therefore his works are of a double nature. Having the human element on him, he did the works of man, but by virtue of the Divine element in him, he did the works of God, i.e., wrought miracles, etc."

Moulvi Muhammad Qasim - Oh! How can two swords fit in one scabbard? The statement of the Missionary is utterly false. Jesus nowhere says that he is God. You elevate him to the position of God, blinded by prejudice."

Rev. Mr. Noble, in reply, read out a verse from the Bible, in which Jesus declares himself to be 'God' and which says that he worked many miracles. The verse did not leave any doubt as regards the fact of his having declared himself to be 'God.'

Moulvi Muhammad Qasim - "If Jesus was God, why could not he save himself from being crucified?"

A native Padri pointed out many inconsistencies in the Quran, and said that a commandment could be annulled but not news or prophecy. The predictions of the Quran had been wrong. The Muslims first bent their head in the direction of Bait-ul-Muqaddas, and the commenced bending it in the direction of Mecca. He then explained many verses, asserting that salvation was impossible "except through Christ." "Your Quran, " added he, addressing the Mussalmans, "enjoins belief in Jesus and God. Why don't you act up to the injunction?"

While the discussion was going on, the shades of the evening, came on, and this brought the meeting to a close.

THE SECOND DAY'S PROCEEDINGS- THE FIVE QUESTIONS

The people assembled at the appointed place, at 7 A.M., and the five questions, which had already been agreed upon for discussion, were again read out. These questions were the following:-

1. When, out of what, and why, did God create the world?
2. Is, or is not, God All-pervading?
3. How can God be just as well as merciful?
4. What proofs are there as to the Veda, or the Quran or the Bible being the Word of God?
5. What is salvation, and how can it be attained?

Some time was spent in settling the point as to who should first reply to the questions.

Christianity Reply to the Questions

At last Rev. Mr. Scott got up to speak on the first question. He remarked that the question was nonsensical, and that therefore it was useless to answer it. But as all had agreed to discuss it, he would take it up. He said: "Although we know not out of what God has created this world, we may affirm at best only this much, that He has created it out of nothing, for there was naught else than God in the beginning. He created the world, yet has a beginning. We cannot know the number of years (that have elapsed since the world was created), God alone knows that. Hence it is not advisable to speak on this subject. As to the third part of the question - Why god created the world? we cannot answer it correctly. All that we may know, is, that He created it for the happiness of men, so that we mortals might live in it, in the enjoyment of felicity."

Islam's Reply to the Questions

Moulvi Muhammad Qasim - "god created the world out of His body. We are not separate from Him. If we were so, we should be beyond His omnipotence. With regard to the question - When the world was created? it is useless to speculate on it, for we are concerned with eating of bread and not with the time when it came to exist. This world was created for human beings, for God has made all things for them, and then He has created him for His worship. If you reflect, you will see that the earth is for us and not we for the earth; for if we did not exist, it would make no difference to the earth. But we should be very unhappy if the earth did not exist. Similarly, water, air, fire and other elements were created for man. Man is superior to all other creatures, and intellect has been given him to bear witness to his superiority. In short God has created man for His worship, and the earth for man."

Swami Dayanand's Reply

Swami Dayanand Saraswati - " At the outset, I desire to call attention of the Muhammadans, Christians and others present to the fact that the fair (meeting) has been held for the ascertainment of truth, and that the object of those who have brought it about, is to find out which Faith is true. That which is proved to be true, should be accepted as such by all. No one should harbor ideas of victory or defeat, for it becomes all good men to see that truth prevails and falsehood perishes. Indulgence in remarks by the Muhammadas, such as that 'the Padris are wrong' and by the Padris, such as that 'the Muhammadans are false', should be avoided.

Wise people should according to their lights, promulgate truth and refute untruth, in mild language. They should always avoid speaking ill of one another, making muse of bitter words and giving expression to painful insinuations, like, 'I am victorious, and your are defeated.' All should give up prejudice, and speak out the truth, going in for mutual recrimination being the work of ignorant persons. No one should, therefore, employ harsh words.

"Now I proceed to reply, in the light of my insignificant learning, to the question - "Out of what, when, and why, did God create the world?' God made the world from Prakriti, which is also called Avyakrita, Avyakata or the atoms. This

Prakiti is the material cause of the world, and is, in the Shastras, spoken of as eternal. As God is eternal, even so is this material cause. As "There is no beginning or end of God, even so there is none of the Prakriti. The various substances are harmoniously proportioned with respect to the atoms of which they are made up, and not one of the primary atoms can be increased or diminished. God makes the primeval root-substance assume various phenomenal shapes. The phenomenal or visible world has a corresponding material cause. God works upon subtle elements, and evolves out of them gross materials which become fit for use.

"Things and objects of various kinds have been created from the primordial, material principle. At the time of pralaya (dissolution) god separates the atoms and beaks things up into their primeval root-form. A thing, as it becomes subtle, vanishes from sight; the ignorant people think that it has been annihilated.

"In point of fact, it remains in space in a subtle form, for the root or cause is never annihilate, and the apparent annihilation means only disappearance. When the atoms are separated, they become invisible, and when they combine, they become visible.

"This process of evolution and involution, under Divine direction and control, is constant and unceasing. It baffles calculation to say how many times God has made the world, and how many times He would yet make it. None can say anything on this subject.

"From this it follows that the position of those who hold that something can spring from nothing, and of those who say that the universe rushed into being as the effect of some words pronounced, is utterly untenable, for the appearance of something out of nothing is impossible. "To assert the contrary, is like saying, 'I witnessed the nuptials of the son of a barren woman with my own eyes.' If the woman in question had a son, why would she be barren, and when her son has absolutely no existence, how could she have been married at all? To assert that creation is the product of nothing, is again tantamount to affirming: 'I was nowhere, but I have arrived here, or that the snake was not in the hole, but yet it has come out of it.' The wise do not attach any value to such affirmations. They are wholly unreasonable, since how can a thing which exist not, come to be? If we were not in our present respective places here, we could not be said to be at Chandapur. Mark what the Shastra

NAASATA AATMA LAABHAH

NA SAT AATMAHAANAM

'Whatever is, shall be in future, and whatever is not can never be!'

This clearly proves that something cannot proceed from nothing, for in this world there is nothing which is without a cause. Something, it is apparent, comes from something; it can never come out of nothing. To admit the absolute non-existence of a taking and then to affirm that it is existent, is VADTO VYAGHAT, a pure self-contradiction. No wise man can ever believe it, nor is it capable of being proved by means of any pramana. The birth of something from nothing is thus wholly impossible.

God created the universe out of the eternal root-matter, and in no other way. In connection with the subject under discussion, two considerations present themselves. One is that if God be the material cause of the universe, He would be identical with the phenomenal world, and consequently knowledge, pain, pleasure, birth and death, profit and loss, heaven and hell, hunger and thirst, fever, bondage, and freedom must all be considered to exist in Him. (According to this hypothesis) the dog, the cat, the thief, the profligate, all are but the various manifestations of the same God!

"The other consideration is, that if it be conceded that the material substratum existed already, the position of god becomes like unto that of a maker or fashioner.

"We observe:

Causes of three kind:

1. Upadan ~ It is that cause which is essential to the formation of a thing, such as earth, which is essential

to the formation of a jar; as gold, which is essential to the formation of an ornament; as cotton, which is essential to the making of cloth.

2. Nimitta ~ It is that sort of cause, which is implied in the agency of the intelligent potter in the formation of a jar.
3. Sadharan ~ Causes such as clay, means, space, time, etc. are called sadharan causes.

"Now if God is to be considered as the material cause of the universe, we are forced to the conclusion that He himself constitutes the world, just as the jar cannot be different from the earth (of which it is composed); if He be the efficient cause, His position becomes analogous to that of the potter who cannot fashion the pot without the earth; and if He be considered to be a general (sadharan) cause, the world cannot arise of itself from Him even as the jar cannot of itself arise from the earth.

"In two of the three cases, god, it would be evident, is reduced to the position of jar (something devoid of consciousness or intelligence.) if the phenomenal world were god, god would be responsible for al sins, such as theft, etc., which is absurd. The substratum of the universe is, therefore, something different and eternal, and God is the maker or fashioner of things, etc., of various forms and shapes. The soul is also, by its inherent nature, eternal, and the gross world is phenomenally eternal. We cannot escape these conclusions.

The Age of Creation

"Now as to the time when the world was created. Listen friends. We can reply to this question, but you cannot. When you affirm that your Systems of Faith came to exist only 1,800, 1,300 and 500 years back, these systems cannot throw any light on the question of the world's age.

The Aryas have been in possession of information on the point since the dawn of creation. Remember that light was carried from this land to other countries - a fact, which is proved by the histories of those countries. Knowledge went from Aryavarta (India) to Egypt, from Egypt to Greece, from

Greece to other countries of Europe, and so none but the Vedic Religion can tell us how old the world is.

"The Aryas know from the verses, bearing on the creation and dissolution of the world, in the Shastras, that a thousand Chaturyugas constitute one day of Brahma, and as many Yugas one night of Brahma. A Brahma-day covers the time from the creation of the universe to its dissolution, and a Brahma-ratri from the dissolution of the world to its next creation, after a thousand Chaturygas. There are fourteen Manvanttraras in one Kalpa and one Manvanttara is equal to 91 Chaturygas. The present is the seventh Manvanttara, the Swaymbhuva, Svarochish, Auttmi, Tamasa, Raivata and Chakshusha having already expired; in other words 1,960,852,976 years of the world's age have passed away, and 2,333,227,024 still remain.

"The histories of our country unanimously corroborate it, and this calculation is to be found in astronomical treatises, and changes are made in the same accordance with the principle just enunciated. The year, as it passes, diminishes the future age of the world, and increases the number of years already passed. All genuine histories of Aryavarta are at one on this point, and the is not least disagreement among them.

"When Jains and the Muhammadans began to destroy the historical works, etc., of the Aryas, the Aryas committed the chronological formula to memory, and they would repeat it daily, on and all, from an old man down to a child, The Sankalpa, describing the age of the world, runs as follows:- Om! Tat Sat (i.e., he whose name is Om, is the true Lord). In the second division of the first half of the Day of Shri Brahma, in the second food of the Kaliyuga of the 28th Vaivaswata, in such-and-such a part of the year, in such-and-such a season, paksha, divas, nakshatra, lagan, mahurat, this act is performed, and it shall continue to be daily performed, in future, by the eldest as well as the youngest, member of the family."

AUM TAT SAT SHRI BRAHMA DWITIYE PRAHARAARDDHA VAIVASVATA

MAVANTATARE AASHTAA VISHATITAMAE KALIYUGE KALIPRATHAMACHARANE

AAYAVIRTTINTARE KADESHE AMUKA NAJARE AAMUKA SAMVATSARAYANARTU
MAASAPAGYADINANASHA TRALAGNA MUHURTE ATRA DE KAARYA KRITAM HRIYATE VAA

"this furnishes a system of calculation in connection with the age of the world. If anyone doubts it, he should know that the mode of counting days, etc., set forth in the Sankalpa, is identical with that given in the astronomical works. No one can gainsay it.

The system of entries in the cash-book and ledger, which are made according to dates, cannot be questioned. If anyone refuses to believe it, he should be called upon to state his believe on the subject, and if he says that the world was created six or seven or eight thousand years ago, and quotes his Scriptures to support his assertion, his statement, we maintain, would be equally open t the charge (which, in his ignorance, he brings forward against the Aryan Chronology.) The science of Geology supports the conclusion already arrived at (namely, that the world is 1,960,852,976 years old.)

"The information which our religion is capable of giving on the point under discussion, is afforded by none else. It is desirable that all should believe it to be true.

Why God Created the World?

"As to why God created the world, we reply, that the jiva (soul) and the material cause of the universe are eternal by nature, and the actions of individual and the visible world are phenomenally eternal. At the time of dissolution some actions of men remain unrewarded and unpunished, and it is with the object of meeting out to them the rewards of their actions that God creates the world and dispenses impartial justice.

"Further, the attributes of knowledge, power, mercy and creation, inherent in God, also call for their natural and legitimate exercise, and hence God creates the world. Just as eyes are meant to see and ears to hear with. Even so the creative power of the Deity exists for creation. God has created the world for the exercise of His powers, so that His creatures may benefit themselves by the innumerable things it contains. He has blessed them with eyes, etc., for the attainment of dharma, arth, kama and moksha. Similarly, there are many other reasons for the creation of the world, and they cannot be all set forth here in consequence of the time at my disposal being short. The wise can think them out for themselves."

Rebuttal to Christianity and Islam

Rev. Mr. Scott - "That which has limit, cannot be eternal. The world is limited, so it cannot be eternal. Nothing can create itself. God has created the world by His power, though no one can know out of what God has created it. The Pandit also has not told us the name of the thing it was created out of."

Moulvi Muhammad Qasim - "If all things exist from eternity, it is useless to believe in a God. No one can say anything as to the time of creation."

Swami Dayanand Saraswati ~ "Rev. Mr.. Scott has not understood me yet. I regard the material cause as eternal; the effect is not eternal.. to give an illustration: My body is 3 cubits and a half (in height). This body was not so long before my birth, nor shall it remain so after my death. But the atoms of which this body is composed, shall not annihilated. They will separate and float in space. The power to combine and to separate inheres in them. Take another example. A jar is made of earth; it had no existence before it came to be shaped into its present form, and it will not continue to exist (as it is) after it has been destroyed. The earth, however, of which it is made, shall not perish or be annihilated.

"The property of adhesion, which renders combinations possible, and which helps in the formation of shape, etc., also inheres in the earth; the atoms are possessed of the property of combination and separation."

"It ought to be clearly understood that this world has been formed of primordial atoms. These atoms exist from eternity; the ponderable substances do not. When did I say that the various things of the world create themselves? All that I said was that God fashioned the world out of the primordial material cause. "As to the Moulvi's remarks on my reply, I beg to say that though the material cause of all things is eternal, yet the very fact necessitates belief in God. Earth or clay has not the power to shape itself into a jar. Matter cannot assume gross forms of itself, for it is devoid of knowledge requisite for the purpose. Nor can any human soul accomplish the result, for no man has yet been able even to make a single hair. No one has ever been able to grasp the atoms and fashion anything out of them by any means. Nor is there anyone in the present time, who can unite every two trisrenus. This shows that God alone has the power to fashion the world.

"Only consider what skill and wisdom have been displayed in the construction of the eye. Great anatomists and doctors have been studying it up to the present time, yet their collective knowledge of it is imperfect. No one can know thoroughly how God fashioned it, and what beauties He has endowed it with. The creation of the Sun, the Moon, etc., and the upholding of these is the work of God, and He it is that dispenses to the souls the fruits of their actions, and none else. Truly, belief in God is a matter of absolute necessity."

A Native Christian - "When there are two things, namely, one cause and other effect, both cannot be eternal. Therefore God has created something out of nothing (with His fiat.)"

Moulvi Muhammad Qasim - "Qualities are to two kinds, - intrinsic and extrinsic. The intrinsic are essential and inherent, and the extrinsic, borrowed from without. The intrinsic qualities, when transmitted to other things, partake of the form or character of those things, but the substance of which they are really the attributes, is distinct from them; as, for instance, the reflection of the sun takes the form of the vessel which it enters, but it does not become the sun itself. Just in this fashion have we been created by the Divine Will."

Swami Dayanand Saraswati (addressing the Native Christian). ~ Why do you object to both the cause and the effect being eternal, for the material cause or the root-matter of which the physical universe is composed, is eternal. The souls, which are past counting are also eternal. Something can never proceed from nothing. I have already made this clear. You ascribe creation to power. Now tell me what is power? If your regard it something real, then being a cause it becomes eternal, since the names, attributes and powers of God are eternal, none of them being the product of time."

Replying to Moulvi Muhammad Qasim ~ "If you ascribe the creation of the world to intrinsic qualities, your contention is not valid, for qualities cannot exist apart from a thing or substance, nor can they lead to the formation of things or substances.

If the world has been produced out of the intrinsic or essential Divine qualities, then the world is effect-God. And if you set it down as the product of the external Divine qualities, you will have to believe in the eternity of those qualities, in addition to believing in God. And if you maintain that creatures sprang out of the Divine Will, then I ask, is will a substance or quality? If substance, then you cannot but believe it to be eternal; if quality, then the world could not have sprang from it. Just as you cannot produce anything from mere will, even so creatures cannot produce themselves simply from will."

Rev. Mr. Scott - "We only know this much that God created something out of nothing, out of what and when, and how, we know not. God alone knows that, man cannot know it."

Moulvi Muhammad Qasim - "God has created this world out of His nur (light)."

Swami Dayanand (replying to Rev. Mr. Scott) ~ "On seeing an effect, we should infer the cause. And an effect is always of the nature of the cause, as an earthen jar of the nature of earth or clay. The jar is composed of the same substance as earth or clay. You say, God created the world out of His power. Is that power, I ask, eternal or created in time? If eternal, then you can believe it to be a substance, and regard as the eternal material cause of the world."

(Replying to the Moulvi ~ "Nur is light. No substance can be produced out of light. It helps the perception of the forms of material objects, and it can never exist apart from that which emits it. It is thus clear that you cannot do without a material cause of the universe. We too do not regard effect to be absolutely eternal, but only the cause of which it is the effect." Anative Christian - "If God evolve the world out of His essence, then the world must be eternally existent in His essence and He must be eternally existing in the world. This makes God limited or conditioned. God, then, is limited or conditioned."

Swami Dayanand ~ "The universe existing in the Divine Essence, was eternal, and the same, assuming a grosser form (from Prakriti), became limited or conditioned, and not God who gave Prakriti or the primary atoms dimensions, - length, breadth, height, etc. Thus the universe came to be limited and conditioned and not God.

"Recall what I said at the outset - that something cannot proceed from nothing, but only from something. Your statement too comes to the same thing, namely, that the material cause of the world is eternal." Rev. Mr. Scott - Hear, my Muhammadan brethren. The Pandit can reply to this question in a thousand ways, and if a thousand men like us were to combine, even then he could reply to them. Hence it is not desirable to prolong discussion in this subject."

The discussion lasted till 11 A.M. and then all men went to their homes. The chief topic of conversation among he people of the fair was the discussion, and everyone said: "We have found a him a thousand times wise than we heard he was."

The Third day of Discussion on Mukti -salvation

The people assembled again at 1 0'clock. Some time was spent in deciding as to which subject should be discussed, since much of the time allotted for discussion had passed away and many subjects yet remained undiscussed. It was settled that the subject of mukti (salvation) should be taken up. Next the question as to who should open the discussion, was considered. The Muhammadans and the Christians excuse themselves, each party in its turn, from speaking on the question first, the one begging the other to make a beginning. Upon this the Swami observed that theprevious order should be followed, namely, that Rev. Mr. Scott should open the discussion, then the Moulvi Sahib should speak, and then he himself. The Rev. gentleman and the Moulvi, however, declined to follow the order suggested. Hence the Swami himself made the preliminary speech:-

Mukti means emancipation, i.e., liberation from pain of every description, and he attainment of bliss in the infinity - intelligent and blissful Supreme Being. It implies release from birth and death. But now is it to be attained? The first means for its attainment is virtuous conduct. As to w2hat is virtuous or righteous, that ought to be ascertained in the light of the approval of God and of the human Soul. That which does not command their approval, is wrong and sinful. as an illustration of what I mean: A person steals a thing, and when caught and questioned by the authorities as to his doing, he denies having committed the crime. But his atma (soul) says from within; 'Yes, you are guilty.' 'Similarly, when a man thinks of committing theft, the internal Ruler speaks to him in the depths of his heart, saying that the act is reprehensible, and that he should not do it, and He (the Ruler) creates in his mind a feeling of shame, doubt and fear. But when a man thinks of doing something virtuous, God gives rise in his heart to a pleasurable sensation, urging him to go on with his pursuit'. The feelings of pleasure that animate the Soul, when it performs a noble act, are conspicuous by their absence when the Soul goes in for something evil. As long as a man, in utter disregard of the Will of God, commits evil deeds, he cannot: in any way, obtain salvation. Such a wicked man is called asur, dusht, daitya. The Veda says:-

ASURYAA NAAM TE LOKAA ANDHENA TAMASAA VRITAA:

"He who destroys the purity of his soul, i.e., who acts in disregard of Will of God and against the dictates of his own conscience, is asur, rakshas, dusht, papi and neech."

"The following are the means of attaining salvation:-

1. Virtuous conduct.
2. The acquisition of true knowledge, i.e., the study of the Divine Word - the Veda; improvement of gyan (knowledge) and love truth.
3. Associating with truthful and virtuous men.

4. Withdrawing the manas, the senses, and the Atam from untruth and leading them towards truth and wisdom by the practice of yoga.
5. Stuti or meditation on the attributes of God.
6. Prarthana or devout and sincere prayer after the following style:

'O lord of the universe! Benevolent Father! Lead us form untruth to truth; lead us, O Blissful Master, from darkness (ignorance and unrighteousness) to light; lead us, all-pervading Lord, from the turmoils (sufferings, i.e., birth, death, etc.), of the world to immorality.'

"When a man contemplates God from the core of his heart he enjoys peace ineffable. When a child wants to come to his parents downstairs, or to go upstairs, the people leave off attending to a thousand urgent and important affairs, and lift him up in their arms to keep him from falling, for they love to keep him happy and in peace. Just in the same manner God, the source of all benevolence, lifts the man, that goes to Him with a sincere heart, into His blissful arms. Such men are happy, and God never permits pain to approach them. The people should cast off prejudice, and, rejecting untruth and accepting truth, strive for the attainment of felicity. Injustice is the result of unrighteous regard for ourselves. This may be illustrated as follows:- 'The clothes of the Moulvi Sahib are good. If I covet them, I should be thinking of my own comfort, and disregarding that of the Moulvi Sahib. This injustice and adharma would be traceable to a feeling of selfishness. This pursuit of selfish ends is also termed anarth. The desire or pursuit of happiness in accordance with the dictates of dharma and arth is kama, and the pursuit of the same by unrighteous methods is designated kukarma. Salvation is obtained by means of dharma, arth and kama. Conformity in life to Divine Will, as has already been stated, constitutes dharma, and its disregard, adharma. These things lead to mukti, and naught else. It is attained by self-exertion, and not otherwise."

Rev. Mr. Scott - "Panditji has defined mukti as emancipation from pain, but I hold it to consist in avoiding sin and attaining heaven. God create Adam immaculate, but Satan tempted him to commit sin. By his fall all his descendants have become corrupt. As the watch-maker does not interfere with the working of a watch, but allows it to go on with its work without imposing upon it any restraint, so has God made man a free agent, andhe commits sin of his own accord. He cannot, by his own exertion, attain salvation or escape pain in any way. Salvation is, therefore, impossible without faith in Lord Jesus Christ. The Hindus say that Kaliyuga is an era of sin and corruption, and that man cannot, in this age, obtain salvation. But I say they can if they will only put their faith in Jesus.

"The people of places which have been visited by Lord Jesus, i.e., wherever his teachings have been disseminated, have been saved. Are there virtue and excellent qualities to be found, in any remarkable degree, in the followers of any religion but those of Christianity? There was in England a man as powerful as Panditji, but he was addicted to drinking, was licentious, and a thief. When, however, he accepted the faith of Christ, he became free from all these vices and sinful habits. Similarly, when I came to believe in Christ as my Savior, I obtained mukti and ceased doing evil deeds. Salvation is impossible of attainment except by conforming to the Will of Jesus. Hence all must believe in him. He alone can give salvation. This the only way of attaining it, and none else."

Moulvi Muhammad Qasim - "We cannot say that all the means enumerated by Panditji for the attainment of salvation are sufficient, for everything depends upon the Will of God. He gives salvation to whosoever He likes, just as the ruler of the time punishes or lets off anybody he chooses. We have no authority over Him, we do not know what He will do. But we must have faith in the ruler of the time (i.e., the Divine Vice-regent on earth.) The ruler of the present time is our prophet; salvation, therefore, depends entirely on professing faith in him. It is, no doubt, true that one can do good acts by means of knowledge, but salvation is in God's hands."

Swami Dayanand Saraswati (in replying to Mr. Scott) ~ "Your statements as regards mukti, that it consists in avoiding sin and not in freedom from pain, is due to a misapprehension of what I said, for I have already said that avoiding doing evil deeds, committing sin, etc., is a preliminary sadhan (means) for the attainment of mukti. The consequence of evil deeds is pain; in other words, when a man commits sin, he cannot escape pain. The sadhans, too, I have enumerate clearly. If the Padri Sahib had kept in mind what I said, he would not have made the remark he did.

"As regards to the second point, that Adam was tempted by Satan to commit sin and that posterity, in consequence, became corrupt, the assertion is without foundation. God, according to Christian belief, is omnipotent. But when Satan disregarded Adam, the immaculate creature of God, and thus, interfering in the government of God, reverse the state of affairs established by Him, god ceased to be omnipotent.

"In point of fact, none can interfere in the ordinances of God. The assertion that the entire race became corrupt owing to the sin of Adam is repugnant to common sense, and whoever commits sin, the same suffers pain, and none else. No wise man will ever subscribe to the Christian idea. Moreover, Adam and Eve alone could not be the progenitors of the human race, for the marriage between brothers and sisters is a sin. Evidently God created a number of men and women in the beginning of creation.

"As regards the assertion that Satan tempts, I would ask - If Satan is everybody's tempter, who was Satan's tempter? If you reply that he was tempted by himself, then I say that the same could be said with equal force in respect to human beings. In such a case, it is useless to believe in Satan as the tempter. If you say that Satan was tempted by someone else, then it would follow that it was the work of none but God. And if this was God's work, then, according to your religion, there cannot by any giver of salvation, nor any receiver of it, for when God himself becomes the tempter, none can be the savior. Such a thing, however, is against the Divine nature, for God is just and true, and His actions are always just, and He can never be a tempter.

"It is noticeable that though Satan works such mischief in the government of God, God does not punish or kill him or throw him into prison. This clearly indicates the helplessness of God. It also shows that God alone is the tempter. But all this is untrue. Nor is there any such being as Satan. As long as belief in Satan is not eradicated from the mind, so long there can be no escape from sin. People must delude themselves: 'As Satan, by tempting Adam, involved him had his posterity in sin, so God, in order to redeem mankind, got His only son crucified.' There is nothing to fear now, for if we commit sin, we, being believers in Jesus Christ, will have our forgiven, for he sacrificed himself for our sins. Verily such men cannot escape sin!

"The illustration of the 'watch' is correct, for all are free agents, but the Will of God consists in the performance of noble acts and in avoiding doing evil ones: the statement that the attainment of heaven is salvation, and that men are unable to shake themselves free from sin owing to the temptations of Satan, is unfounded; for every man is free to act, and Satan is a myth. You can, by shaking yourself free from the hold of sin and by the grace of God, attain salvation. Adam ate wheat - the only sin he committed - and was driven away in consequences from paradise. I ask, when the mere eating of wheat involved Adam in sin, and resulted in his expulsion from heaven, will you, who long for the attainment of heaven, abstain from the use of these things in that place? If not, won't you be sinners and driven away from paradise in consequence?

"Your conception of God appears to be anthropomorphic, i.e. as man is not omniscient, even so is God according to your belief, for you speak of intercession and advocacy, in connection with Him. Such a thing is a reflection on Divine omnipotence. God knows everything. He does not stand in need of an advocate, nor in that of intercession from others, for intercession can be necessary for him only who has not knowledge of the person whom it is to benefit. Further, God, according to your belief, becomes essentially dependent, for He cannot bestow mukti on anyone except through the intercession of Christ. That is to say, His knowledge is limited, which (you must admit) is inconsistent with His knowledge attributes of omnipotence and omniscience. You must see that if God is just, He cannot go against this attribute of His at the intercession of anyone; for if He does, He ceases to be just. Similarly, if you believe that angels, etc., are ever present in the Divine court, as there are officers in human courts, you make Divine nature defective and faulty in my other respects for, in such a case, God cannot be all-pervading and All-encompassing. And if God be not omnipresent, He must be corporeal, and in the event of His being corporeal, He cannot be all-controlling and all-grasping.

And further, a corporeal being must be subject to birth and death, but this is against the attributes of God. Hence, such a belief, it is evident, can never gain currency, for it circumscribes God.

"Observe how, without a proper study of Arya Shastras , men are apt to believe in wrong ideas. The statement of the Reverend gentleman, in connection with the Kaliyug, is also wrong, since we do not believe in it, in the light of the Vedic Teaching. The Aitareiya Brahmana says:-

KALIH SHAYAANO BHAVATI SAMJIHAANASTU DWAPARAH

UTTISHTHAMSTRE TAA BHAVATI KRITAM CHARAN

'It means, 'The person who is adharmi (unrighteous) and nominally dharmi (righteous) is kali; he who is one-half dharmi and one-half adharmi, is dwapar; he who is I one-fourth adharmi and three-fourths dharmi is treat; while he who is entirely dharmi, is called satyuga.' It is not proper to indulge in any assertions on this point in disregard of facts.'

"Those who commit evil deeds, cannot escape their painful consequences; they alone will, who do noble acts, no matter what country they may belong to.

"Cannot God save His devotees by His own power and without the intercession of Jesus? The answer must be in the affirmative, for He does not stand in need of prophets. This, however, is true, that dharmatmas (good and virtuous people), in whatever country they may be, serve as saving agencies, reclaiming individuals from sin, and such a country attains prosperity and glory. And this desirable result it essentially due to virtuous conduct, it has but little to do with creeds. "In olden times there were good arrangements for updesh among the Aryas, and consequently the condition of the Aryas was good. If, at the present time, they are degenerate, owing to the absence of updesh among them and for various other reasons, their degenerated condition cannot, in any way, detract from the nobleness of their religion. The Arya Religion alone has been preserved pure since the dawn of creation, it has not been corrupted at all.

The degeneration that has taken place among our community during 1,960,852,976 years is but insignificant compared with that which had taken place among the Muahmmadans during 1300, and among Christians during 1800 years. The prosperity of the Christians is due to good organization (of which the British Parliament is an example) and not to their religion. If organization among you became extinct, you would not be able to make solid progress through your religion. The example which the Reverend gentleman has given of a wicked man in England, likening him to me, was unworthy of him. I suppose he did it unintentionally.

"As regards the remark of the Moulvi Sahib on mukti, that God may do what He desires, it is not grounded on reason, for God is all-knowledge and ever just. He is partial to nobody. Moreover, the remark implies that it is God that does evil, and that the evil in the world is the outcome of His desire, a thing which cannot be true. Whoever performs acts conducive to the attainment of salvation, it is to him that salvation is granted and not to those who do not perform such acts, for God never does injustice.

If He were to bestow happiness upon men, or subject them to pain and suffering arbitrarily, His conduct would be open to the charge of partiality and injustice. Indeed, He never so acts. Just as the fire cannot be false to its property of burning, even so God cannot go against His own nature, which is for universal justice. He can never do anything fraught with injustice in the remotest degree.

"God alone is the ruler of all times for purposes of salvation, and none else; whosoever sets down any other as such, is in the wrong. "Salvation is impossible of attainment by a mere belief in another individual, for when salvation is the result of intercession from without, God has virtually no power to grant it; in other words, God is not independent in the matter. Such a being cannot be God! The true God can never stand in need of anyone's intercession, for He is omnipotent. I believe all wise men regard Him as such, and if, influence by prejudice, some do not, that is a different matter. It is strange that you believe Him to be 'one without a second'. And yet associate prophets with Him as His indispensable counsellers in the matter of determining as to who should get salvation and who should not.

"The truth is that God grants salvation to righteous people, who perform noble acts fro the attainment of that exalted position. He does into require the assistance of anybody in the matter. It is man who stands in need of the help of his fellow-beings. God wants no one's help. Nor is He of a capricious nature, and were He such, He would be perpetrating gross acts of injustice. He does not, in point of fact, deviate from His nature at all. He gives salvation to His truthful, righteous devotees, and keeps them in a state of perpetual bliss."

In the meantime it struck four (P.M.). The Swami said that he had yet much to say. The Mussalmans said that it was their prayer-time. The Rev. Mr. Scott told the Swami that he was desirous to a private talk with him. Both of them, therefore, retired to a separate place for the purpose. While they were away, one of the Moulvis mounted the table and began to harangue the people on his faith, while just a few yards from him the Pandits began to hold forth on their own doctrines.

Some men began to give out that the fair was at an end. On hearing this the Swami asked the Padris and Aryas if the Moulvis had returned from their prayers. The reply was that the fair was over. The swami enquired who had declared the fair to be over without previously having secured the consent of the parties concerned, and whether the discussion would be proceeded with or not. When there was confusion and noise, and no chance of a further discussion was left, some gentlemen requested the Swami to return to his resting-place as the fair has terminated. The Swami observed that he wished it had lasted at least for five days. Rev. Scott replied that he could not stay for more than two days. Upon this the Swami returned to his lodgings and commenced discoursing on the "Principles of Dharma".

TRANSMIGRATION OF SOULS

The same day the Rev. Mr. Scott, in company with two other gentlemen, visited him at his place, asking if the doctrine of the transmigration of the souls was true. The Swami answered in the affirmative. He said that migration was proportionate to one's karma; those who did noble acts, became human beings; but those who did evils ones, went down into the bodies of birds, animals, etc.; while those whose karma was of a very high order, become devatas or saints and sages. As an illustration of the truth of the doctrine, the Swami said that the moment a child was born, he commence sucking at his mother's breasts. The reason of this was that the child was impelled to do so because of the impressions of the previous birth. Further, inequality, in the degree and extend of riches and happiness, and difference in social status, showed that all these were the results of karma. The karmas determined the body. The souls were eternal, without a beginning or end. The impressions of preceding birth clung to the spiritual body, and this was why there was such a variety of human temperaments.

Similarly, there were many other proofs of the truth of the doctrine of transmigration of souls, but there was none in support of the assertion that the soul was a creation, which might ultimately become extinct in the world. The doctrine of sleep after death and of the day of judgment was not true.

After talking so far the Padris went away.

The Moulvis, on reaching Shajahanpur, wrote a letter to Munshi Indramani, inviting him to a discussion there; but when the Swami and Munshi reached the place, no one would come forward

The Brahmo Samaj

The lectures were on the "Revealed character of the Vedas" and the "Transmigration of Souls". In these the Divine origin of the Vedas was fearlessly upheld and thoroughly proved and the arguments put forward in support of the doctrine of the transmigration of souls were unanswerable. The Brahmo Samaj does not believe in a Revelation, nor has it's faith in the doctrine of the transmigration of the souls and it would, under the circumstances, be perfectly natural on its part to desire that some building, other than the Brahmo Mandir, should be made available for the Swami's speeches and discourses. At the same time, the orthodox, smarting under the rebuke administered to them, and the exposure to which they were subjected, pressed round Lala Bhagwan Das, son of Diwan Rattan Chand, with the request, given expression to in grieved and indignant tones, that he would turn the atheistic Sanyasi out of his garden.

"The man condemns idol-worship and runs down your and our deities, and as such, no true believer should, in the slightest degree, be helpful to him.' Lala Bhagan Das judged discretion the better part of valor and forthwith notified the Swami that his house was to be vacated without delay. There was no other alternative but to comply, and the Swami's well-wishers waited upon Dr. Rahim Khan for the loan of his kothi, situated in the Anarkali. The doctor was duly informed for whom the kothi was wanted and to what use it would be put, but he was a large-hearted gentleman and cheerfully acceded to the wishes of the Deputation. And the Swami removed to the Doctor's kothi, an it was found to be sufficiently spacious and commodious to allow of lectures being delivered there also.

The Koh-i-Noor Reports Again

The Koh-i-Noor, speaking of these lectures, said, in it's issue of 5th May, 1877:-

"Swami Dayanand Saraswati is still in Lahore, and residing in Dr. Rahim Khan's kothi, situated in Anarkali. He now and then addresses the public on the Vedic Dharma, when he feels an inclination to do so. These lectures of his have split the city people into two parties. One of these believes that that what the Swami teaches is right and useful, the other looks at his preaching as unorthodox and false, and hence inimical to the interests of religion.

The first party is composed of young men who have received Western education, and of those who are in Government employ; the other of men of the old type and old ways of thinking, advanced in years. We are not in a position to say what the result of all this will be. We notice, however, that the party in sympathy with the Swami is gaining strength, and the other one faring in just the opposite way. Whatever is going on here, is very much the same as was described in some past week."

The Biradar-i-Hind Reports on the Swami' Visit

The Biradar-i-Hind, a monthly journal, edited by Pandit Shive Narain Agnihotri, a prominent member of the Brahmo Samaj, contained, in its number fro June, 1877, the following in connection with the Swami's work at Lahore:-

"Starting from Ludhiana on 19th April, 1877, Pandit Dayanand Saraswati reached Lahore the evening of the same day, and took up his quarters in the garden belonging to the late Ratan Chand Sarhiwala. The people here had already been waiting for his arrival. When they heard of the arrival of the Pandit Sahib, they streamed forth from their houses to see him. The Brahmos were particularly delighted at his coming, for they had specially exerted themselves to induce him to come here. For four days the people continued to gather around the Pandit in the very garden (where he put up). After the expiration of the period it was thought advisable that the Pandit (the principal object of whose life is to preach and to teach the people) should address the public in a suitable place within the city. At a general meeting held to consider this proposal, the conclusion was arrived at that the Baoli Sahib, being situated in the heart of the town and being, at the same time, a spacious and commodious building, was specially suited for the Pandit's lectures. In conformity with the decision of the meeting, printed notices were issued, and on the date appointed, the Pandit delivered a lecture on the 'Vedas' (in the building in question). People had come together in large numbers to hear lecture, but inasmuch as the Pandit is a dead enemy of idol-worship (wishing to exterminate it altogether) men of the old school, - Brahmans, who, for a living, are largely dependent on idolatry, and who had, long before the lecture came off, assumed an attitude of hostility towards the Pandit, made a terrific noise, and otherwise behaved most shamefully on the occasion of the lecture. But for the presence of the police in attendance, there was every chance of disturbance taking place. But one took place, and the Swami once more addressed the public in the very same building. However after the two lectures in question, it was resolved that, inasmuch as there was apprehension of a disturbance in the Baoli Sahib, and inasmuch as there was a great deal of noise there, the Swami should henceforward lecture in the Brahmo Mandir. Accordingly the Pandit delivered two lectures in the Brahmo Samaj, perfect order, as might be expected, prevailing there on each occasion, and the people hearing the updesh with patience and attention.

"In the meantime, however, the gentleman, in whose garden the Pandit had to put up, and who had, of his own free-will invited him to take up his quarters there, yielding to prejudice and wholly regardless of the fact that he was a Reis, desired the Pandit to vacate his house. Well, there was not dearth secured for his residence another building, better and far larger than the first, and the Swami vacating the Reis's house, removed into the new kothi. This new kothi belongs to Dr. Rahim Khan, Khan Bahadur, whose courtesy and large-heartedness may be gauge and judged from the fact that, though a Muhammadan by faith, he most cheerfully made over his house to the Pandit the moment the people asked him for the loan of it. This act of generosity on the part of the Khan Sahib was such that the well-wishers of the Pandit would ever consider themselves beholden to him for the same. The house was so big and possessed such a spacious compound, that it was thought that it was suitable not only for his residence but for his lectures also. This being the case, his lectures commenced to be given in the kothi instead of in the Brahmo Mandir, ever since his leaving his old lodgings.

"On reaching here the Swami commenced speaking against idol-worship so strongly that the Brahman community in particular, and the other people in general, came to be in a state of excitement. When the Brahmans saw that many of their 'sheep' had left them and many were daily leaving them, they could contain themselves no longer. Recognizing the necessity, they convened a meeting, which was attended by the best-known and select Pandits of the town. These Pandits summoned Pandit Bhanu Datta, Acharya, Sat Sabha, Punjab, to the meeting also, and inasmuch as the Pandit was an acharya of a Sabha whose chief object was, admittedly and in effect, to proclaim to the people the worship of the one formless, and inasmuch as he himself had helped the educated community to entertain about him the impressions that he did not look upon idolatry as anything commendable, and further inasmuch as he was frequently seen with the Swami when the latter arrives at Lahore, the Pandits, with one voice, declared to his face that they thought he too was of the religion of Dayanand Saraswati. Now sooner were these words uttered than Pandit Bhanu Datta, in trepidation and alarm, replied that he was at a loss to understand how such a thing could be predicted of him. 'My faith,' he added, 'is the same as yours and, if you desire to say anything against the Swami, my services are your disposal.' Hearing his answer the Pandits were pleased, and Pandit Bhanu Datta was appointed 'Secretary of the Sabha organized by them.

"When the people came to hear that Pandit Bhanu Data had joined a Sabha whose object was to uphold idol-worship and to prove the same from the Vedas, they, the educated portion of them especially, who were fully acquainted with his religious views, were extremely surprised. We, in particular, were not only surprised to hear the news but very much grieved also, for the Pandit was friendly-disposed towards us in a remarkable degree. Whenever we had occasion to converse with him on idol-worship, he never supported idol-worship. Indeed, only a few days ago, he told us that Pandit Dayanand Sarawati wanted him to remain with him and to assist him in this national work by becoming a missionary and giving updesh to the people; but,' said the Pandit, 'I am so very much attached to my family and household that although Swami Dayanand is willing to provide amply for my family, and although I myself like the work proposed very much, I have not sufficient moral courage to close the with the Swami's offer and to work with him in the furtherance of his mission.'

"Our readers will see from this that Pandit Bhanu Datta joined the idolatrous Pandits and became the Secretary of their Sabha through motives of 'policy'. Indeed, he went so far as to stop seeing the Swami from the day he joined the Pandits, and to issue a notice under his signature that a certain Pandit would, on behalf of his Sabha, deliver a lecture in 'idol-worship' and prove that the Vedas allowed the adoration of idols. In addition to this lecture, the Pandit himself, in the meantime, delivered two lectures,-in which he explained the nature and character of the gods, and actually supported idol-worship. So far we have spoken of the Lahore Pandits and of the opposition of the Pandit Sabha. As to what are the views of Swami Dayanand, what the nature of the reform which he wishes to bring about by his updesh in different places, how far his teaching produces its effect on the minds of the educated youth, to what extent the principles of the Brahmo Samaj are in conformity with his religious ideas, wherein they differ and why, what is the measure of success which the noble efforts of the Swami have already achieved, and what success they are likely to achieve in future; - on these points we shall speak in a future issue:"

And in fulfillment of the promise made in the foregoing article, Pandit Shive Narain Agnihotri, wrote in his journal (1st July, 1877):-

"The views of Swami dayanand are catholic and mostly in accordance with the advance ideas of the present day. His mind appears to be capable of vast improvement, and hence it is that although he is conversant with no literature other than that embodied in the Sanskrit language, he has yet, by the help of this literature, and by mixing enlightened and educated gentlemen, liberalized his ideas and made them clear in such an eminent degree that, rising far above the level of bigoted and narrow-minded contemporary Pandits, he has developed into a model of a truly learned and enlightened Pandit, his views are ahead of those of the general mass of English educated people of our country. This man, to all outward appearance, seems to be an enthusiastic advocate of national reform, and an enthusiastic lover of his nation, although it is utterly impossible for us to declare at present how for this enthusiasm is free from the alloy of selfishness. For it is only time and experience that can furnish conclusive evidence on this head one away or the other. For all this, his personality, as far as we can judge of him at the present time, holds out great hopes of progress and reform in the country. As a religious reformer, this man is an inveterate foes of idol-worship. Really, contemplating him side by side with those who are at present body undermining the foundations of idolatry, it would not be improper to set him down as the greatest iconoclast of the age.

On Child Marriage and Education of Women

"Viewed in his capacity as a helper of the Brahmo Samaj, in pushing forward the interests of the of the religious crusade undertaken by that body, whose fundamental principle of belief requires that idol-worship in all its phases should be uprooted and the worship of the one only true God should be spread in the world, the man has so much of the angel in him that it is impossible to over praise him. It is not only religious upheaval which this man is desirous of bringing about: he has also in view the reformation of the evil customs and usages such as child-marriage, etc. which are prevailing in the land. He is, above all, an advocate of female education and emancipation, believing that so long as the Indian woman remains ignorant and does not obtain freedom from domestic thralldom, the hope of seeing India make an appreciable progress will never be realized. To be brief, the destruction of ignorance and prejudice from among the nation, the diffusion of knowledge, the creation of national union, and evolving, out of this union, an all-embracing civilization, which will make the Indian Community a model community, is thee first and final aim of this man."

Excerpt from the Koh-i-Noor

The following excerpt from the Koh-i-Noor, 16th June, 1877, describes the effect on the public mind of the Swami's utterances at Lahore:- "The truthful words of the Swami have turned the hearts of numbers from idol-worship. Many have packed up their idols to be put away and never to be thought of again, many having gone to the Ravi quietly have consigned them to the waters, while many others, more daring than the rest and wholly indifferent to the threats of the Biradari, have flung them hero-like into the streets. The result of these herculean efforts of the Swami had been of the highest advantage not only to his followers but to the other party also. A body of young men, educated and imbued with new ideas and impatient of restraint, has given their whole-hearted allegiance to the Swami, and such has been the effect of his preaching that during the current week, a man, taking up his Chauki of idols, threw it into the bazaar."

Swami Dayanand had hardly been little more than two months in Lahore, when the enlightened community of the town came to recognize the absolute necessity of establishing an Arya Samaj in their midst. Strange that over a dozen years, updesh in the N.W.P. should have failed to produce in these Provinces the result which a couple of months' stay in the Punjab was sufficient to bring about!

No doubt, the educated people of Bombay had been prompt in perceiving an organization which should, on systematic lines, work for the good of mission; but in the vigor and intensity of feeling, - the earnestness with which the Punjab took up the Swami's work, in the comprehensive realization of the stupendous significance of the Samajic propaganda, and in the prevision of its far-reaching and enduring consequences, for which the Punjabis distinguished themselves, our good brethren of Bombay were far from bring up to the mark. And they were not to blame.

Dealing with Sikhism in the Punjab

The conditions under which they lived were different from those which prevailed in the Punjab, and they had not the traditions which the Punjab had cherished for the last three hundred years. They still were hemmed in by a conservatism whose power had long been broken in the land of the Five waters. The pure and sublime theism of Guru Nanak and his successors, and the liberal social code which they had promulgated in their writings and utterances, had but little affected Southern India, and, under the circumstances, it as too much to expect that they would rise quite up the height of the Punjabis in their appreciation and grasp of the high character of the doctrines (several of them at least) offered for their acceptance, doctrines which, before they came to reiterated by the Ten Gurus in the troublous times of the Muslim Rule, had, we must remember, been elaborated in this very region by the ancient sages in the light of the Revelation.

Arya Samaj and its Ten Principles

As to why the Arya Samaj came to assert its distinctive being in spite of the theistic bodies like the Sat Sabha and the Brahmo Samaj already in existence, the reason is to be sought in their recognizing and teaching truth only in part. At the same time, it must mot be lost sight of that one of these bodies had, in the lapse of years, degenerated into an eclectic System of Faith which sought for strength and nourishment in the dogmas of an alien creed, and such a System of Faith was bound to give way before an indigenous Faith of an all-embracing character, philosophical and scientific, in the highest degree.

The self will prefer its own to what is foreign or but partially its own, and this was the reason why Brahmo Samajists and the Sat Sabhaists, as well as numerous other educated gentlemen, whom these bodies had wholly or partially failed to satisfy, and who were drifting into materialism, gathered under the banner of the Arya Samaj. They saw Dayanand one who was their own, one who offered them once more the legacy left to them by their ancestors.

It will be remembered that the principles of the Arya Samaj proclaimed at the Bombay were a collection of principles and bylaws mixed up. It was evident that they needed a thorough revision before they could be adopted.

This was pointed out to Swami Dayanand, and he, in conjunction with the late Lala Sain Das, Lala Mul Raj, M.A., District Judge, Lala Jiwan Das, and few other gentlemen, remodeled and recast them, separating the niyams from the upniyams (by-laws), and at the inaugural weekly meeting of the Arya Samaj, which tool place on 24th June, 1877, at the kothi of Dr. Rahim Khan, had them duly announced. These principles and by-laws were recognized and adopted by the Bombay Samaj, as well as by all the after-coming Arya Samajes, in the whatever part of the country they came to be established, and they remain in force in all Samajes down to the present time. These principles were:-

1. "The primordial Root - the Eternal Unseen Sustainer - of all true knowledge, and of objects made known by true knowledge, and of objects made known by true knowledge - aye of all these - is the Supreme God.
2. "God is All-Truth, All-Knowledge, All-Beatitude. He is Formless, Almighty, Just, Benevolent, Unborn, Endless and Infinite, Unchangeable, Beginningless, Incomparable, Fearless, Eternal, Holy and Maker of the universe. To him alone is worship due.
3. "The Veda is the Scripture of true knowledge. It is the paramount Duty of every Arya to learn and teach the Veda, to hear and preach it.
4. "We should ever be 'ready to accept Truth, and to renounce Untruth.
5. "All acts should be done in accordance with Dharma, after a thorough investigation of Right and wrong.
6. "The prime object of the Arya amaj - Vedic church - is to do good to the world, that is to promote the Physical, Spiritual and Social good of every sentient being.
7. "Our conduct towards all should be guided by Love, Righteousness and Justice.
8. "We should destroy avidya - Nescience - and promote vidya - Science, spiritual and physical.
9. No person should be content with promoting his own good only; on the contrary, he should look for his good in the good of all.
10. "All men should abide by the laws of Society calculated to promote the well-being of all; but everybody is free

in regard to the laws affecting his individual well-being." We may be sure that it was no tame affair - that of the establishment of the Arya Samaj at Lahore. We have reliable information that the excitement and enthusiasm created and evoked by the function were at their highest pitch.

The following is the list of office-holders and members elected at the preliminary meeting:-

1. Lala Mul Raj, M.A., Prem Chand Rai Chand Scholar (at present member, the Anarkali Samaj, Lahore) President.
2. Lala Sri Ram, M.A., Headmaster, Normal School Lahore, Vice-President (since dead).
3. Lala Sain Das, Translator, Government Gazette, Punjab Secretary (since dead).
4. Lal Jiwan Das, Translator, Finanacial Commissioner's Office, Punjab (at present an Office-bearer of the Vachhowali Samaj, Lahore) - Secretary.
5. Babu Sarda Parsad Bhattacharya, Secretary. (The gentleman has ceased to take interest in the Arya Samaj.
6. Lala Bishen Lall M.A. Joint Secretary. (Probably member of no Samaj at present)
7. Lala Kundan Lal, Treasurer. (Member of no Samaj at present).
8. Lala Ballabh Das, Librarian (since dead).
9. Pandit Amar Nath, Translator, Chief Court, Member. (Has ceased to be a member of an Samaj.)
10. Dr. Bhagat Ram Sahni, Member. (Has ceased to be member of any Samaj.)
11. Dr. Khazan Chand, Member. (At present member of the Gujrat Samaj.)
12. Lala Madan Singh, B.A., Member (At present member of the Amballa Samaj.)
13. Lala Mungoo Mal, Member. (At present a member of the Lahore Arya Samaj, Anarkali.)

14. Lala Hans Raj Shani, Member. (At present Secretary, Arya Samaj, Rawalpindi.)
15. Lala Dwarka Das, M. A. Member. (At present President, Arya Samaj, Anarkali.)
16. Lala Gobind Sahai, Member. (At present member, Lahore Arya Samaj, Anarkali.)
17. Dr. Sada Nand, Member.
18. Lala Ishwar Das, B.A., Member (deceased).
19. Bhai Nihal Singh, Member (ditto).
20. Lala Balak Ram, Member. (ditto)
21. Lala Ram Sahai, Member.(At present member, Arya Samaj, Lahore, Anarkali.

A gentleman writing to the Koh-i-Noor gave expression,in a letter, to the following sentiments regarding the Arya Samaj - sentiments which echo the innermost ideas and feelings of the advanced section of Lahore community of the time.

Aryavarta until the Muslim Invasion

The letter ran as follows:-

"The updesh which Swami Dayanand has been giving during the last two or three months moved the hearts of the people so strongly and roused the national sympathies so far that they established and Arya Samaj on 26th June, 1877. The Samaj has very nearly three hundred members at present, and it is progressing day by day. The real object of the Samaj is to revive and spread the old Arya Dharma - Vedic Teaching - and to give an impetus to the study of Sanskrit Literature. With this object in view, the Samaj has established a School fro imparting instruction in Sanskrit and for the study of the Vedas. It is, at present, attended by one hundred men. The establishment of the Samaj is mainly due to the arrival of Swamiji here.

"History bears witness to the fact that during 2,500 years after Swami Shankracharya, no leader or Vedic Scholar or Rishi (except Swami Dayanand) has appeared to show the right way." "Is this not an occasion for us to congratulate ourselves upon, that the Swami is doing so much for our good and guidance? Brethren! Ye who profess allegiance to the Arya Dharma, why don't ye awake from your sleep of forgetfulness now? Praised be the Lord! - the Saschchidanand, who, out of His infinite mercy revealed the Vedas to mankind, and most praiseworthy were the Arya people who adopted and follow the Vedic Religion. They were strong in their armor of knowledge and affluent in virtue, and lvied and treated each other as a brother lives with a treats a brother.

"This is fully evidenced by the fact that no foreign nation, from the dawn of creation to the time of Rao Pathaura, could invade Aryavarta"

"But bethren, from the time when the Arya nation made progress in 'disunion', the state of Aryavarta underwent a change. Form that time commenced the invasions of Mahmood of Ghazni and others, till at last Shahab-ud-din Gauri became master of the land. The result of our disunion was, that our sacred Veda and our Arya Faith and works were utterly lost to us. And instruction in the Veda disappeared utterly that we could not light upon traces of it, even if we set about finding them with a lamp in hand.

"However, thanks are due to that merciful God who, taking pity on our miserable condition, gave us Swami Dayanand, filling his mind with a noble ambition, which urged him to uproot creature-worship and belief in the marvelous, and to establish, in their place, the worship of one God and a love of the Vedic Teaching. We are deeply beholden to the Swami who, after under going untold suffering and studying the Vedas, chose to consecrate his life to the work of leading us to the right path.

If the entire country were to appreciate the efforts he is making for us, there van be no doubt that a single day would suffice to drive away poverty and ignorance from among us, and to bring back the Vedic Dharma and Vedic karma and the worship of the true One, which once our seers and sages followed and practiced. But, alas! There are people who not only make not effort to extricate themselves from the pit of ignorance in which they are fallen, but dissuade others in like circumstances form doing so.

"My advice to you is 'Follow your true Dhama and worship your true Creator, and exhort your brethren to com to the right. You are your own masters, and hence choose for yourself. Brethren, in my opinion, disunion should be exterminated root and branch at once, and all should follow the teaching of the Veda only. Whatever the Veda teaches, by following that alone can we save ourselves and in no other way." Although the inaugural meeting of the Samaj was held in Dr. Rahim Khan's khoti, it was felt that the place was not exactly the place for the purpose. Hence, the second meeting was held in the premises of the Sat Sabha, but a scathing criticism on the Puranic teaching so upset the authorities of the Sabha that they refused to lend their building for another meeting. A building in the Anarkali was, consequently, rented, which long remained in the possession of the Samaj.

On the 29th July, 1877, a library was opened in connection with the Samaj, the late Lala Sain Das, than whom the Samaj has bee no greater patriot or thinker, giving a donation of two hundred rupees, a sum which far exceeded his means, considering his salary at the time was no more than Rs. 130 a month.

Some Interesting Facts and Anecdotes

As the reader is aware, the Swami would not let women come into his presence. The ladies of Lahore, however, accustomed to a different order of things, and wholly failing to appreciate the Swami's attitude towards members of their sex, thronged to the Swami's lodging in numbers and insisted upon having an updesh.

Unwilling to disappoint them, he had separate accommodation provide for their benefit, and in his lecture strongly emphasized the fact that it was improper for women to take part in the meetings of men, adding; "Women generally go to the Sadhus and Faqirs for children and for the acquisition of wealth. But the Sadhus and Faqirs, who promise such things to women are great scoundrels. It is meet that women should have their own Sabhas or hear updesh from their husbands, who, according to the Shastras, being their gurus, should be alone served and waited upon by them. They should never go to the Faqirs, either for offspring or for wealth." And he also said: "the men who permit their women to go anywhere and everywhere, and have no control over them, are worthless."

One day Pandit Shiv Narain Agnihotri asserted that the Sama Veda contained the story of owls. The Swami, taking up the Book, quietly handed it over to the Pandit, and asked him to find the story for him. The Pandit kept turning over the leaves for some time, but finally returned the book, observing that he could not find the story!

One day Babu Sarda Parsad Bhattacharya proposed, in a public meeting, with the full occurrence of the other Arya members present, that the title of "Patron of the Samaj" be conferred upon the Swami. When the proposal had been thoroughly approved by the meeting, the Swami smiles and observed:

"The word 'patron' is suggestive of 'gurudom', my mission is to weaken and break up sects which recognize 'gurudom', and not to found a new sect and become a guru myself. If my head is turned by the title tomorrow, or if my successor becomes proud and haughty by reason thereof, you will be confronted with a great evil, and this evil will be the same as the new creeds have been confronted with! Hence, the proposal that has been made, should never be repeated in the future."

The Babu still insisting that the Swami should at least accept the title of parama shaik (supreme helper), and latter answered:

"If you call me parama Sahaik, by what name will you call the almighty Paramatma?

This anecdote contains lessons of the highest value for the Arya Samaj, and may Heaven help us never to lose sight of these. Slavery and thralldom of the worst kind ever follows in the train of 'gurudom', it utterly enfeebles men morally and intellectually and spiritually, and of what use is a community that is undone in so many ways?

Once Pandit Manphool said to the Swami: "If you give up refuting and denouncing idol-worship, the people would cease to be angry with you and what is more, the Maharaja of Jammu and Kashmir will also be pleased with you!" The Swami answered:

"Shall I strive to please the Maharaja of Jammu and Kashmir, or shall I strive to carry out the mandates of Ishwara - the Sovereign of sovereigns - embodied in the Vedas?"

This reply was conclusive for the Pandit, and it is said he never saw the Swami after this.

While putting up in the kothi of Nawab Nawaszish Ali Khan, the Swami one day delivered a lecture on Islam. While the lecture was going on, the Nawab walking about at a distance, listening to it, a person approached the Swami and said: "Maharaj! None will lend you his house to step in, neither Hindus nor Muahmmadans nor Christians. Now that the Nawab Sahib has kindly placed his kothi at your disposal, you would run down Islam even in his house!" The reply of the Swami was,

"I cannot barter my religion for the luxury of staying in comfortable lodgings. In declaring the truth I fear no one, though the declaration might cause me trouble and inconvenience."

During his stay a Lahore, Swami Dayanand had interviews with Colonel Holroyde, Director, Public Instruction, Punjab, and one with Sir Charles Egerton, Lieutenant-Governor, also. In the course of conversation with His Honor, the Swami observed that:

"I could not understand how Englishmen, with all their boasted civilization, could believe in such a book as the Bible"

His Honor begged to be excused from making a reply, as (said he) he was not prepared to talk on religious subjects with the Reformer. The Swami, of course, did his duty.

During the days when prachar-work was being pushed on in the garden belonging to Nawab Ali Raza Khan, near the Masti Gate, a Padri and his lady visited the Swami.

A conversation ensued, during which the Rev. gentleman said: "What proof have you that the Aryas were originally wealthy and in the enjoyment of comfort, and degenerated and fell in to poverty afterwards?" In reply the Swami observed that the annals of ancient Aryavarta bore witness to the truth of his assertion, and that the Rev. gentleman, being conversant with history, could verify the fact for himself. As to the cause of the fall of the ancient Aryas, it was their great wealth that brought them down.

"I have been', said the Swami, "an early riser from my childhood. In the beginning I saw that Englishmen would get up early in the morning, and, taking their children with them, would go out for a walk. The excess of wealth, however, has made them indolent since. They are seen stretched on their beds in their Bungalows till the sun is up, and I cannot but perceive that, like the old Aryas, the days of your fall is also coming."

Dr. Hooper came one day to hear the Swami's lecture at Dr. Rahim Khan's house. On the termination of the lecture, the missionary put the Swami a question in Sanskrit. On the termination of the lecture. The audience who were about to disperse, retained their seats. The Swami requested the Doctor to come forward and take a chair. The latter replied that it did not become him to sit on a chair in the presence of such a man as the Swami, for the Swami was the "sun of knowledge." The question which he (the Doctor) wanted to ask, he had come to ask in the capacity of ajigyasu (enquirer), and not in the spirit of one who would discuss and argue. Having said this, the Doctor remarked that since the Vedas spoke of Ashvamedha and Gomedha Yajnas, it was evident that in the Vedic period, the people were in the habit of offering sacrifices of horses and cows. What had the Swami to say about it? The Swami's answer, in substance, was:

"All these stories have been invented by the Vamamargis. The Vedas nowhere speak of doing Yajna by sacrificing kine and horses. Ashvamedha, according to the Shatapatha Brahmana, Nirukta and so on means the just and impartial treatment of his subjects by a king; while Gomedha means the cleaning of grain, the purifying of the five senses, the mind, and so forth."

The second question which the Rev. gentlemen asked was: "What have the Vedas to say on Caste?" the reply was that caste-distinction, according to the Vedas, rested on worth and merit. Upon this, the Missionary asked: "If I be a possessor of noble qualities and virtues, can I become a Brahman?" The Swami answered: "Most certainly. If your worth and actions are such as to entitle you to claim the position of a Brahman, you can become one."

One day a Padri hearing his criticism on the mantra - Hiranyagarbha, etc. remarked that the ancient Aryas knew nothing about God, adding that the spiritual upheaval of the word was due to the Bible. "Wherever," the Bible has been carried, the people there had become civilized, and the teachings of the Bible influence an area of land over which the sun never sets." The Swami replied that it was not due to the Bible that the results of which the Missionary spoke had been achieved, but to the teaching of the Veda which the Western people practically followed. The non-recognition of early marriage, observing of brahmacharya, love of knowledge, monogamy, traveling of distant countries, patriotism, etc. (inculcated in the Vedas) had made the Western people what they were. The people of India had made the Western people what they were. The people of India had come to mistake for the Vedic religion a totally different faith which was worthless, and had ceased following the behests of the Vedas. But the Europeans, though not acquainted with the Vedas, yet followed their commandments. This was the reason why the Indians were going down, and the Europeans 'going up.'

The Swami was in Lahore when the anniversary-festival of Brahmo Samaj came round. The Swami was invited. He went in company with a large number of Arya gentlemen after the proceedings of the weekly meeting of the Arya samaj wer over. When the Swami entered the Brahmo Mandir, Pandit Raghu Nath Gupta, pracharak of the Brahmo Samaj of India, who was at the time conducting the Service, descende from the pulpit and falling at the Swami's feet, embrace him and said: "In reality the Brahmo Samaj and the Arya Samaj are one." The Swami replied:

"Although there is a difference between the Samajees at present, the day will come when the two will become one."

The upaniyams (by-laws) of the Arya Samaj were passed on 6th November, 1877. the Swami happening to be present in the Samaj at the time, the members requested him to give his opinion on some points. The Swami replied that he had no right to do it, as he was not a member of the Antrang Sabha. And he never gave his opinion till, for special reasons, he had been elected a member of the Executive Body!

The body that had suffered most by the establishment of the Arya Samaj was the Brahmo Samaj. Its ranks were considerably thinned, and, in their annoyance, the remaining members of the Samaj called upon their brethren of Calcutta to help them. The Calcutta Brahmo Samaj sent the Lahoris a number of mantras with their interpretation, claiming to prove that the Vedas were not revealed. The Lahoris lost no time in holding a public meeting and asking the Swami to explain the mantras. The Swami accepted the challenge. As the Brahmo gentlemen were ignorant of Sanskrit, they constituted Pandit Bhanu Datta their representative. The Pandit read out the mantras, with their interpretation. Before rising to reply, the Swami asked the Pandit if he too, who unlike the Brahmos, knew Sanskrit, thought the interpretation to be right. The Pandit replied in the negative, adding that the objections which the Brahmo gentlemen had brought forward, had no weight in his opinion. The answer sent the audience into roars of laughter, and it ws a 'stunner' for the Brahmos. As Brahmo gentleman then undertook to repeat the objections, and after he had done speaking, the Swami got up and explained how the words, Ganga and Yamuna, were not proper names, but the names of two arteries, paling a conspicuous part in Yoga to convince his hearers thoroughly, he read the chapter from the beginning, explaining each mantra and proving conclusively that the chapter dealt with the Science of Yoga, and not with the so-called rivers, Ganga, Yamuna, etc.

AT AMRITSAR

Lahore was, for several months, the head-quarters of the Swami, and during months he would be frequently away from the station to the neighboring towns and cities in the interests of prachar. He visited Amritsar twice during 1877, and again on 15th May, 1878, staying up to 11th July, 1878. During his first visit h put up in the kothi near the Ram Bagh Gate of the town, being the guest of the late Sardar Dayal Singh of Majithia, who had hired the kothi in question at a rent of Rs. 40 a month. The interested priesthood had not been sparing in their efforts to give currency, at Amritsar, to the false and ridiculous rumors which their kith and kin had been so assiduous in spreading at Lahore. But the charm of novelty had worn away and, believing the idle reports set afloat by the advocates of idol-worship as nothing better than old women's tales, the people came pouring daily to the reformer and listened, with the deepest attention, to all he had to say to them.

His exposure of the Puranas and his lectures on other subjects displayed a vastness and depth of learning and a power of reasoning which absolutely surprised and fascinated his hearers, and made many of them set him down as an "incarnation" of the Deity Idol-worship became an object of hatred to the intelligent and thoughtful, and the scenes enacted at Lahore were repeated, the idols and images being handled unceremoniously and either put away in lumber-rooms or 'shied' into the thoroughfares. A month's preaching was sufficient to establish an Arya Samaj, with about fifty Members, Babu Ghanya Lal, Pleader, being elected President, and Bawa Narian Singh, Pleader, Secretary. The exact date of the establishment of the Samaj was 12th August 1877.

The champions of idolatry did all they could to persuade the famous Pandit Ram Datta of Amritsar to hold a shastrarth with the Swami, but a clear refusal was the reply. The Pandit frankly acknowledged that he had not studied the Vedas, nor had the ability to enter into a contest with a man of the stamp of Dayanand. Pandit Tulsi Ram, another well-known and able Pandit was also approached, he too begged to be excused from acceding to the wishes of his admirers. Indeed, the Pandit meeting the Swami one day, in the bazaar, prevailed upon him to accompany him to his house, where, on arriving, he extended to him a most cordial welcome and treated him with the greatest respect.

On visiting Amritsar the second time, the Swami has notices circulated, challenging the orthodox Pandits accepted the challenge, and several days were spent in settling the conditions of the proposed shastrarth should take place in the tawela of Sardar Bhagwan Singh, and, long before the hour fixed for the commencement of the discussion, the place was full to overflowing, there being over five thousand persons present. The Swami waited and waited, but no Pandit put in an appearance, and at last thinking it advisable to spend the time for some purpose, he rose to address the meetingl.

He had not, however, proceeded far in his lecture, when Babu Mohan Lal, Pleader, coming into the meeting, announced that he was a messenger from the Pandits and that they desired to come into the meeting. "They should be welcome," was the reply, and the Pandits came, surrounded by a pageant indulging in loud shouts of triumph (Jai! jai!). One might expect that the shastrarth would begin without further delay; but no, the paper embodying the conditions of the shastrarth was again taken in hand by Pandit Chandra Bhan, and heated discussion as to the merits of the conditions ensued. While the time was being uselessly wasted, some bad characters, hiding themselves behind the multitude, took to shying stones and pieces of bricks at the "unorthodox."

One of these came directly towards the Swami, but as he was seated surrounded by several gentlemen standing, the progress of the missile was intercepted, and it failed to do him any injury. Being unable to throw the stones with precision, it was natural that the miscreants should often hit those they did not intend to, and the result of this was that the entire assembly was transformed into a disorderly mob. Many were seen covered with blood, and a fray seemed imminent. Such a contingency was wholly undesirable, and the friends of peace, taking in the situation, exerted themselves as they had perhaps seldom exerted themselves before, and the apprehended disturbance was prevented. Ever mindful of his mission, even in the midst of trials and suffering, the Swami had a fresh challenge went to Babu Mohan Lal for a shastrarth, but the Babu replied that he was the representative of the Pandits only for a few hours of the of the previous day and that he had nothing to do with them now. "They are," he added "wrangling and disputing among themselves, and nothing appears to farther from their intentions than to hold a shastrarth." The Swami waited for twenty days more for a more satisfactory answer on behalf of the Pandits, but it was waiting in vain. At last, he saw no other alternative than to have al the circumstances connected with the promised but enventually-shirked shastrarth printed and published for the information of the general public.

Mr. Perkins was the Commissioner of Amritsar during these days, and, either of his won free will or in the interests of state policy and under instructions from the higher authorities, he expressed a wish to see the Swam. The interview duly came off, and a conversation ensued. Among other things, the Commissioner, who was a thorough Christian, and who, on retirement from service took up preaching work, observed that the Hindu Religion was a like a 'weak, untwisted cotton thread,' read to snap in two at the slightest pressure and on the slightest tension.

The Swami replied that the fact as otherwise, that the Vedic Religion (misnamed Hindu religion) was strong as iron, yea even stronger than that.

There is reason to believe that before the interview came to an end, the Commissioner was fairly convinced that the mission of the Swami was perfectly harmless, and that it was not, in the remotest degree, of a character to justify the reckless manner which the orthodox chose to behave while expressing their disapproval of it.

At Amritsar too individuals were not wanting who, not understanding the Swami, often made him requests which he could never grant. One gentleman besought him not to be so hard on 'idol-worship,' and, of course, the request had to be refused. Another wanted him to become his son's guru, and begged him to give the young fellow the guru-mantra. The Swami expressed his inability to comply with this request also, adding,

"Let your son and yourself repeat the the Gayatri Mantra, for there is no greater mantra than that. You may become a member of the Samaj and learn how to do it." Lala Murli Dhar, Drawing Master, at present President of the Gurdaspur Samaj, and certainly one of the noblest men belonging to the Arya ranks, was also among those who wanted, the Swami to become the their guru. In this instance too, the Swami's reply was fully characteristic of him, and the Lala was told to accept the 'Paramata as his guru and to repeat and recite His guru-mantra only - the Savitri!

Amritsar had long been a center of the Missionary activity, and it might be presumed that the Padris would no mind risking a discussion with the Swami specially as the Swami was yet new to the Punjab and the Padris did not know (as Mr. Foreman and others came to know later) what sort of man they had to deal with. They put forward Pandit Kharak Singh, but judge of the surprise of his supporters when, instead of arguing against the Swami, he commenced assenting to every proposition and admitting the force of every argument which the Swami laid down and advanced!

Seeing how matters stood, the Missionaries wired to Dr. A.M. Bannerjee of Calcutta, but he final answer from that erudite gentleman was, that he could not obey the mandate. Of course, under the circumstances, no discussion could be held!

Criticizing Darwins Theory on Evolution

He refused the Darwinian theory that man was descended from a monkey, He said that the thing was impossible, and brought forward unanswerable arguments in support of his contention. One of these was, that if man was really a descendant of monkey, then it was, as it were, a fact - a law which according to the followers of Darwin and other philosophers of his school, was unceasing in its operations under any conditions whatsoever. If the law was of a constant and permanent nature, ever working itself out, how was it that for thousands of years past, no monkey's young one had developed into a human being? If in times gone-by a money copulating with a fish (for instance) brought into being a strange creature, and if that strange creature copulating with some other creature brought forth another strange creature, and if the process of copulation on the same principle continuing, the last strange creature helped to bring on the scene, as the result of copulation with a nameless creature, a human being; if all this happened formerly, why was it that similar result had ceased to be brought about in the later ages? Did the last strange creature leave a will that no animal in future, especially a monkey, was to act after the fashion of his ancestor.

The Swami further observed that the copulation of an animal of one species with that of the another, did not result in off-spring. Similarly he advanced many other arguments. The English-educated young men of the station were surprised on hearing the Swami's arguments, confessing that they had never heard such arguments before. And these young men were also under the impression that the principles of physics, chemistry and of other sciences, which they studied in their colleges, had been discovered and brought to light by the Europeans, and that no other people were aware of these before.

When however, the principles in question were dwelt upon by the Swami in language remarkable for its connectedness and its intellectual depth, as if the speaker was reading from a scientific treatise, the wonder was all the greater. When a gentleman observed to the Swami that the principles and theories he had spoken of were the discoveries of modern times he deplored the fallen state of India and added: "Any (true) theory or principle which you think to me of modern origin, name the same, and I will prove to you that it is taught and set forth in the ancient Shastras."

Upon this the people commenced asking him many questions as to the fixedness of the sun and the motion of the earth, as to the nature of rain and clouds, of elements , of chemical simples, of fixed and moving stars, of the heavens, of the planetary system, of the moons, of earthquakes, hurricanes, etc. etc., and the Swami would reply to them from the Shastras, with incontrovertible proofs in support of his replies. His answers were so absolutely convincing as to remove all doubts on the points touched from the minds of the questioners. For no sooner was a question uttered than a shloka in reply was forthcoming. The mere literal meaning of the shloka was sufficient to satisfy the enquirer, and to impress the greatness of the Shastras on his mind.

On the Law of Gravitation

"My own contention, in particular, was, that the law of gravitation was a discovery of Newton, and that nobody was aware of it before. When, after expressing my idea in two words, I had done speaking, the Swami asked me to repeat the whole story. I related how the falling apple had attracted Newton's attention (and led him to make the discovery he had made). Upon this the Swami repeated a shloka and translated it. The shloka was clear, and I could follow the literal interpretation.

I was perfectly convince that the author of the shloka thoroughly believed in the law of gravitation. The Swami quoted many Vedamantras also, dealing with the law of gravitation. Although the language of the mantras was too difficult for us to understand, yet we could grasp and appreciate the Swami's rendering of the passages.

On Contemplation of God

Lala Ghanaya Lal, Engineer, observed that in a state of intoxication, the mind became concentrated, and that whatever the attention was directed to, even in that it remained absorbed. This being the case, God could not be contemplated better by a person than when he was in a state of intoxication. The Swami, while admitting that intoxicating liquors did tend to produce a kind of mental fixity, declared that:-

"The concentration of attention thus obtained could serve no useful end whatever in reference to God as an object of contemplation. The mental concentration needed for the purpose must partake of the holy nature of the object contemplated, it must be pure, the result of pure action, of righteous practice."

Taking the Bible to Task

"One day Colonel Mansell, Commanding Officer, Roorkee, accompanied by Captain Stuart, Quarter-master, came to hear the Swami's lecture. When the Swami, in the course of his remarks, began to take the Bible to task, the Colonel was very much excited and, without waiting for the speaker to finish his lecture, commenced asking questions.

The Swami to each as soon s it was, put and his answers were so reasonable that the Colonel could not see his way to find fault on them. His mortification was complete, and at last finding that he was unable to carry on the contest longer, he took his leave, remarking that he would reply to the Swami's objections on them morrow, the Captain alone came, and, unlike the Colonel, hear the lecture that was being delivered, with evident pleasure."

An Open Challenge to Islam

The Muslim community sent for Moulvi Muhammad Qasim Devabandi, with the object of pitting him against the Swami. The Moulvi came, but after a great many letters had passed between the parties as to conditions of the would-be discussion, and after a set of conditions had been agreed to several times and several times cancelled, it was discovered that he Moulvi had no intention of coming forward, and, of course, further correspondence with him was stopped.

The people clearly saw where the truth lay, and as the result of this perception, an Arya Samaj came to be established on 20th August, 1878, with the following office-holders:- Lala Shanker Lall, Master, President; Pandit Umrao Singh, Master, Secretary; Lala Rangi Lall, Master, Treasurer.

AT ALIGARH

Leaving roorkee on 22nd august, 1878, the Swami proceeded to Aligarh, where he stayed for four days, and delivered only a single lecture. Mr. Moolji Thakursi, Mr. Harish Chandra Chintamani, and Pandit Shyamji Krishna Varma had come from Bombay to meet the Swami, and the Swami was extremely pleased to see them.

Sir Syyad Ahmad, who was extremely cordial and hospitable, gave a feast in honor of the Swami's arrival to his friends. The Swami, being indisposed, could not join in the entertainment.

AT MEERUT

From Aligarh, the Swami went to Meerut (August 26th, 1878), where he put in Lala Damodar Das's kothi, near the quarter of the Native Calvary. The Hindus and Muhammadans alike made preparations for a discussion, issuing hand-bills and exchanging letters with the Swami as an evidence of their earnestness of the Swami, but no discussion actually took place, the opposing parties no doubt, being convinced in their heart of hearts that the wisest plan for them to adopt was to rest content with making a reasonable amount of fuss and show.

The Muhammadans would hold a shastrarth on the condition that it should not be reduced to writing, and to this demand of their would-be representative and spokesman the Swami found himself unable to agree.

Meritoriousness of bathing in the Ganges

The Sanatanists, after they had sent a few questions to the Swami for a reply, declared their willingness to publicly face the Swami. The question of conditions was taken up and half settled, when lo! The announcement came from the upholders of orthodoxy that they could never hold a shastrarth with Dayanand till it was satisfactorily determined what varna and ashrama he belonged to? The uselessness of holding a shastrarth with such a man as Dayanand, was further pointed out in the following words, appended to the announcement:- "Our Pandits are profound scholars, and you are an ignorant man. It is ridiculous for the learned to hold a shastrarth with the illiterate."

The questions which the assembly of "profound scholars" had sent to the Swami for an answer were:-

1. "We hear that doubts have arisen in you mind in respect of 'idol-worship'. If the report is true, then quote from Shruti and Smriti in support of your contention; but if the report is unfounded, then declare the fact in clear words.
2. "If you have any doubts in respect of the Gangamahatam (meritoriousness of bathing in the Ganges), then quote authorities in support of your contention.

3. "Is the doctrine of incarnation right? If otherwise, cite authorities to prove your case."

Replying to the questions in his public lectures, the Swami said that he was absolutely convinced that idol-worship was opposed to the teaching of the Veda. The mantras like the third and the eighth of the thirty-second and fortieth chapters of the Yajurveda proved this beyond the shadow of a doubt, showing further that the worship of idols and images could only be productive of suffering. As to the Gangamahatam, the Swami quoted the well-known shloka (109th) from the 5th chapter of the Manu Smriti, and further repeating a passage from the Chhandoagya Upanishad, showed how tirtha was a name from mental purification - the cleansing of the heart from envy, hate, etc. According to the true Shastras, therefore, bathing in the Ganges or any other river or pond was fruitful of no moral or spiritual merit. It could only benefit or harm the body.

INCARNATION OF GODS

As regards the question of incarnation, the Swami's answer was, that there were no incarnations of God. God , as taught in mantras like the first mantra of the thirty-first chapter of the Yajurveda, was all-pervading, infinite, omnipotent, free from the bondage of corporeity of every conceivable kind, indivisible, unharmable, absolutely immaculate, the knower of all hearts, and so forth, and, as such, He could not assume a material form.

The beings looked upon as "incarnations" of God by the orthodox, added the Swami, were only mortals, men of an exalted and lofty type, who deserved to be reverenced and followed, and by walking in their footsteps, we too could make ourselves good and virtuous.

The Swami's lectures, which were delivered in three different places in succession, in Lala Geneshi Lal's Press, at the house of Lala Ram Saran Das, Reis, andint he kothi of Babu Chhedi Lal, Commissariat Agent, had their effect on unbiased minds, and an Arya Samaj was established at Meerut on 29th September, 1879, with the following gentlemen as Office-bearers:- Pandit Kundan Lal, B.A., President; Lala Ram saran

Das, Ries, Vice-President; Babu Anand Lal, Secretary; Babu Chhedi Lal, Treasurer; Pandit Jagan Nath Pershad, Librarian; Pandit Amba Shanker, Assistant Secretary.

AT DELHI

Departing from Meerut, the Swami reached Delhi on 9th October, 1878, and stayed there nearly a month. The effect of his updesh and lectures given and delivered in Shahji's Chhatta, was that an Arya Samaj was at last established in the city. Lala Makhan, Lal became the President, and Lal Hakumat Rai, the Secretary, of this Samaj.

AT AJMER AND PUSHKAR, ETC.

Starting on the 6th November from Delhi, the Swami arrived at Ajmer on the 7th. His visit to this place is associated with an act of under-hand dealing which deserves a mention. It was, while preaching in the Punjab, that the Swami received a letter from certain gentlemen, resident in Ajmer, embodying a request that he would pay them a visit, the inviters of the letter undertaking to defray all expenses in connection with the visit by means of a subscription they intended to raise. The Swami replied that he would come.

A subscription was duly raised by the Ajmer, gentlemen on the receipt of the news that the Swami was coming to them. Before, however, the reformer had time to reach Ajmer, some member of the priesthood, probably in his desire to "settle old scores, sent him a letter in the name f an admirer of the Swami, telling him that it was unnecessary for him to come, since no subscription could be raised in the interest of his visit! The Swami communicated the contents of the strange epistle to Munshi Samarthdan at Ajmer, and the Munshi instituting enquiries and ascertaining the real facts, submitted his report to the Swami. The villainy was apparent, and the Swami duly came to Ajmer, reaching there on the date already specified.

Without making a halt at Ajmer, the Swami proceeded direct to Pushkar, a famous tirtha of the Hindus, situated at a few miles' distance from Ajmer. The annual fair was taking place, and the work of prachar could not be neglected on an occasion like the present one. The Swami put up at the ghat of Maharaja Jodhpur, popularly know as the "Window of Nathji," and he stayed at Pushkar as long as the fair lasted. Notices were issued, inviting all true enquirers to come and hold religious conversations, but nobody came forward for the purpose. The updesh, however, was regularly given, and we may be sure that it did not fall on deaf ears. As soon as the fair was over, the Swami returned to Ajmer, and kept lecturing here till 1st December. 1878. His lectures were attended by the gentry and nobility of the town, and by the local Officials, such as Rai Bhag Ram, Extra Judicial-Assitant; Sardar Rai Bahadur Amin Chand, Judge; Sardar Bhagat Singh; Rao Sahib Masooda, etc. The first named gentleman was long a member of the Ajmer Samaj.

The following lines are form a gentleman's diary regarding the Swami when at Ajmer:- Swamiji must be about fifty years of age. I saw him lying on a bed with his langot on. It appeared that he was suffering from dysentery. For all this, however, his appearance, by virtue of his brahmacharya was such as to furnish little ground for anyone to suspect that he was ill; he possesses a well-knit body, and is tall of stature".

One of the lectures the Swami delivered at Ajmere was on the teachings of the Bible. Mr. Rev. Grey, and some other Missionaries, were present at this lecture, and being anything but pleased with what was being said, they, finding their opportunity, intimated to the Swami that they were ready and willing to hold a discussion with him in connection with any objections he might bring forward against the Biblical teachings provided that he had these objections handed over to them in advance for consideration.

The Swami agreed to the condition, and getting some sixty-four out of the numerous objections he could raise against the dogmas of Christianity, had them sent to the Rev. gentleman, through Rai Bhag Ram. After the Rev. gentleman had considered them for full ten days the 28th of November, 1878, was fixed for the discussion. The public announcement that a discussion of such a character was going to take place between the Missionaries and Swami Dayanand attracted thousands of men to the place of meeting. Three reporters were in attendance.

When the objections against the bible were read out to the audience, Rev. Mr. Grey insisted that only two or three objections should be made the subject of discussion, and that no objection should be spoken upon, if possible, more than once. It was pointed out, in reply, that the restriction imposed was unfair, and that, though it did not signify much what objections were discussed and what left out, it was material that the objections that were selected for discussion should be discussed thoroughly. The Rev. gentleman would not listen to this, and so the discussion being nominal led to no definite result; the more so as the Missionary declined to resume it after the first day had closed. Whatever, however, was said by the parties, was published in the Theophist.

An Invitation for a Shastrath by the Hindus on the Vedas and Shastras

"Salutations to the sacred Ganesh! We, the Sadhus and Pandits and other Sabhasads, in council assembled, write to Swami Dayanand Saraswati, and beg to inform him that for the last three or four days we have been daily holding meetings, from 4 P.M. to 6 P.M., at which religious subjects are discussed for the differentiation of truth from falsehood.

Be it known to you that ever since the Aligarh Sat Dharmavlambi Sabha came to be established near Jhona Akhara, in the vicinity of Mayadevi, invitations have been sent to you regularly, asking you to come over. Now we send you the present letter. If coming into this meeting, you speak, it will lead to two results. In the first place, you, who have hitherto been lecturing on the Vedas and Shastras, in retirement, would, by speaking in the presence of learned men, enable them to judge whether your utterances are in conformity with the teaching of the Vedas and Shastras, and, in the second place, if your utterances turn out to be in accord with the teaching of the Vedas and Shastras, you would find us ready to accept and preach the doctrines you promulgate. The union this brought about will materially conduce to the well-being of Aryavarta. Do please attend Sabha, and if you cannot come, kindly mention the reason.

The Swami's Reply

To this letter the Swami replied as follows:-

"I have never declined, and can never decline, to hold a shastrarth: I am ready for one at all times. But the shastrarth which you propose should be arranged for by some Magistrate, and it should be attended by Pandits only and by no illiterate men. The place where it should be held, should be such as might not be regarded as especially yours or mine. The place where your Sabha is being held, is one by coming where I apprehend personal violence.

The thought of losing my life does not grieve me at all, but it grieves me to think that in case I loose my life, the work of reform I am carrying on will cease, and it is only for this that I guard my body; hence I don not think it advisable to attend your Sabha."

The Swami further had the writers of the letter informed that he should hold a shastrarth with them only if Swami Vishuddhanand should declare that hey could understand and grasp the Vedas when pitted against him (Dayanand) and that, in the extent of such a declaration forthcoming, he would choose Vishuddhanand as Madhyastha. The orthodox took Swami Dayanand's letter to Swami Vishuddhanand. Lala Jamiyat Rai, Master, Normal School, who was present at the time of their arrival at Vishuddhanand's quarters, says that as soon as that sturdy Sanyasi reas the epistle of his great opponent, and knew the errand on which the representatives of the orthodox Sadhus and Pandits had come, he fell to abusing the messengers, Pandits Shardha Ram and Chaturbhuj, in a violent manner, declaring it to their face that, compared with Dayanand, they did not understand so much, as a single letter of the Vedas! Swami Vishuddhanand also wrote a letter to Swami Dayanand, and it was to the following effect.:-

"Many ignorant and illiterate persons have gathered together with the intention of creating a disturbance. You should not at all listen to what they say."

Pandit Bhim Sen read out this letter in the evening in public to an audience of some ten thousand men, and what the effect of the communication must have been on the minds of the hearers, may be better than described. Pandit Shardha Ram, however, was not going to take his discomfiture to heart. On the contrary, he had the hardihood to write a letter to the Koh-i-Noor, saying that Dayanand had refused to hold a shastrarth with his party. More that this, he prevailed upon some creatures of his to declare in his Sabha that though they had, by bearing Swami Dayanand's updesh accepted his faith, the were now as orthodox as ever. "We have found out our mistake," said they, "and we beg that we may be readmitted in the Sanatan Dharma." Their repentance, was, of course, accepted, and they were conducted to the steps of Haridwar with great pomp, to be purified and reclaimed. No pains were spared to give the expiation as wide a publicity as possible, but alas for the clever Pandit! The trick was expose by a member of his own fraternity. It was Pandit Gopal Shastri, who did the thing. Truth came out!

THE SWAMI ON HIS HEALTH

The Swami's health during the period the fair was at its height, was anything but good. He was suffering from acute dysentery. Writing in a letter dated 2nd April, 1879, he said "that he was having as many as ten or twelve motions every day, and in another (dispatched 12th Baisakh, 1936), that he had had 400 motions up till then. But though afflicted with the terrible disease and considerably weakened, he would never let the interest of updesh suffer in any way. Lala Jamiyat Rai, noticing the amount of his daily work on the occasion of the fair, says that that he would get up early in the morning and, after an hour or two spent in bathing and prayer, etc., would take his seat under the Shamianas and converse on the Shastras and Dharma with the Pandits, Sadhus and other people that came to him till 11 A.M., and sometimes till 12. then the Sabha was held at 1 P.M., continuing till 5 P.M. After that the Swami, the Pandits and other Arya gentlemen would meet together and hold religious conversations among themselves. In a word, almost the whole day was passed in teaching and preaching." Probably it would have been better for the Swami if he had left the fair early; but whatever the state of his health, he chose to remain almost to the last, to preclude the possibility of men like Pandit Shardha Ram getting a chance to workd any real mischief, for he was aware that if he left Haridwar before the termination of the fari, the Puranic Pandits would not fail to make capital out of it; they would proclaim to their admirers that Dayanand had run away from the field!

While at Haridwar, the Swami was not unnoticed by the Officials. The Commissioner of Meerut Division, the Collector of Saharanpur, and the Conservator of Forests one day came to see him. The Swami being engaged in upasna at the time of their arrival, they had to wait till he was free. His devotions being over, the interview came off. A long conversation on the "Nature and attributes of the Deity" took place, and the European gentlemen were highly delighted with the arguments and observations of the Swami, and before taking their leave, they saw, of their own accord and free will, that the Swami had the benefit of Police attendance, so that there might be no disturbance at his lectures.

Some more Interesting Facts and Anecdotes

One or two interesting facts and anecdotes in connection with the work (Vide Vidya Prakash, June, 1879) at Haridwar may be given here:-

- Rao Ivaz Khan, Hakim and Reis, Jwalapur, often came to see him. Among other subjects gauraksha (protection of the cow) formed the subject of conversation between the two. Whatever arguments the Rao could bring forward in support of his contention, were easily dispose of by the Swami. The discussion finally resulted in the Rao's becoming a convert to the Swami's views, and he gave him a solemn promise to further the cause of gauraksha to the best of his power.
- Some orthodox Pandits and Sadhus, waiting upon the Swami one day, besought him to desist from denouncing idolatry, shraddh and other Puranic institutions and practices. "We have not the slightest doubt as to your profound scholarship," said they; "if you grant the request we have made, the whole of India will worship you as

an incarnation; and we too will bow before you, and help you in every way." The request was accompanied by the threat that if he rejected their request, they should deal with him as with an enemy, and make him repent. The reply the Swami made to this was the repeating of the well-known shloka of Bhartrihari, upholding devotion to principle.

- A European Doctor of Nianital, in an interview with the Swami, pooh-poohed the idea that the burying or burning of human excreta could produce cholera. However, the very thing came to pass only three or four days after the interview. The gentleman saw the Swami again and asked his opinion as to the best way of disposing of the night-soil. The Swami advised him to have it thrown at some place fairly distant from the area occupied by the pilgrims and where the wind blew in the direction opposite to human habitation.

The doctor saw there was sense in the advice, the interment of filth was stopped, and arrangements were made for its transportation to, and deposit in, the kind of locality specified. At the same time, the Swami did not forget to exhort the people in his lectures to leave for their homes before it was too late, for not even the wisest sanitary measures that could be adopted in an assemblage so vast and so unnatural, could shield it from the attacks of one epidemic or another. Many profiting by the counsel betook themselves to their native places several days before the breaking up of the multitude Arya Samajists departing a day before the Swami did.

Vedantism

- When the report was being assiduously spread by the enemies of reform that Swami Dayanand had refused to hold a shastrarth, some Sadhus elated by the report hastened to the Swami's quarters, and coming into his presence, said that they had sought him out with the view of holding a discussion with him. The Swami, who weakened by dysentery, was laying down, sat up and replied that he was ready.

- Vedantism," was the reply of the leader of the band, a man of learning.

Swami ~ "To begin with, please explain what do you mean by Vedantism?"

Sadhu - "Vedantism is that which teaches that the world is false and that God is the only true existence."

Swami ~ "What do you understand by the 'world' (jagata)? What things are included in your 'world' and what do you mean by the term 'false' (mithya)?"

Sadhu - "Whatever there is from atoms up to the sun, is called the 'world' and all that is in it, is false and unreal."

Swami ~ "Are or are not your body, speech, moving about, updesh, guru, and books included in this world also?

Sadhu - Yes they are."

Swami ~ "And is your religion also included in this, or is it outside of it?"

Sadhu - "Verily, that too is included in this."

Swami ~ "When you yourself admit that you and your guru, your faith and your books, your speech and your updesh are false, what can I say to you? The case, according to the statement of the claimant himself, deserves to be dismissed. There is no need of witnesses here."

- One day, a Parmahansa Sanyasi, a man eighty years old, visited the Swami in company with his disciples. At the sight of him the Swami hastily rose, and advancing as far as the door of his khema, conducted him into a tent and seated him on an elevated masnad (seat). The old saint was a Vedanti, and the discussion between him and the Swami, conducted exclusively in Sanskrit, lasted till 2 P.M. All the time the discussion was going on, the Swami would take up one book after another and show his opponent the required parmanas (authorities) in support of his position. On the termination of the shastrarth, which had been absorbing enough to make the disputants forget that they were hungry, the two great Sanyasi rose, and the Parmahansa, addressing his disciples, said: "I accept Dayanand's faith, you also do as I do."

TOUR IN THE N.W.P. - OUDH, BIHAR AND DEHRADOON

Having done with the Kumbha Fair Swami Dayanand, in response to an invitation received, left for and arrived at Dhradoon on 14th April, 1879. the place was a Sanitorium, and the Swami was anything but unwilling to lose an opportunity which, while it would enable him to attend to the interests, of prachar in a new locatlity, would give him a chance to recoup his health. He reached Dehradoon so weak that he had to be helped to get up to answer the calls of nature, and these calls were frequent and sudden, coming when he was engaged in conversation.

The exhaustion consequent on the frequency of motions was so great that for two or there days public preaching had to be gone without, and the updesh to be addressed to a small number of select gentlemen. When, after all, the number of motions seemed to be decreasing, and the strength returning, the Swami had notices issued, announcing his lectures. The lectures delivered at a European Lady's Bungalow, where the Swami had put up, drew large audiences.

Offending an European Missionary

In one of these which was on the "Existence of God"' the Swami commented freely on the Biblical idea of the Deity. Doctor Morrison, a Padri Colonel and there other Europeans were among the listeners. The Missionary was deeply offended at the Swami's strictures, and, on the termination of his speech, got up in a passion and explained: "The Pandit Sahib has done nothing but kick up dust, hiding his Vedic Faith in that dust." After giving utterance to these words, he began to dispose of the objections which the Swami had, both directly and indirectly brought against the Christian conception of God.

The Swami listened to him patiently and perfectly unmoved, and, after he had done speaking, rose to reply. This was too much for the irate Missionary, and, in the excess of his rage and disappointment, he commence interrupting the speaker every second. The other European gentlemen at last could not help remonstrating with the Doctor on his strange conduct observing that the lecturer was proving his contention in temperate language and in a perfectly rational manner, and that the Doctor should give him the same patient hearing as he himself had been accorded when speaking. This only added fuel to the fire, and, in angry tones, he answered: "I am replying to the man in a proper way. If you thing my answer is not proper, you had better go and join him." Saying this, he turned his back upon the crowd and disappeared!

After he had gone, Mr. Palmer and Mr. Cartlaine, two of the European gentlemen still present, approached the Swami and wished to have some talk with him in private. The Swami agreeing to this a conversation ensued between the parties in the verandah of the bungalow. But he had hardly made a commencement when Mr. Bose, Master, Mission High School, came edging in and began speaking in favor of the Bible. This interruption and intrusion was unwelcome to Mr. Palmer and Mr. Cartlaine. And the discussion took place between the latter gentleman and Mr. Bose, and it lasted till midnight.

It was not only the Christians that had taken umbrage at the Swami's remarks, the Muhammadans and Brahmo Samajists also were in a state of great excitement, for the Puranic conception of God as the Brahmanic, had not been left unexamined and uncommented upon by the apostle of the Vedic Faith. The Mussalmans (Muslims) in particular looked desperate, and it was feared that the thatch-work of he bungalow would be set on fire. But better counsels seemed to have prevailed, and the night passed off peacefully. On the following day, however, a very large number of Muhammadans came hurrying into the bungalow, in none of the best of moods, but soon cooled down and there was no disturbance. After a short time spent in discussing the conditions in view of a probable shastrarth which however, never came off, the retired.

The Swami delivered nine lectures in all a Dehradoon. These and the labor entailed in other ways brought on a relapse, and the motions again commenced. Not liking to make a longer stay at Dehradoon, the Swami left for Saharanpur on 30th April, 1879, and it was some two months after his departure from this station that an Arya Samaj came to be established here. One of the members was a Muhammadan gentleman, and he is still a follower of the Vedic religion. Ever since his conversion, he has called himself Alakhdhari.

At Meerut accompanied by Madame Blavatsky and Colonel Olcoot

At Sharanpur the Swami halted only for two days, and then in company with Madame Blavatsky and Colonel Olcott, who were waiting for him there, he left for Meerut, arriving there on 3rd May 1879. the Swami's first installment of updesh during his present visit to Meerut was a lecture on the "Existence of God."

At the conclusion of this lecture he said a few words about Colonel Olcott and Madame Blavatsky also. On his resuming his seat, Colonel Olcott made a short speech in English, suited to the occasion. Next day the Colonel's lecture proper came off. Ti gave some account of America, dealt with the tenets of Christian religion, and set forth the aims and objects of the society which Madame Blavatsky and her friends had established.

He stated, in words clear and unmistakable, that they had come to India accepting the Swami as their guru and guide. After the substance of the Colonel's lecture had been given to the audience in Urdu, the Swami spoke a few words in connection with what had been said by the lecturer, and Madame Blavatsky also said something. The meeting broke up in a very happy mood.

A grand feast given to the Americans at the station and they left for Bombay on 7th May, 1879, the Swami, however, stayed her up to the 25th of the month, on which date he left for Aligarh, proceeding thence, in company with Thakur Bopal Singh and Thakur Manna Singh, to Chhalesar, there to place himself under the treatment of a competent physician and take a little rest.

AT MURADABAD

Leaving Chhalesar on 3rd July, 1879, the Swami arrive at Muradabad anything but improved in health. This was his second visit to the place. The Arya Samaj established here during his first visit had ceased to exist, and a new one had to be established on a firm footing, and such a one came on 20th July, 1879. The orthodox priests gave out that the Samajists had eaten the leavings of the Swami, and the idle rumor proved so mischievous that the Biradiries commence persecuting all who had embraced the Vedic Religion.

The weak-minded left the Samaj, but there were others who were not in the least move by the threats indulged in by their enemies. Munshi Indramani, the great Arabic and Persain Scholar, who had been a member of the defunct Samaj, was nominated President of the present one; Kanwar Parmanand and Thakure Indra Singh were appointed Secretaries; Sahu Shyam Sundar and Raja Jaggan Nath, Treasurer and Librarian, respectively. In addition to these, the Samaj had 38 members.

though the Swami stayed for 27 days at Muradabad he could deliver only three lectures during the period. Dysentery had robbed him of his strength, and he found it rather irksome to work. One of the lectures was delivered in the Cantonment, under the presidency of the Collector, on Rajniti (political wisdom). The collector was highly pleased with the remarks which fell from the speaker's lips on the subject and on the termination of the speech spoke of him in very high terms.

The well-wishers of the Swami at Muradabad finding how weak he was, placed him under the treatment of a Vaid, summoned specially for the purpose from Badaon., but the Vaid's medicines did him no good. At last the European physician, Dr. Dane was called in. His treatment proved highly beneficial, and before long the Swami was restored, evidently, to perfect health. On the completion of the recovery, Rs. 200 were offered to the Doctor, but the good man refused to receive any remuneration, observing that he could not accept anything from one who was laboring for the good of humanity.

A remark which fell from theSwam's lips at Muradabad, no doubt as a protest against words, intentionally or unintentionally uttered by some one, ought to yield a lesson to al who are, or who may become, members of the Arya Samaj. Addressing the Samajists the Swami said:

"It is wrong for anyone of you to say that you believe in the religion of Dayanand; what you should say instead is, that your religion is Vedic."

BADAON

A Sabhasad of the Badaon Samaj had come over to Muradabad to take the Swami to Badaon, and although the Swami was still weak, he did not like in the interests of reform, to disappoint the gentlemen who wished to see him so much. He reached Badaon on 30th July, 1879, and stayed there till 13th August, lecturing almost daily. The City Pandits one day waited upon him, and a discussion took place between himself and them on the "Nature of God, Incarnation, and the right to study the Vedas."

The Pandits repeating the well-known mantra of the Yajurveda - Sahasra Shrisahpursha, etc. declared that God, having so many heads, etc., was not merely incorporeal, and that He could incarnate Himself at will. The Swami's reply explained the true meaning of the mantra, saying that there were in the all-pervading God innumerable heads, innumerable eyes, innumerable feet, and so on. Similarly, he brought forward various arguments, proving that Divine incarnations were an impossible thing, and he quoted authorities showing how the Vedas were meant for entire mankind and not for any particular class.

The Salono festival came off while the Swami was yet at Badaon. Seeing the Brahmans going form house to house with red thread and asking largesses the Swami sorrowfully remarked:"Ignorance has brought about the extinction of all our sankars. This festival had for its object the raksha (protection) of Vidyarthis (students), and the enforcement of righteous practice. But today all men, old and young, are tying the red thread round their wrists!"

AT BEREILLI - THE SHASTRARTH

From Badaon the Swami repaired to Bereilli (14th August, 1879), where he became a guest of Lala lachhmi Narayan, Treasury Clerk. His lectures commenced, and they were largely attended, the local European officials and the lical Missionaries often forming par to the audience. One of the lectures was on the Puranas and similar other books. Mr. Edwards, the Commissioner, Mr. Reid, the Collector, and the Rev. Mr. Scott were present.

So long as the Puranas were being exposed, the European gentlemen felt delighted and went into rears of laughter; but when the turn of the Bible came, and the birth of Christ and similar other mysteries where commented upon, the became sober and serious, and not unoften frowned. According to Lala Munshi Ram, Editor-in-Chief of Pandit Lekh Ram's Life of Swami Dayanand, the Commissioner, shortly after the lecture was over, sent for Lala lachhmi Narayan and told him to warn the Pandit not to be very strong in his language; "for," said he, "if the ignorant Hindus and Muhammadans get excited, the lectures of your Swami Pandit will be stopped." The treasury Clerk in hesitation and fear carried the message to the Swami, but while he was trying to express himself in a round-about fashion, not knowing how his communication would be received, the Swami grasping his meaning burst out laughing, and bade the Lala be easy. The evening lecture for the day was on "the Nature of the soul."

In importance of truth, the Swami observed:

"People say - Don't give expression to truth, the Collector will be displeased, the Commissioner will be annoyed, and the Government will make you suffer? O ye simple ones! Let the Chakravarti Raja himself be displeased, if he will, I will give expression to truth alone." and then reading a passage from the Upanishad, which says that the soul defies the attack of fire, water, weapon and of everything else material, however subtle, he resumed in a voice of thunder:

"This body of mine is perishable, and nothing can be more ridiculous for me than to commit acts of unrighteousness for the preservation thereof. Whoever wishes may destroy it. But show me a warrior who claims that he can destroy my Soul. So long as such a warrior is not forthcoming in the world, so long I am not prepared even to think that I shall suppress truth."

The Rev. Mr. Scott had been regular in his attendance at the Swami's lectures from the first, but one day he did not put in an appearance. The Swami, who used to call him by the name of Bhagat Scott; asked those around, about the cause of the Missionary's absence. The reply was that it was a Sunday, and the Missionary had to attend the Church. Upon this the Swami said that since the Bhagat had not come, he should himself go and see him in the Church. So in the company with some tow or three hundred men he walked off to the sacred building.

When he entered the edifice, the Reverend gentleman, who had but just finished his sermon, came down at the sight of him from the pulpit and conducted him to it, offered him the seat there, and requested him to say something. The Swami complied, and, without taking the preferred seat, spoke fa a few minutes on "Man-worship."

The Missionaries of Bereilli came to the determination of holding a discussion with the Swami, and it was at last settled that is should come off on 25th august, 1879. The subjects to be taken up were:

- 'Transmigration of Souls,' the Swami speaking for, and the Rev. Scott against.
- The doctrine of 'Incarnation,' the Rev. gentleman upholding, and the Swami refuting;
- 'Forgiveness of Sin,' (the attitude of the parties in this case being the same as in respect of the doctrine of Incarnation).

The discussion came off in the building of the local Library; in the presence of large gathering, most of the gentry and nobility of the town being among them.

Debate with Christianity on Transmigration of Souls

As agreed upon, the doctrine of the Transmigration of Souls was taken up first.

Swami ~ "The inherent qualities, activities and tendencies of the Soul are eternal, and the divine, attributes, Justice, mercy , etc., are also eternal. Whoever does not believe this but holds that the Soul and its attributes, etc., are born and accidental, he must also concede that they are perishable.

And he must furnish satisfactory and convincing proofs, to himself and others, in respect of the origin and cause of the Soul and its attributes, etc.; for the birth of an effect in the absence of a cause is absolutely impossible. (The fact is, that the good and bad actions of the Soul, by virtue of their regularity of succession, are eternal, and the Deity, to be true to His nature, metes out, rewards and punishments for the same). And be it known that it is impossible for the Soul to taste of pleasure or pain, except through a body, be it gross, or subtle or elemental.

This being the case, the soul must assume a body over and over again, for a free agent is ever doing new actions, and these accumulate and go on forming new destinies (Prarabha). Were a person to contemplate this world with eye of knowledge, the laws of nature in operation and the Pratayaksha and other parmanas would soon convince him that the doctrine under discussion is true. Only think that Monday, i.e., to day, comes over and over again; the months, the days and nights also are perpetually recurring. The wheat-seed that is sown, reproduces itself in continual succession.

Rev. Scott - "The teaching that is being now offered to us, means that we are to believe that all the Souls that there are, are being constantly born, sometimes in the body of man, sometimes in that of a bull, sometimes in that of a monkey and anon in those of worms and insects. But this teaching is being gradually repudiated by the enlightened communities.

The ancient Egyptians originally believed in the doctrine of transmigration, but subsequently they gave it up. Similarly, the Greeks, the Romans and the English at the outset believed in it and abandoned it in the end.....My question to the Pandit is, what are the arguments in support of this doctrine? When any specially remarkable proofs are given in support of the doctrine, I shall raise objections in refutation of the doctrine. In the meantime, I have to ask a few questions in connection with what has been said, and they are:

- Are Souls other than that of God also from ever?
- Shall we ever be free from birth?
- As regards your contention that all that we see in the world, is there as punishment, it may be asked: Is re-birth only for punishment, or does it proceed from some other cause?
- Another question is: Is the Deity always sagun or does He become nirgun also? Is this perpetual rebirth the result of a special exertion of His power, or is it traceable to the operation of some natural law? - some such law, for instance, as regulates the growing of a seed, the ripening of a fruit, or the coming down of rain, etc.?

Swami Dayanand ~ "Three things are eternal: God, the Material cause of the universe, and the Soul. There will never be freedom from birth. Re-birth is for punishments as well for rewards. God is always sagun as well as nirgun. His natural law is only this, that He punishes or rewards, in compliance with the dictates of His absolute justice, everyman in proportion to the amount of sin or righteous action committed or performed. The admission on the part of the Padri Sahib that the doctrine of re-birth was originally believed in by his nation proves that it was an article of faith n all lands in ancient times.

As to his assertion that every community that is progressing in civilization is gradually abandoning the doctrine, I would put him the question - Are all ancient things false or are some of them true also? And further, Is modern teaching true in all its entirety, or is there something untrue in it too? If the Padri Sahib should assert that the old teaching is not fit to be believed in, then the teaching of the Old Testament - the Pentateuch, etc., as well as that of the New Testament being old, when contemplated in connection with the present age, should no longer be believed in now, does not prove the thing to be true or otherwise....

"As to the Padri Sahib's words, that I should furnish proofs in support of the doctrine of Transmigration of Souls or rebirth, I got the reporters to write down at the outset that the actions, etc., of the Soul, and the attributes of justice, etc. of God are eternal. If the doctrine of Karma is to be rejected, then how would you account for God's creating in this world the wise side by side with the obtuse, the poor and indigent side by side with princes? For, doing such thing as a mere matter of whim savors of partiality, and partiality on the part of the Deity would utterly defeat the ends of His justice. When action has fruit, God is certainly just and otherwise: he never commits an act of injustice."

Rev. Scott. - "According to the assertion of Panditji all the Souls are eternal. This being the case, there is no difference in the eternity of the Souls and that of God; in other words, two existences are eternal, which, in away, means, that there are two Gods. My objection is, that this teaching is totally oppose to what is taught in the Old Testament - Pentateuch and the Gospel, and I want to inquire, in what teaching there is greater comfort: whether in the consciousness that our Souls will keep wandering, through eternity, in a state of bewilderment - sometimes in the bodies of oxen, sometimes in those of monkeys, sometimes in the repulsive frames of worms and insects, and occasionally in tenements of higher type, in a never-ending succession; or whether it is more consoling to believe that people who are striving after righteousness and do become pure, will, at last, reach a resting-place, where they will be safe form re-birth and secure from all suffering.....How, again, can God be nirgun and sagun both at the same time - with attributes and without attributes? What thing is there that is wholly destitute of properties or attributes?

"If (according to this position of yours) God does not possess the attribute of justice, how He exercise this attribute....? Moreover, if re-birth is for punishment, what punishment can there be in being made to be born again? The monkey, for instance, does not know what sins he committed (that brought down his soul into the frame of a monkey). Similarly a Padri or a Pandit, coming to assume the repulsive shape of a worm or insect, has really no punishment inflicted upon him, for it is wholly unknown to him what sins he had commitied. Has anybody ever been able to remember, or can he remember, that he was a monkey at such and such a time, or that he was a jackal on such and such a occasion? When nobody in the whole world is conscious of ever having passed through such bodies, how can re-birth serve as punishment in the case of nay one whatsoever? We believe that pain is sometimes for punishment and sometimes not."

Swami Dayananand ~ "The fact that both (God and Soul) are eternal, does not make them equal so long as they are not equal in their attribute, powers, and so on. As it is, God is infinite, the Soul is finite; God is omniscient, and the Soul is partially knowing; God is ever pure and in a state of salvation, the Soul is only occasionally pure and sometimes in bondage and sometimes free; this being the case, both cannot be equal.

"The fact that a thing is opposed to the teachings of the Bible, does not prove that, if really true, it is false. For in the Old Testament, etc., the things that are true have, through delusion, been often declared as false, and vice versa. The teaching of that book alone can be true, in which from its beginning to its end not a single untruth is to be found. Such a book is nowhere to be found in the world except the Veda, of Divine Origin, because the teachings of the Veda alone fits in with the attributes, actions and nature of God. ..God, by virtue of His own attributes, such as omniscience, etc., is sagun, and He is nirgun when viewed as destitute of the properties of unconsciousness matter and of the characteristics of the Soul, - such as birth, death, doubt, delusion, ignorance, and so on. From what has been said, it follows as something indisputable, that there is nothing in the world which is not sagun and nirgun at the same time. "When the sin committed by the soul exceeds the amount of merit (punya), it has to assume the body of a monkey, etc. when its merits and demerits are equal, it is born as man; and when merit exceeds demerit, it appears in the world as a sage, etc."

Rev. Scott - "Not all the ancient teaching is false, nor is the new teaching true in all its entirety. But when enlightened communities, after prolonged though and reflection, give up a thing as false, the proof is conclusive that it is false. The Old Testament is not all new compared to the Vedas. It does not at all speak of re-birth. the point at issue at this time is not whether the teachings of the Old and the New Testament is or is not false. For all that, however, the fact is insignificant that while civilized communities are firm in their belief in the Old and the New Testament, the Hindus, in proportion, as they are advancing in education, are abandoning the Vedas. If necessary, I could cite a thousand instances. If, it be asserted that all His actions are good, then where is the impossibility that the Soul also, through His grace, be so fructified as not to go down into the bodies of monkeys and jackals. As is written in our sacred Book, man has to die only once, and after that he is to be regenerated (for everlasting life).

"As regards nirgun and sagun, I have no faith in the explanation which the Swami has given of the words. Nirgun does not imply in a thing the existence of gunas. When God is nirgun, He cannot be sagun, and the case being such, who arranges for births then? I ask again: if the Soul's re-birth is for punishment, it ought to be in a position to remember why it is being punished, otherwise the purpose of punishment is utterly defeated. I inquire again, Why it is that nobody remembers that he was a monkey or a jackal in his previous birth?"

Swami Dayanand"As to the first question of the Padri Sahib, the Soul is alpagya (possessing partial knowledge, etc.), and hence it cannot remember thing connected with the previous birth or births. The Padri Sahib ought to ask himself, 'Why do I put such a question?' For even in the present birth, a person cannot remember things connected with the first five years of his age. And when a person is in sound sleep, he cannot remember even a single thing connect with his waking-hours. And from perceptions of an effect one may be sure about the cause of that effect; the wise without an exception, concede that such is the law.

"When the fruit of merit and demerit (pap-punya) is clearly observable in the world in the form of happiness and suffering, of elevation and degradation how can one deny the existence of cause - the actions of previous birth, of which all these are the result?

"I can site the names of hundreds of men who have told me themselves - the author of the Bible in India and other scientific men of the present day, that they have given up believing in the Bible. Colonel Olcott and others also say that they do not follow the teaching of the Bible. An our educated people - F/A.'s, B.A.'s, M.A.'s, LL.D's thousands of them have no faith in the Bible, and they are all educated. This will show that the illustration the Padri Sahib gave in the interests of the Bible, does not meet the requirements of the case. There is no birth of God, for He is infinite and all-pervading, and no material frame can contain Him. He is ever in a state of salvation, and never does aught of which bondage is the result."

Rev. Scott - "The illustration of a child which Pandit gave, asserting that (when grown up) he cannot remember anything, is false, for a child does remember something at least. And the question that naturally suggests itself in this connection is, since our Souls are from eternity and since, like the child, we have become grown-up (through the lapse of years), why should not we remember something like him? But in point of fact we remember nothing. This argument deserves consideration.

"It is impossible that, being from eternity, we should have, on assuming a body, forgotten everything. And re-birth in such a case can serve no end. And a regards sleep, it appears from the (Swami's) reply that things connected with sleep are remembered. Some people hit upon great idea in sleep. Here I want to bring forward a strong objection. This teaching or re-birth encourages the commission of sin. For people say to themselves, - 'Let us do whatever we like, it will be some time before we suffer for it, and after all, a desirable kind of re-birth may fall out lot. And they further way to themselves (in their helplessness), "This succession of births is everlasting, what are we to do?" We do admit that there must be some reason for the suffering which comes to people in the world. Sometimes it is sent to the wicked as punishment, and sometimes to the wise that hey may have training of different kinds."

Swami Dayanand ~ "By citing the example of a child, I meant to say that the pleasure or pain which he enjoys or suffers, he cannot re-call to memory of himself; he remembers it occasionally when reminded of it by somebody else.

"And the inherent qualities of the soul remain ever unchanged, it is only the accidental ones that increase or decrease. Hence the Souls is always the same, but the stock of its knowledge and information grows and grows after the fifth year (from the date of its birth) has expired. If anyone were to ask the Padri Sahib or myself now, What did you talk with such a one ten years ago? Can you re-call the words and the letters you sued in their proper order?" the reply will be, that 'we can't remember or reproduce what we said, correctly'.

"If the Souls are not from ever, where have they come from? Although people do not know, for certain, what and what crimes this and that prisoner committed, yet they can infer that it must be for some crime or other that the prisoners in question are in jail, and they can take the lesson from the condition in which the prisoners are, that they (people) should never do what the prisoners did, as otherwise their state would be that of the prisoners. The Padri Sahib has not grasped my meaning. I spoke of Sushupti, and not of the ordinary sleep in which one dreams. Sushupti is profound slumber in which nothing is remembered and no idea is hit upon or re-called. Those who have faith in no re-birth, their teaching increases sin in the world, for 'there is not re-birth,' say they, 'let us do what pleases us.'

"And this postponement of the case of a departed non-believer in birth is something hard and unreasonable. His departure from this world takes place to-day, and his Soul remains in custody uncared for till the day of judgment. The door of the Court is shut, and God is sitting idle. The Soul that goes into Hell, is Hell's time to come, and the actions performed by the Soul are limited, but the rewards and punishments meted out for the same are eternal in duration! This is very unjust of God. And suffering, in the absence of hope, cannot generate man. What is the cause of suffering? If suffering is sent to man as a warning, then it is for his good, but the lesson from that suffering comes only through wisdom. As to the assertion of Padri Sahib, that the Souls will enjoy bliss in a certain place for ever, will he specify the place and its geographical position?"

Rev. Scott - "As to the assertion that some qualities are retained by the Soul and some disappear and that hence it is that things in connection with re-birth are not remembered, I maintain that since some qualities are retained by the Soul, we should remember something at least in connection with our previous birth. if I had a talk with Panditji somewhere during the current year, I could not fail to remember some things at least. The illustration of sleep is out place, for if things are sometimes not remembered in sleep, they are still very often remembered. This being the case, why don't we remember things connected with our previous birth? the example of jail that ha been given, that too does not meet the requirements of the case, for it implies that punishment has only one object. In point of fact, punishment has two-fold object, - the improvement of the sufferer and to serve as a warning to the spectators. But re-birth furnishes warning only to the spectators: the man show is suffering the punishment, does not know at all why he is suffering it.

As to the question where the Souls have come from, the civilized nations of the present day hold that just a seed proceeds from a seed, a tree from a tree, and nobody says that the tree existed previously, even so is one Soul born of another Soul, and one body of another body.

For all this, however, it is incomprehensible in what particular manner the body comes into existence, and in what the Soul. But is not a fact that the Soul which occupies a body at present was in some other body before; it of recent birth. And when the Soul departs from this world, it will be dealt with impartially, according to the character of it actions. Hence God is not unjust: on the contrary, the fact proves Him just. As to the question where the Souls stay, we don't pretend to be omniscient that we should specify the locality where bliss is to be enjoyed. The almighty God can give the Soul a resting-place, what does it signify if we know it or not?

Swami Dayanand ~ "There is a stock of accidental qualities present in childhood, but it is small; the essential qualities of the Soul, however, are always the same, never varying. This fact the Padre Sahib has not been able to thoroughly grasp. To illustrate, the heat that comes into the water from fire, that is naimittic or accidental, but the heat that is in fire, that is essential or inherent (swabhavik) to it. The essential qualities or attributes of the Soul neither increase nor decrease, but the accidental qualities do increase and decrease. As to the observation of the Padri Sahib that although the sight of the prisoners in jail produces a fear in the minds of the spectators, warning them not to do what brought the prisoners in their present sorry plight, this lesson is not at all conveyed to the souls that are made to be re-born (by the Deity), for these Souls do not remember what they are suffering for, I beg to say that when people can infer a cause form an effect, why can't a sufferer draw a similar inference in regard to his sufferings.

"Suppose that a physician gets an attack of fever, and an ignorant man also. The physician, by the assistance of his knowledge, will know the cause of the fever, but the ignorant man will be unable to hit upon the right cause. Both however, are conscious of suffering, nor can even the ignorant man fail to conclude from his suffering at least this much, that intemperance or imprudence in some way or another has given him the fever. Hence the punishment he is suffering is for his future benefit. For he says to himself; 'If I do anything objectionable, the result of this will be pain to me, as it is to such and such a one.'

"If the Souls are born from Souls and bodies from bodies, the it's not God that is your Maker. This shows that what you say is far from being true. And, according to your theory, the Souls and bodies that came to be in the beginning, from what Souls and bodies did they proceed? If you assert that the proceeded from God, then God must be like unto horses, trees and stones, for an effect is always of the nature and character of its causes. And then effect is always of the nature and character of its cause. And then the postponement of the departed Soul's case for an indefinite period. The suffering with which this delay must be fraught must far exceed the pain that could come from actual punishment. If the Soul is to undergo the suffering inseparable from a postponement of its case, for what actions then can it be sent to Heaven or condemned to Hell? - there are virtually no actions to receive a reward or punishment for.

"If you are not omniscient, why do you contend that there is no re-birth? all this does not prove your theory of single birth, but does prove the doctrine of re-birth."

The Debate Continues on 'Incarnation'

The discussion on the 2nd day, 26th August, was on 'Incarnation.' The opening speech was from the Missionary, and the upshot of what he said was, that whoever pretended that he knew everything about God was in error, and such being the case, no one could reasonably maintain that God could not assume a body if it so pleased Him. In reply the Swami observed that in saying what he had the Padri Sahib had done anything but proved his contention, which was, that God does incarnate Himself. The real questions that should be answered were:

- 'what necessity is there for God to take a body?
- Is it or is not, His pleasure subject to any restriction?
- Is He incorporeal or corporeal?
- Is He all-pervading (witnessing all), or is He confined to a particular locality, etc.?"

The missionary 's answer, stated the popular belief as to the omnipresence or all-pervading character of God, adding that no one could positively say what Divine omnipresence really meant. What he (the Missionary) affirmed and maintained was that God did incarnate Himself, He passed in all His entirety into the body assumed, and yet remained outside of it also, for He could do it, and there was nothing to be wondered at this. To entertain the idea that the assumption, by God, of a body was something that detracted from His greatness and glory, was to labor under misapprehension. To this the Swami made answer, that if God was all-pervading, His entering a body or coming out of it was an impossibility. The Missionary (he said) had not shown how it was necessary for God to assume a body. As to the assertion that God had made man in His own image, it was worth knowing in whose image He had made other creatures, - lower animals, etc.

There were further questions and replies, till at last the Missionary leaving the point of issue remarked that the incarnation of Jesus Christ fulfilled a Divine purpose, which (he said) was fully evident from the fact that the Bible was being gradually accepted by the civilized nations. He added: "The Bible has been translated into hundreds of languages, and millions of copies of this book are printed and distributed. Who says 'I don't believe in this book?

And Finally on "Forgiveness of Sins"

" Hence it is clear that an incarnation of God was possible. Belief in such an incarnation of God was nothing oppose to reason: on the contrary it was only proper that such an incarnation should take place. The great necessity of such a thing coming to pass he (the Padri) had described, and the words of the Bible were true!

The Third discussion on the subject selected for the purpose came off on 27th August, 1879. the contention of the Missionary was, that Divine forgiveness of sin was possible under certain circumstance, for instance, when a man came to have faith in Jesus Christ; while the Swami maintained that forgiveness of sins was impossible, for to hold the contrary view was virtually to declare that God was the encourager of sin in the world. But, indeed, God was no such thing. Hemetedout punishments and rewards for all actions in all their fullness.

SHAHJAHANPUR

From Barelli the Swami went to Shahjahanpur, where he satyed till 17th September, 1879, delivering during the period six lectures. The updesh, however, was daily given, the enquires coming in large numbers. The orthodox sent for and prevailed upon one Pandit Angad Shastri, who had at one time served as a teacher in the Pililbhit School on a salary of Rs 15 a month, to hold a shastrarth with the Swami.

The Pandit proved an ideal orthodox disputant. He would not come forward, declaring that the conditions of the would be shastrarth were unsatisfactory, and that till they were amended and altered so as to be perfectly acceptable to his friends and brethren, the shastrarth could not commence. What the Pandit seemed to be rally striving for was the bringing about a publicjalsa, in which the mischievous element at his beck and call should have a chance to display their activities and should accomplish, by dint of noise and abuse and force, that which he had not the learning and the brains to achieve in a fair contest.

The Swami perceived his aim and would not give him a chance to carry out nefarious purpose, insisting that the conditions of the contemplated discussion should be, in an equal degree, cognizant of the interests of both the parties. The Pandit's letters to the Swami were generally full of unparliamentary expressions, but the Swami could bear fouler language than that, and his replies were always thoroughly courteous in tone. Of course, the shastrarth never came off.

It was at Shahjahanpur that the Swami conceived the idea of writing books of a purely educational value, and it was also here that he gave the idea a practical shape.

Shahjahanpur already boasted an Arya Samaj, of which Lala Bakhtawar Singh, Editor and Proprietor, The Arya Darpan, was the Secretary, and the Swami left the station for Lucknow on 18th September, 1879.

AT FURRAKHABAD

The Swami did not stay long at Lucknow. After a week's halt during which the updesh given die not appear to have led to any definite and tangible results, he left for Furrakhabad. An Arya Samaj already existed here, but it was markedly strengthened by the Swami's presence. The members, with a view to securing permanency to the religious institution which had been founded in their midst, came forward with liberal donations for the purpose, each individual subscription ranging from Rs. 200 to 1,000. Over and above this they subscribed Rs. 1,000 in the aid of the Veda-Bhashya. A new building having been secured for the use of the Samaj, the Swami delivered his lecture on 5th October, 1879, in the premises of the same. We may be sure that the orthodox Pandits were in none of the most enviable of moods at finding thousands of rupees going in to the coffers of the Samaj, and at seeing that Body making itself perfectly at home in their midst.

When the Swami was about to leave Furrakhabad, the champions of idolatry had as many as 25 questions, duly written and subscribed, sent to the Swami for an answer. It was a clever move on their part. They thought that the Swami would not stop to answer them, and if such a thing actually came to pass, they would have a chance of proclaiming with the beatof drums that the Swami had given them the slip! The unexpected, however, came to pass. The Swami answered their questions on the 7th October, and the Dharma Sabha has to gulp down its disappointment as best as it could.

One of the questions was: "Can a Muhammadan or Christian join your faith, and are you and your followers prepared to eat the food cooked by his hands?" To this the Swami thus replied: "My religion is none; whoever follows the commandments of the Vedas, the same is a follower of the Vedic Religion. Have you, falling into darkness, come to identify Dharma with eating and drinking, with answering the calls of nature, with wearing shoes, dhoti, angrakha, etc.? Listen and reflect, such things are mere usages and customs, peculiar to one country or another?"

While at Farrukhabad, the Swami assisted at many Yajnopavit sankars, and it is noteworthy that his lectures here were frequently attended by English Officials also.

MIRZAPUR

Starting from Furrakhabad on 8th October, 1879, and making brief hlats at Cawnpur and Prayag, the Swami arrived at Mirzapur on 23rd October, 1879, and lectured there for dour or five days. He was far from being in the best of health yet, but for all that, the updesh was given without fail, and religious conversation with the enquirers was being daily pushed on. A Samaj already existed here, doing by itself and others what it was in duty bound to do.

The Swami left Mirzapur for Danapur (Behar) on 30th October, 1879, in company with some members of the Danapur Samaj, who had come to fetch him. He delivered on different subjects some fourteen lectures during the seventeen or eighteen days he stayed there. the lectures were attended by the Missionaries and by other European gentlemen also. Being full of criticism on the Hindu, Muslim and other creeds, they created considerable excitement, and threats of vengeance were forthcoming freely. A Muhammadan youth, thrown into a state of frenzy by the reformer's comments, warned the Swami not be so free with his creed, but the only reply which the Swami gave to the menace was that in is public lecture when he said:

"So long as Muhammadans had their way, they spread their religion by the sword, but now that India had a better Government and the people enjoyed the blessing of freedom of speech, there was no reason why men like him should not expose absurdities and abused, like rational men, with their tongue!"

At one of the lectures delivered on the teachings of the Bible, General Roberts, the Commander-in-Chief, with his staff, was present. The comments were as strong as ever. On the termination of the speech the General shook hand with the Swami, remarking: "When you can speak in this fashion on the Bible in our presence, you must care but little for others."

A Real Sanyasi will fear Nothing

The local Dharma Sabha, in its desperation, sent for its famous Pandit Chaturbhuj, to hold a shastrarth with the Swami. The Pandit obeyed the call, but he would not come forward, insisting that the shastrarth,if it was to take place, should take place in a building to be specified by the Dharma Sabha. The Swami suspected foul play, but at last he agreed. His suspicions proved to be true.

Pandit Chaturbhuj did not put in an appearance at al in this new building either, the Secretary of the Dharma Sabha only attending and declaring that he should speak in place of the Pandit. The Swami refused to have anything to do with him, on which that truly excellent man extinguished the lamp, and, giving admission to a large number of Muhammadans from the other entrance to the house, prepared to set upon the Swami and his companions, but he was playing a losing game. There was that in the voice of the Swami which sent terror into the hearts of the miscreants. The party forcing their way through the crowd emerged into the open, safe and sound, although the Dharma Sabha-followers and the Muslims in combination had sen after them showers of stones and bricks.

The Missionaries and other Europeans saw the Swami when he was comparatively at leisure. Mr. Jones one day urging an objection against the Arya Religion, on the ground that the Hindus observed chhut-chhat, the Swami replied:

"We do not believe that Dharma lies in eating or drinking with this or that man. All these things have to do with the usages and customs of a country or a nation. They have no bearing on the true Dharma. Those who are wise, they too will not infringe the national usages unnecessarily." At the same time, the Swami, in the course of further observations made on the point, assured the European that the real religion of the Hindus (Aryas) was not 'idol-worship.'

People were not wanting at Danapur, who would misrepresent the reformer through the press. One good man sent a telegram to the Indian Mirror, Calcutta, saying that the Swami had kicked an idol! But what sensible man could ever believe such idle and unfounded reports? The unbiased minds at Danapur gave the lie to the telegram by an increased faith in the Swami and in the true and enduring character of his mission. One person, who, through the fear of the priests and the biradiri, has not the moral courage to hear the Swami's updesh openly, one day waited upon him early in the morning, in a secluded spot, far from human habitation, when the Swami was returning from his "constitutional." Giving the Swami an insight into his inmost feelings, he touched his foot with his head, in spite of the Swami's declaration that it was useless doing so, and then went his way.

The Danapur Arya Samaj had now been in existence for over a year, having been established in April, 1878, when the Swami was yet in the Punjab. In fact, it was a development of the Hindu Sat Sabha, which the station had possessed for some time past.

AT BENARES

Returning to Mirzapur the Swami proceeded to Benares, which he reached on the 19th November, 1879. He stayed here for six months. During this period the Vedic press was established, and much was accomplished in connection with the Veda-Bhashya and other works on hand, nor was the updesh-work neglected. The orthodox Pandits were challenged to come forward for a discussion over again and again, but there was no response there was, however, no dearth of men the exact prototypes of excellent Pandit Shardha Ram, in Benares. One of these, by name Jugal Kishore, had a printed notice put up, saying that the gentlemen, whose names were given at the bottom of the notice, had waited upon Swami Dayanand, but finding that his conversation was oppose to the teaching of the Vedas and to the lessons which practices of men of righteous conduct yield, they thought of having their doubts removed by the Brahm Amrit Dahrshini Sabha. "The accordingly, (said the notice), waited upon the Sabha, and their doubts having been thoroughly removed by the same, they underwent and expiation by the advice of Pandit Jugal Kishore, and got rid of their sins by being face to face with the gods....."

In due course the notice came to be read at a meeting of the Bradm Amrit Darshini Sabha, and how far it was relished by that Body will be clear form the following article which appeared in the Arya Darpan, May, 1880:-

"Bawa Narian Singh, Member, Arya Samaj, Benares, asked Pandit Jugal Kishore to produce the men whose names appeared in the notice. The Pandit, livid with rage, answered that he should produce them at the next meeting of the Sabha,. But as the men referred to in the notice were merely creations of the Pandit's fancy, imagined into realities solely for the sake of amusement, where could he produce them from for the

Sabha? The Pandit was in a dilemma, and at last began to look out for and train stray lads to his purpose, telling them to accompany him and depose so-and-so before the Sabha. But who could accede to the Pandit's request in connection with such an ugly business? The very mention of the word Prayashchit is sufficient to frighten people out of their senses, the more so as the confession on a person's part that he performed a prayashchit gets him an ill-name. However, the Pandit made a shift to produce one man at the next meeting of the Sabha. When his name was asked, he said, it was Ram Krishn Doobe. (The Pandit must have put him to say that he was called Ram Krishn Doobe, but how long can one remember an assumed name? It slipped from the man's memory).

They next asked him, whether he had gone to the Swami? The reply was in the negative. This reply exposed Pandit Jugal Kishore's nefarious trick, and the people now asked him why he had got a false notice printed and circulated. The Pandit was red with anger and began to talk incoherently, uttering, among others, the words, 'he who ahs seen Dayanand's face, he is not from the seed of a Hindu!"

Upon this Bawa Narain Singh observed that at the Kashi shastrarth of Samvat 1926, there were thousands of Hindus present, among others, the Maharaja of Kashi, Pandit Balshastri, Swami Vishuddhanand, etc., and that the Pandit and virtually offered them a gross insult, in saying what he had.

"The result of this was that the Sabha, passing a resolution for the expulsion of Pandit Jugal Kishore, turned him out. The Pandit, when being expelled, raised a hue and cry, and mutual thrashing was about to commence; but God be thanked, matter did not take a serious turn, and all ended well." The Swami delivered at Benares some twenty lectures in the beginning of 1880. an Arya Samaj was established on 15th April, 1880, and it continues to exist down to the present day, having a fair Mandir of its won, the result, in a great measure, of the zeal and efforts of Rai Bahadur Surjan Das, Executive Engineer.

The Press was established largely by subscription, the members of the Arya Samaj contributing each a specific sum. As the contributions had been accepted on the distinct understanding that they should be considered as a loan, the money was in time returned to the donors. The late Lala Sain Das, however, who had contributed about Rs. 250, declined to receive back the sum, which anything but pleased the Swami, who insisted upon repayment, remarking that the donor could spend it in charity in some way or another.

AT MAINPURI

On May 5th, 1880, the Swami left Benares for Lucknow, where he preached for about two weeks and then left for Furrakhabad, staying there till 30th June. From Furrakhabad he went to Mainpuri, whence he departed to Meerut on 6th July, arriving there on the 8th, and five days after he had left Mainpuri, an Arya Samaj was established there (11th July, 1880.)

AT MEERUT

At Meerut the Swami came across Pandita Ramabai, who had purposely come there to see him. The Swami presented her with a copy of his works, and counseled her to preach the Vedic Faith to women, adding that if she had doubts on any doctrinal points, he would remove them and convince her of the truth of the doctrines.

The Pandita begged to be excused from following the counsel, though she did deliver some lectures on "Female Educaiton" at Meerut. When she was leaving the station, the local Samaj presented her with Rs. 125 in cash, and a full piece of cloth. Colonel Olcott and Madame Blavatsky also paid a visit to the Swami at Meerut. In the course of conversation with the Americans on "God," the Swami, on hearing their views on the subject and discovering that they were not prepared to change them under any circumstances, drew the line of demarcation between the Arya Samaj and the bold declaration of facts on his part led to the creation of a gulf between the two Bodies which has never been bridged, nor is likely to so long as the Theosophical Society does not give up, among other things, the atheism or materialism to which the Americans, in Swami's time, were so partial.

While at Meerut the Swami received a letter from Lala Nihal Chand, Resis, Requesting him to come to Muzaffarnagar. The Swami accepted the invitation and spent about a fortnight at Muzaffarnagar, delivering during the period, some ten lectures.

Professor's Monier William's view on the Sanskrit Language

It was from Meerut that the Swami indited a letter, in Sanskrit, to Shyamji Krishna Varma, assistanat Professor of Sanskrit at the Oxford University. This letter was published by Professor Monier Williams in an English paper, with his own comments. In this interesting letter the Professor said a great deal in praise of Sanskrit, declaring that it was the lingua franca of India, and that those who thought it was now a dead language, were laboring under a delusion. Could a language, he asked, be called 'dead' which was drawn upon to such and extent in the daily talk of the Indian people, and which was the invariable medium of commnunication among the learned of the land? To quote his own words:

"Some individuals entertain the idea that Sanskrit is no longer in use, while others think that it is on the decline. But can anybody justly consider a language defunct or extinct which still exists and is full of life, in which thoughts are exchanged and conversation is carried on, whose permanency gains strength from daily correspondence, and, whose living influence, as displayed from Hindukush down to Ceylon, in literary composition and in matters of religion, in enduringly complete?"

Speaking of Swami Dayanand, the Professor referred to an article published in the Athaeiem a year back in which the famous Scholar was mentioned as a person who, while was well-versed in the Classical Sanskrit of ancient days, was one who, by his denunciation of heresy, infidelity and idol-worship, had produced a commotion in all the modern religious sects of Aryavarta. The writer added:

"The Swami is a believer in the pure theism of the true religion of the Arya nation, and takes his stand upon the Vedas s the basis of his religious beliefs. The name of this generator and reformer is Swami Dayanand Saraswati, to whose eloquence of speech, faultless (or weighty) composition, I can myself bear witness."

To convince the readers of the Athaenium that he did not praise the Swami on the strength of second-hand evidence, the Professor informed them that he was present at a lecture of the reformer at Bombay, and further, that the Sanskrit letter, a translation of which now appeared in the paper, was fully worthy of the man whom he had occasion to hear in the Commercial Capital of India - a model letter, in the highest sense of the word model.

Never for a moment oblivious of the interests of his mission, the Swami did not forget to ask his pupil, among other things, if he was doing anything to disseminate the principles of the Vedic Religion among those he now came in contact with, had whether the attitude of his (Dayanand's) friends - Professor Monier Williams and Professor Max Muller, towards the Vedas and the Shastras, was the same as before. 'How do they like the Veda-Bhashya?' he further asked, and how far are they disposed to give encouragement of the interpretation of the contents of these works (Samhitas)? And is it true that the Theosophical Society, as a branch of the Vedic Religion, has been established in London?"

From Meerut the Swami went to Dhradoon, where he stayed up to 20th November, 1880, giving updesh throughout the period of his stay. The Muslims and Hindus kept back as usual, declaring, just to pass off time, that they could not come forward for a discussion till such and such terms were granted to them. A Missionary gentleman, however, came, but finding that argument was not his forte (when pitted against the Swami), he went his way.

From Dehradoon the Swami left for Agra, arriving there on 25th November, 1880. He stayed here for some three months and- a -half, the first series of his lectures ending on 22nd December. The result was that here also a Arya Samaj was established on 26th December, 1880. the second series of lectures commenced on 23rd January, 1881, and was continued during February. The orthodox Pandits bestirred themselves after their fashion, their leader, Chaturbhuj, making two men undergo Prayashchit. One of these men had broken in two his kanthi on hearing the Swami's updesh, and the other had committed the great sin of teaching Sanskrit to Aryas!

At Agra the Swami, at the request of the Archbishop, visited the local Cathedral, and had a long conversation with His Lordship.

At Agra ends the last tour of Swami Dayanand in Upper India.

THE ARYA SANMARG DARSHINI SABHA

While Swami Dayanand was a Agra, a Sabha, called the Arya Sanmarg Darshini Sabha, was established at Calcutta, with the object of having it decided and settled, once for all, by the most distinguished representatives of orthodoxy in the land (that could be got hold of for the purpose, of course), that Dayanand's views on Shradhs, Tiraths, Idol-worship, etc., were entirely unorthodox and unjustifiable. Sanskrit Scholars and Reises to the number of three hundred responded to the call of the Sabha, and a grand meeting, composed of the local men and of he outsiders, came off in the Senate Hall on 22nd. January, 1881.

It is significant that not one of the numerous distinguished Pandits present thought of suggesting or moving that the man upon whom the Sabha was going to sit in judgment, should also, in fairness, be summoned before the august tribunal, to be condemned or acquitted after he had been fully heard. It may be urged that the Sabha was not in a homor to acquit Dayanand under any circumstances, but still he should have been permitted to have his say before he was condemned. Surely, one man could be dealt with very well by assemblage so illustrious and so erudite. But the Pandits and their admirers were wise in their generation.

Dayanand, though one, had proved too many for a still more 'earned and august gathering at Benares. His powerful intellect and the still more powerful truth, which he was called upon to defend and advocate, had carried everything before them, and left the formidable and unique multitude opposed to him no other alternative than to resort to a mean trick if they would extricate themselves, from their most embarrassing position and make the ignorant mass believe that the victory had been theirs.

It was, thus, wholly inadvisable that Swami Dayanand should be present. "Lord! Who could miss the man when we are present?" must the great Pandits have said to themselves. Among the great ones in evidence and gracing the occasion, were:- Pandit Mahesh Chandra Nyyaratna, Pandit Tara Nath Vachaspati, Pandit Banke Bihari Lal of Cawnpur, Pandit Jamna Narayan Tiwari, Pandit Bindraban Sudarsdnachari, Shastri Ram Subramania of Jaunpur, Maharaja Jotindrao Nath Tagore, C.S.I., Maharaja Kanwal Krishna Bahadur Mukhopadhya, Junwar Debindrao Mulluck, Hon'ble Babu Krishna Lal paul, Babu Charu Chandra Mulluck, Lal Narain Das of Mathura, Rai Badri Das Lakhim Bahadur, Seth Jugal Kishore, seth Nahar Mal, etc. , etc.

The proceedings of the meeting opended by Pandit Mahesh Chandra Nyyaratna explaing the object of the Sabha, and laying before his brother Pandits the following questions for consideration;-

1. Are or are not the Brahmanas entitled to be as much believed in as the Samhita portion - the Vedas, and are or are not the other Smritis as much worthy of being accepted as the Manu Smriti is?

2. Are or are not we allowed, according to the Shastras, to worship Shiva, Vishnu, Durga, and other gods and goddesses; to perform the Shradhs, in honor of the departed ancestors; to reside at and bathe in Tiraths like the Ganges, living and bathing at Kurushetra, and other Tiraths and Kshetras?

3. Does not the word 'Agni' occurring in mantras like Agni mile prohitam, etc., mean God or Fire?

4. Are Agnihotra and other Yajnas performed for the purification of oar and water, or for obtaining heaven (swarga), etc.?

5. Is or is it not a sin to belittle the 'Brahmana portion of the Veda?'

Pandit Ram Subramania Shashtri replied to the questions, seriatim, and we give the substance of what he said:-

- 'In the Veda Samhita it is written that whatever Manu said, is worthy of acceptance; hence the Manu Smriti is worthy of acceptance then the Veda, which enjoins the acceptance thereof, will also become unworthy of acceptance. Dayanand Saraswati has accepted the Manu Smriti (as authoritative), and he ahs declared as such in his Satyarth Prakash also. And similarly, there are many arguments which prove that the Brahmana portion is fully as worthy of being believed in (i.e. is authoritative) as Samhita, and that the Vishnu, Yajanavalk and other Smritis are, in every way, on a level with the Manu Smriti.
- 'all these (worship of Shiva, etc.), are allowed in the Shastras. The worship, the establishing, etc., of the Shivalinga, according to the well-known shloka of the Purana, bear all the fruit attendant on worship (pujan). There are many other shlokas (the speaker cited these too) which say that the worship of Shiva, Vishnu, and Durga is allowed in the Shastras, and that whoever neglects the worship, commits a sin for which prayaschit has to be performed. The worship of idols also is supported by a passage in the Brahmanas. Dayanand is wrong in interpreting the passage as meaning that it speaks of the dwellings of the sages and of Brahmaloka, etc. As to Shradhs, the word pitriman occurs in the Vedas and it proves that Shradhs in honor of the departed are allowable.

The Smritis say that whoever say does not perform Shradhs in honor of the departed is born in the race of Chandals for thousands of generations. This shows that Shradhs and Tarpans are allowed both by Shruti and Smriti. And the Tiraths are mentioned in the Rigveda. It is said there that bathing in the Ganges etc., gets one heaven (swarga) and destroys one's sins in the Manu Smriti it is said that bathing in the Ganges and living at Kurukshetra is an expiation for lying.'

'The word Agni in such Mantra means Fire

- 'The object of the Yajnas is to secure Swarga to the Soul, and the performance of the same does obtain one Swarga.
- 'The Brahmanas being part and parcel of the Vedas to belittle them is to belittle the Vedas: in other words, it is a sin to speak disparagingly of the Brahamanas.'

7

Last Days and Death

Swami Dayanand comtemplated leaving Jodhpur at, or towards, the close of September, but, as we have already informed the reader, he was unable to do so before the next months had half expired, and we have further informed the reader that when he bade farewell to the Rathore sovereign and his people, he was in the very reverse of the best of health. Only five days after the letter, reproduced in English in the proceeding chapter, had been sent to Maharaja Pratap Singh, the Swami caught a bad cold, but it was, after all, nothing very serious, especially in the case of a person of the Swami's build and physigue, and the 28th and 29th September passed off without giving any indications of the fact that great, almost frightful sufferings were in store for the Swami, finally terminating in death.

He did not at all appear to be in any danger whatsoever, when, after his usual draught of milk, he retired to rest on the night of the 29th. He had not, however, slept much when he felt a violent pain in the region of the stomach, and a dull, heavy sensation in the chest, as if it was choked up with something which struggled to get out. To relive the pain he left his bed several times. And threw up matter thrice; but though he suffered much, he waked no one.

The violence of the pain abating at last, he thoroughly rinsed his mouth with water and went to sleep. The morning was far advanced when he rose on the following day (a very unusual thing for him), and as soon as he rose, he threw up again. He felt suspicious, and, as the painful heaviness was still present in the chest, and a feeling of utter uneasiness pervaded the whole frame, he thought he would repeat the practice which he had formerly resorted to with success. Drinking a good deal of water, he thrust his too fingers into his throat, and brought on vomiting again, being under the impression that if poison had got into the body, no matter how, it would be cast out, moreless, in this way. But there was little relief still. The Swami caused fragrant drugs to be thrown into the havan-kund, and drank a decoction of ajwain, (lighusticum ajwain) etc., but with no beneficial results. On the contrary, he became worse, the colic pains having commenced to add to his sufferings. Dr. Suraj Mal was at last called in, who administered some medicine that would stop vomiting, and also allay the patient's thirst. The medicine failed to do any good. The colic was as bad as ever, the breathing became rapid and painful, and there was coughing besides. Maharaja Pratap Singh, who heard of the illness late on the 30th, sent Dr. Ali Mardhan Khan to attend the Swami. The Doctor had the region of the abdomen tightly bandaged, and had the patient cupped on 1st October.

This relieved the cough a little, but failed to produce any desirable effect as far as the colic was concerned. On 2nd October, he administered some pills, and on the 3rd gave a purgative, but till 2 O'clock in the night there was not motion. At ten the motions commenced, and continued the whole night. By morning the Swami had thirty, nor did they cease during the day, and he was now so weak that with every motion he fainted. The case did not improve on the 5th, indeed he had now a hiccough in addition to be tormented with. Day after day of intense suffering passed. There was a constant looseness of the bowels, an unbearable pain in the pit of the stomach, frequent vomiting, and a continued hiccough and over and above all this, his face, throat, tongue, palate, forehead, etc., become covered with blisters.

On the 15th of October, Doctor Adam came to see the Swami by desire of His Highness. The Doctor evidently saw that the case was hopeless, and he advised the Swami's removal to Abu, observing that change of climate might do him good. The Swami, already disposed to leave Jodhpur, approved of the advice, and communicated his intention to the Maharaja. His Highness, on hearing the nature of the Swami's resolve, came in person to the great teacher's lodgings and besought him to postpone his departure, urging that he was not fit to move in such a condition, and that if he went away as he was, it would give the State and its Ruler a bad name. The Swami, however, was not be turned from his purpose, and the Maharaja had to ultimately agree. A sum of Rs. 2,500 was presented, and the 16the of October was fixed as the day of departure.

As the hour of departure drew near, the Maharaja with his brother, Maharaja Pratap Singh and other dignitaries of the State, made his appearance, to pay his respects to the Swami, and to see him off. Some royal tents, six camels, three chariots, one phaeton ere to accompany the Swami, who himself was to travel in a Palanquin, attended by a number of courtiers, on of these being Doctor Suraj Bhan. The parting moment came, and it was clear to al present that His Highness, as also his brother, was in real distress. Who could say how the disease would terminate and if His Highness's worst fears were realized and the illness had a fatal ending, neither he or his descendants could, for generations, hold up their heads when the sad event was mentioned in their presence. His Highness felt after th noble race from which he came.

What has not the true Rajput done and dared to prevent a slur being cast upon his fair name. His Highness with his own hands tied his own special belt round the Swami's waist, and mark his appreciation of the invaluable lessons he had received from the Swami and of the profound respects in which he held him by reason of his lofty virtues and his unique attainments, he walked some two hundred paces by the side of the palanquin before he eventually tool leave of its occupant.

The shades of the evening had already fallen, but in spite of the breeze, in spite of the fact that a pankha-coolee was incessantly fanning the Swami, in spite of his having a dripping cloth, in several folds, on his head, he felt as if he were on fire. After a whole night's traveling, the party reached, Ropat, where the next twenty hours were passed. On the 18th the Pali station was reached, and the tents were pitched near a Mandir, which turned out to be the dwelling of some Sanyasis. On hearing who had arrived all these came out, and touching the feet of the Swami retired. The Swami discovering that he was in the immediate vicinity of Sadhus and Sanyasis, caused his tent to be removed to a distance, to prevent his proving source of inconvenience to the individuals in question in any way.

A man was sent from this place to Ajmere to consult the local physicians, and to bring from there any medicine that the best native skill could suggest and prescribe for a case like the Swami's. The Ajmere Samaj consulted the well-known Yunani Hakim Pirji, and the medicine which he prescribed was got prepared without delay and handed over to the messenger, who rejoined the Swami at the Karachi station, hours before he had time to resume his journey, along the Abu Road, for the Mount Abu, which he did on the morning of the 21st October. The medicine was taken. It did bring some relief, but it was not much.

While the party was on its way to its destination, it fell in with Doctor Lachhman Das, Assistant Surgeon, who was proceeding on duty to Ajmere. Seeing the Swami in the State he was in, he at once turned back and followed him to the Abu, which was reached on the evening of the 21st, and where the Doctor treated the patient for two days. The treatment appeared to be doing good from the very first, stopping the hiccough and removing the looseness of the bowels within forty eight hours, but it was not to be continued longer.

His officer coming to know what the doctor had done, was extremely put out, and after reprimanding him severely for having returned to Abu in defiance of his orders, to the contrary, directed him to be off at once. The brave Mohyal, indignant that his deepest feelings should have been so slighted and disliking the preemptory nature of the order now issued, tendered his resignation on the spot, but the officer refused to accept it at such a short notice. The Doctor had no option but to set off to Ajmere, his faced bathed in tears. Before taking his leave of the Swami, he entreated him in most earnest tones, to come to Ajmere, where he himself should be constantly by to see him and to direct everything.

The Swami thanked him, but said that he could not follow his suggestion. The doctor, however, actuated by the best and most patriotic of motives, was resolved to do all he could to have the Swami near him. On the way the encountered several gentlemen, from the Punjab and elsewhere, hurrying to their beloved teacher, and he besought them, one and all, to exert themselves to the utmost to induce the Swami to leave for Ajmere. The Swami was going down, those by his bed-side. - Munshi Lakshman Saroop, Pandit Lakshman Datta, Lala Shiv Dayal, Seth Sevak Lal Krishn Dass, and numerous other gentlemen, professional as well as laymen could not clearly but perceive. His condition on the 23rd was that of man in the utmost state of exhaustion. He could speak with effort, and could not turn in his bed without efficient assistance.

The blisters were still present, and as bad and ugly as ever. Though retaining complete possession of his sense, his hands and feet were always cold. During the next three days, at the desire of His Highness, Maharaja Jaswant Singh, Dr. Adam and Assistant Surgeon Lala Gurcharan Das came to see the Swami several times, but neither could do nay good. Maharaja Pratap Singh came on the 26th, but his influence and wealth, though he was willing they should b4e fully pressed into service for the Swami, were as powerless to bring about any good result as those of lesser men. His brother was willing to make a present of two thousand rupees (and of more if need be) to anyone who should restore the Swami to health! Finding how matter stood, and to try as were, a last chance, the attendants of the Swami, big and small, came to the determination of removing him to Ajmere. Dr. Lachhman Das had given them hope, and who could say but he might, after all, be able to save the Swami?

The Swami was unwilling to go, but the united representation of his well-wishers present, had, at last, its way, and to Ajmere he suffered himself to be taken, reaching that station on the morning of the 27th. Ti may be mentioned that while being conveyed to Ajmere, the Swami felt a strong desire to eat dahi (tar or curds). The article was supplied, and it is affirmed that it would have been better if he had not eaten it, being injurious for a person suffering from dysentery (sangrahni). As contemplated, the Swami was again placed under the treatment of Dr. Lachhman Das, but it would not do. The disease began to assume a still more alarming aspect, foreshadowing, in an unmistakable manner, the end that was near. On the 29th the entire body became covered with blisters, and the restlessness became considerably greater.

But for all that the Swami, with the help of two or three gentlemen, sat up in bed, and unsupported by anyone, remained in a sitting posture for some time, deep in SamadhiOn the 30th Hakim Pir Imam Ali (popularly known as Pirji) came and saw the Swami after having thoroughly examined the Swami, he gave it as his opinion, that he had been poisoned (the arsenic having been administered to hime, he could not say how), and he said that if the Swami, instead of going to Abu, had come direct to Ajmere, the fatal substance would, very probably, have been got out of the system. This, in other words, meant that the poison had, by this time, been fully absorbed into the system, and that it was now beyond the reach, of human skill.

After the departure of this celebrated physician, Dr. Newton was called in. the cough at this time being most troublesome, he had three or four seers of poultice (linseed, boiled in milk), prepared and applied to the chest of the sufferer. But no good came of it. The Doctor declared that he had seldom come across any man who under such suffering was so calm and resigned, and so self contained. As the Swami threw the poultice away, he remarked: This is worse than useless now."

It was a just remark, considering the change that was coming over him. The color of the urine, at this time, was black as coal. At 11 A.M. the Swami was seated on a chair to answer the calls of nature for the last time. When he was clean, he took the water with his own hands, and performed his ablutions, thoroughly cleansing his mouth with a datan. After this he lay down on the bed. The regulation of the in-going breath, the result of no little effort at such a moment, clearly showed that the Rishi was in communion with his Maker.

At 4 P.M. the teacher desired the Swami Atamanand and Gopal Giri to be brought before him, and as soon as they made their appearance, he asked them to sit down, and then said: "What do you want?" the answer was, that all they desired was that he should be restored to health. The Swami replied: 'What is left of this body now to get well? And extending his hand he placed it on the head of each in turn, and said "Live in peace." A few minutes after this, he directed that one hundred rupees, in cash and a shawl be given to Swami Atmanand and a similar present to Padnit Bhim Sen, but both the gentlemen humbly begged to be excused from accepting the gift, and they had their wish.

At about 5 P.M., the Swami, who had, now and then, give his loveful glance to the arrivals from various parts of Upper India and Rajputana, now beckoned them, one and all, to come and stand before him. They came, and stood contemplating the noble figure lying prostrate before them, but not for long. At a signal from him they retired behind him, and set down silence. The doors of the room and the sky-lights, in deference to his wishes, were thrown open and looking at the ceiling he asked: "What paksha is it now? What is the tithi and what day?" the reply was that it was the end of the Krishna-paksha and the beginning of the Shukla-paksha and that the day was the Tuesday.

Upon this he composed himself for contemplation, and began to chant Veda-mantras, following the same with Ishwara-stuti in Sanskrit and in Bhasha. When repeating the Gayatri-mantra he remained wrapt in trance for some minutes, after which opening his eyes, he exclaimed: "Merciful and almighty Lord, such is Your will, yea, such is Your will, and let this Thine will be fulfilled!

And simultaneously with closing the prayer, he turned in his bed and controlling the out-going breath after the manner of Yogis, cast it out utterly with one vigorous effort! It was at 6. P.M. the 31st of October, 1883, the Dipali Day, that India's greatest savior of modern times expired. Were the preparations for a universal illumination in Aryavarta at this moment in honor of the departed soul? And was the universal illumination that came off almost synochrously with the exit of the departing soul, a representative of the inconceivably bright and glorious light of which the latter part of the following mantra speaks, and in which the spirit of the Rishi was to range and to dwell:-

"ETAAVAANASYA MAHIMAATO JYAAYAA-MASHCHA PURUSHAH

PAADO AASYA VISHVAA BHOOTAA NI TRIPAADASYAAMRITAM DIVI"

Swami Dayanand was 59 years of age at the time of his death. As soon as it was known that Swami Dayanand was no more, two Sanyasis made their appearance, claiming the body and declaring that they should, in accordance with the usages of their Order, inter it.

The claimed was refused. Maharaja Sajjan Singh, longing to have last look at his departed guru, suggested, through this representative, that he cremation of the body might be postponed for a couple of days, but His Highness was informed that that this could not be done, since it was the unanimous opinion of the gentlemen in attendance that the sanskar should be performed without delay. In pursuance of this resolved, the body was washed and bathed early on the morning of 31st, and having been wrapped in a shawl of the geru color, placed on a baikunthi (a kind of bier) and borne towards the place where it was to be cremated, soon after it had struck ten. The procession, perhaps the grandest and most representative of its kind ever witnessed at Ajmere, moved on with bowed heads and with hearts weighed down with grief. Four Vepathis preceded the hearse, chanting hymns from the Vedas.

On arriving at the spot Rai Bahadur Pandit Bhag Ram, pointing to the body deposited in from of him, spoke of the undying achievements and singular virtues of the soul which had tenanted it, and of the irreparable loss which the country had suffered by the early departure of that soul. After this the body was placed on the Vedi, and burnt with two maunds of Sandal-wood, ten maunds of pipalwood, four maunds of ghee, five seers of camphor, one seer of saffron.

In less than an hour the frame that had been instrumental in doing so much for the world, was a handful of ashes!

Bibliography

Arun, Pseud.: *Testament of Subhas Bose*, Delhi, Rajkamal Pub., 1946.

Bose, S. C., *The Indian Struggle, 1920-1942,* Bombay, Asia Publishing House, 1964.

Calvocoressi, Peter, and Guy Wint: *The Total War: the Story of World War II,* New York, Pantheon Books, 1972.

Chakrabarti, Mohit : *Fire Sans Ire : A Critical Study of Gandhian Non-Violence,* New Delhi, Concept, 2005.

Chaudhuri, Kali P.: *Netaji and India,* Shillong, Kali Prasanna Chaudhuri, 1956.

Das, Hari Hara: *Subhas Chandra Bose and the Indian National Movement*, New Delhi, Sterling Publishers, 1983.

Datta, Asit Kumar : *Aesthetics and the Poetic Image of Rabindranath Tagore*, Delhi, Abhijeet Pub., 2007.

Dhawan, S.K. : *Discovery of Indira Gandhi : A Select Chronology,* Wave Pub., Delhi, 1986.

Edwardes, Michael: *The Last Years of British India*, Cleveland, World Pub. Co., 1964.

Gandhi, P. Jegadish : *Dr. Abdul Kalam's Futuristic India*, Deep and Deep, New Delhi, 2006.

Gaur, Mahendra : *Indian Political Parties Annual*, Delhi, Kalpaz Pub., 2006.

George, Davis : *Dynamics of Power : The Gandhian Perspective,* New Delhi, Frank Bros. & Co., 2000.

Ghosh, K. K.: *The Indian National Army: Second Front of the Indian Independence Movement*, Meerut, Meenakshi Prakashan, 1969.

Gordon, L. A.: *Bengal : The Nationalist Movement 1876-1940,* New York/London, Columbia University Press, 1974.

Gupta, Om : *Encyclopaedia of India Pakistan and Bangladesh*, Isha Books, Delhi, 2006.

Gupta, S.P. Das : *Rabindranath Tagore : Thought Relics: New Expanded Version*, Kolkata, Sadesh, 2007.

Hunter, Sir William Wilson : *Encyclopaedia of Indian Rulers*, Cosmo, New Delhi, 2001.

Kumar, Ravindra : *Gandhian Thoughts : An Overview*, New Delhi, Gyan, 2006.

Majumdar, R. C.: *Jibanera Smritideepe*, Calcutta, General Printers and Publishers, 1978.

Mishra, Anil Dutta : *Challenges of 21 Century : Gandhian Alternatives*, New Delhi, Mittal Pub., 2003.

Murthi, R.K. : *Discovery of Nehru*, Indian Pub., Delhi, 1993.

Nair, A. M.: *An Indian Freedom Fighter in Japan*, Bombay, Orient Longman, 1983.

Narula, Sanjay : *Indian Politics*, New Delhi, Murari Lal and Sons, 2007.

Nehru, Jawaharlal : *The Discovery of India*, Oxford University Press, New Delhi, 2003.

Noorani, A.G. : *Indian Political Trials : 1775-1947*, New Delhi, Oxford University Press, 2005.

Patel, Asha : *Gandhian Vision of Rural Development : Its Relevance in Present Time*, New Delhi, Decent Books, 2005.

Pruthi, R.K. : *Indian Political Thought*, New Delhi, Mohit Pub., 2007.

Sanghavi, Nagindas : *The Agony of Arrival : Gandhi : The South Africa Years*, New Delhi, Rupa & Co., 2006.

Sharma, S.R. : *Gandhi : Ahimsa and Non Violence in Practice*, Delhi, Cosmo, 2001.

Sivaram, M.: *The Road to Delhi*, Rutland, Vt., C.E. Tuttle Co., 1967.

Toye, Hugh: *The Springing Tiger: A Study of a Revolutionary*, London, Cassell, 1959.

Index

❑❑❑